On Edge

CULTURAL ⚘ POLITICS

A series from the Social Text collective

Aimed at a broad interdisciplinary audience, these volumes seek to intervene in debates about the political direction of current theory and practice by combining contemporary analysis with a more traditional sense of historical and socioeconomic evaluation.

On Edge

The Crisis of Contemporary Latin American Culture

George Yúdice
Jean Franco
Juan Flores, editors
(for the Social Text collective)

Cultural Politics, Volume 4

University of Minnesota Press
Minneapolis and London

Portions of Howard Winant, "'The Other Side of the Process': Racial Formation in Contemporary Brazil," first appeared in "Rethinking Race in Brazil," *Journal of Latin American Studies*, 24, part 1 (1992); reprinted by permission.

Published by the University of Minnesota Press
2037 University Avenue Southeast, Minneapolis, MN 55414
Printed in the United States of America on acid-free paper.

Library of Congress Cataloging-in-Publication Data
On edge: the crisis of contemporary Latin American culture / George Yúdice, Juan Flores, Jean Franco, editors.
    p. cm. — (Cultural politics; v. 4)
Includes bibliographical references and index.
ISBN 0-8166-1938-7 (alk. paper).
ISBN 0-8166-1939-5 (pbk.: alk. paper)
    1. Latin America — Cultural policy. 2. Privatization — Social aspects — Latin America. 3. Intercultural communication — Social aspects — Latin America. 4. Culture diffusion — Latin America.
I. Yúdice, George. II. Flores, Juan. III. Franco, Jean. IV. Series: Cultural politics (Minneapolis, Minn.); v. 4.
F1408.3.05   1992
306.4'098 — dc20   91-41743
                                              CIP

Contents

Introduction

George Yúdice, Jean Franco, and Juan Flores

"A new dawn in the New World" is the tune that several Latin American presidents have been singing as backup to George Bush's lead on his December 1990 promotional tour for the Enterprise for the Americas Initiative.[1] "To fulfill the New World's destiny," Mr. Bush crooned, "all of the Americas and the Caribbean must embark on a venture for the coming century: to create the first fully democratic hemisphere in the history of mankind."[2] On the flip side of the democracy label is the Brady plan, "an Administration proposal that developing debtor countries sell state-owned industries and cut spending while commercial banks forgive some debts and lower interest payments on others." The aim is to create "a free trade zone from the North Pole to Tierra del Fuego."[3]

These lyrics, with all their promise of novelty, are of course just a jazzed-up remake of an old standard that has variously been billed over the past two centuries as the Monroe Doctrine, Pan-Americanism, the Big Stick, the Good Neighbor Policy, Alliance for Progress, the Caribbean Basin Initiative, and so on. The lyrics' double entendre was already understood by José Martí as early as 1889. On the occasion of the First Pan-American Congress, Martí wrote: "From Independence onward, there has never been an issue calling for more prudence nor needing more caution nor a greater and detailed scrutiny than the invitation made by the almighty United States, a country overflowing with unsaleable products and determined to extend its dominion over America, to the less powerful American nations. The purpose of this invitation is to ask these American nations, which have useful and free trade agreements with Europe, to form an alliance against Europe and make trade agreements with the rest of the world."[4]

The tune that set Martí's teeth on edge a century ago is even more out of sync today. Democracy and capitalism have proved time and again to sing a poor duet because they elide questions of social justice. Dramatic changes in the past two decades have put developmentalism and social justice in an inverse relationship. The widely publicized economic "miracles" produced by the military regimes of the 1970s made Latin America into an area beset by debt, informal economies, mass migration, and narcotraffic. Latin America has been transformed in a matter of decades from predominantly agricultural and peasant economies to highly urban societies with the attendant problems of mass unemployment, homelessness, and starvation. This has had a direct effect on people's everyday lives, especially in the increase of environment-related diseases and urban violence; the criminalization of entire sectors of the population, such as the *pixotes* of the shantytowns; the increase of repressive surveillance; and the bunkerization of the rich. The poor can no longer depend on the old-style system of favors from local caciques, nor are they integrated into the consumer society that is represented in the media.

On the one hand, the space of the nation, and even that of the continent, is transcended by global economic and communications networks. On the other hand, in the interstices of these networks there develop local, quite specific and ephemeral, protests, resistances, and social movements, even national movements of a new type. For example, transnationalization and narcotraffic have spawned a broader-based and more ostentatiously vulgar jet set than ever before, with its hub in Miami. But globalization leads not only to new elites; it also gives rise to new particularisms: the indigenous population of Ecuador, for the first time, has organized on a national basis; the Afro-Brazilian movement contests the definition of a Brazilian national identity that excludes them in matters outside of samba and soccer; squatters' movements in Chile and the movement of earthquake victims in Mexico have provided social services that the state either cannot or refuses to offer; a new Mexican-American border culture openly defies geopolitical frontiers.

Globalization implies greater possibilities of social control. The pervasive reach of the media — especially television — into politics and everyday life, and the breakdown of political culture in the new social movements and in informal economies (whose most notorious example is narcotraffic), have made it impossible to interpellate convincingly the entirety of the socius on the basis of traditional master discourses. Identity and subjectivity are no longer articulated on a national or continental basis by discourses of civilization, hispanicity, *indigenismo*, *mestizaje*, anti-imperialism, working or *campesino* classes, and so on.

This book starts from the assumption that there is no point in attempting to rewrite the old polarities, especially as a substantial body of scholarship and thinking has emerged in Latin America after the rise of the debt crisis, the collapse of the welfare state, and the struggle for redemocratization. The cultural consequences of this are far-reaching. Within Latin America it has produced debates not only on the meanings and possibilities of implementing democracy but also on the historical vicissitudes of modernization and around questions of privatization, free markets, and pluralism. This book owes a great deal to the work of Latin American intellectuals — Beatriz Sarlo, Carlos Monsiváis, Néstor García Canclini, to name a few — often working under very difficult conditions, and whose work does not reach the U.S. public.[5] These writers, like the authors of the essays in this book, are trying not only to understand the limitations of past ideologies, but to discern the cultural spaces within this new and very difficult situation, in which oppositional practices are no longer very well defined.

The current "integration" of Latin American economies into the "new world order," with its emphasis on phasing out the welfare state, privatizing national enterprises, and placing the management of political matters in the hands of technocrats, has provoked new thinking on questions of modernization, modernity, and postmodernity, and particularly on the meaning of pluralism as the ideology of contemporary neoliberalism. Pluralism camouflages itself behind an egalitarian mask, whereas it in fact neutralizes class conflict and the claims of the new social movements. The chief of staff of the president of Chile, for example, is able to declare that "our main accomplishment has been to lay the foundations of a stable competitive, nonconfrontational political system,"[6] that is, to retain competitiveness in the economic sphere while making it possible to *disregard* the claims of diverse social groups in the social and political spheres.

Pluralism also manifests itself in international relations, with the attendant projection of the national image in cosmopolitan capitals, as a means of salvaging national pride and distracting attention from local problems. Mexico, for example, has organized an unprecedented exhibition of its ancient culture at the Metropolitan Museum in New York City — *Mexico: Splendors of 30 Centuries*; the catalogue has a foreword by Emilio Azcárraga, CEO of Televisa, and an introduction by Octavio Paz — at enormous "private" expense while resources for desperately needed public services have been slashed. Privatization is not just an economic issue. It deeply affects culture and displaces it from national to transnational arenas as advertising for entry into the "new world order." The Mexican state, by itself, could not have put on such a lavish display.

As culture becomes privatized, intellectuals and artists increasingly act as salespersons for free enterprise, hawking and making wares of "otherness" familiar to transnational culture. Octavio Paz's inaugural lecture for the Mexico exhibition at the Metropolitan Museum emphasizes this ready translation of difference into sameness for the Western consumer:

> The radical "otherness" of Mesoamerican civilization is thus transformed into its opposite: thanks to modern aesthetics, these works that seem so distant are also contemporaneous.[7]

In short, the ideological veneer of pluralism admits difference without that difference constituting a threat to state and market systems. In fact, pluralism has mobilized difference in the service of these systems. It has even enabled some revolutionary movements to "go legit," as in Chile and Colombia, thereby changing the rules of contestatory practice. The eclecticism of cultural production — there are no current defining literary or cinematic movements in Latin America — is also part of the articulation of pluralism and consumerism. Increasingly, artists are forced to seek out commercial funding as state resources dry up. In 1990, for example, President Collor de Mello's government abolished Brazil's Ley Sarney, which provided funding for artistic endeavors through tax incentives. As cultural products are integrated into a (global) market rationality, with their effectivity measured in sales receipts and media ratings, they are less articulated to social movements that express the negotiated meanings that give a social formation its distinctive cultural politics. Market rationality fosters segmented audiences that need not, in turn, relate to each other. This explains, in part, why there are no current defining literary, artistic, or cinematic movements comparable to *realismo maravilloso*, Cinema Novo, the "Boom," and so on.

Intellectuals and artists have found it necessary, therefore, to seek opportunities in the media and in private enterprise. Televisa provided the funds for the establishment of the Tamayo Museum in Mexico. Established writers like Vargas Llosa, Octavio Paz, and Juan José Arreola have all had their television programs. New personalities have also become influential; many politicians are now recruited from among media celebrities. Owners of the media like the Azcárraga group in Mexico, TV Globo in Brazil, and Mercurio in Chile have played the largest role in electing politicians.

The new uses of the media have not, however, replaced long-standing intellectual traditions in Latin America; they have, instead, been transformed or "reconverted," as García Canclini calls this process of adapting traditions to new circumstances:

> Not all traditions or all forms of modernization are in crisis. Old and new symbolic products still offer attractive investment opportunities. At the same time, there is the growth of electronic cultures and also of museums and their publics; artisans and popular singers prosper and expand their audience. Instead of the death of traditional cultural forms, we now discover that tradition is in transition, and articulated to modern processes. Reconversion prolongs their existence. . . . To reconvert cultural capital means to transfer symbolic patrimony from one site to another in order to conserve it, increase its yield, and better the position of those who practice it.[8]

It is true, on the one hand, that privatization has led to the extinction of alternative outlets for cultural production. Argentina and Brazil no longer have film industries, which provided crucial funding for contestatory representations, such as the films of Cinema Novo and many works produced by Embrafilme, the Brazilian state production company. Television and video production are now almost exclusively funded by private enterprise, like MTV Brazil, which demands high consumer appeal measured in Nielsen ratings.

But, on the other hand, are we to believe that transition from state-sponsored culture to private control has had only negative consequences? Or have spaces emerged for alternative political and cultural practices? According to García Canclini, we should no longer expect to find the hegemonic and the contestatory in their familiar guises; reconversion has shifted their context of operation and their significance:

> High, popular, and mass are no longer to be found in their familiar places. The traditional and the modern are mixed together all the time, even in cities where the disposition of neighborhoods and institutions has been governed by criteria of social strata. Artisans sell weavings and native pottery in front of art museums. Painters who might once have been classified as elite incorporate quotes from comic strips in their works, or work in industrial design. Designers of commercials borrow images from popular artisans and painters of high art. In London and New York, rock music is being transformed by the melodic structures of African, Asian, and Latin American music. In these new settings, our cultural capital is reconverted. Through cultural exchange, we are making the most of what we have and are trying to say something more or different.[9]

As the state and traditional intellectuals withdraw from the advocacy of social causes, new kinds of intellectuals — organic to ethnic, gender, and class experience — emerge to articulate the particular demands of new social movements such as indigenous rights groups in Central America and the Andean countries, women's movements throughout Latin America, an emerging black consciousness in Brazil, and worker-intellectual alliances such as the Brazilian Workers party (PT) or Cuauhtémoc Cárdenas's PTN in Mexico. Their political and cultural activism has provided, throughout the seventies and eighties, reasons to hope for change in social consciousness. Testimonial literature, the literature surrounding the activities of the Mothers of the Plaza de Mayo in Argentina, the popular poetry and music of marginal peoples, and so on, have indeed expressed the will to change the social order and challenged traditional thinking about the aesthetic and its important role in shaping public culture.

The urgent question arises, however, as to whether in the face of intensified class stratification, the posturing of intellectuals and the recycling of traditional genres do not point up the irrelevance of public culture. The power of the "new world order" to shift the terrain of the political to an international framework weakens the usefulness of a national, public culture for much-needed change. This "new world order" is heralded by three negations: the obsolescence of traditional aesthetics and its concomitant public sphere; the superfluousness of the avant-garde or the counterculture; and the extinction of the future — socialism, like the master discourses of the nation and hispanicity, has fallen on hard times and no longer projects the new horizon for the Latin American masses. Whether or not we accept this state of affairs, we must recognize the changes the new transnational hegemony has induced throughout Latin America. We must focus on the present and come to terms with the many dispersed practices unleashed by reconversion. The challenge in Latin America's *fin de siglo* is how to think of these dispersed and heterogeneous particularities.

No one book can aspire to capture the whole picture of a cultural formation; this book is no exception. The following essays are, rather, exploratory forays into this rather changed terrain of Latin American culture. This altered terrain requires rethinking the traditional disciplinary constraints imposed by social science methodologies, historical interpretation, or aesthetic analysis. These essays may be seen as contributions to the evolving paradigm of cultural studies, which emerged as a critique of controlled knowledge production under traditional disciplines and as a means to bring to the surface alternative histories and aesthetic practices. Our particular focus on *cultural politics*, on the social and political struggles waged in and through intellectual and aesthetic practices as well as all kinds of everyday matters such as racial or gender identity, is more suited, we think, to the current situation in which no one master discourse sets the agenda for understanding self, society, and the world.

NOTES

1. Quoted in Maureen Dowd, "Bush Begins His Latin Tour in Brazil Amid Worry Over Argentina Strife," *New York Times*, Dec. 4, 1990, A14.

2. Quoted in James Brooke, "Debt and Democracy," *New York Times*, Dec. 5, 1990, A16.

3. Clifford Krauss, "Bush Leaves for South America to Push Trade," *New York Times*, Dec. 2, 1990, 29.

4. José Martí, "Contra el Panamericanismo," in *Política de Nuestra América* (México: Siglo XXI, 1977), 152.

5. See Beatriz Sarlo, *Una modernidad periférica: Buenos Aires 1920 y 1930* (Buenos Aires: Ediciones Nueva Visión, 1988); Carlos Monsiváis's cultural history and chronicling of social movements, collected in *Entrada libre: Crónica de la sociedad que se organiza* (México: Era, 1987); and Néstor García Canclini, *Culturas híbridas: Estrategias para entrar y salir de la modernidad* (México: Grijalbo, 1990). An excerpt of García Canclini's book is included in this volume as "Cultural Reconversion."

6. Quoted in Shirley Christian, "Pinochet, Under Fire, Seems Willing to Yield Army Command," *New York Times*, Jan. 22, 1991, A17.

7. Octavio Paz, "The Power of Ancient Mexican Art," *New York Review of Books,* Dec. 6, 1990, 19.

8. García Canclini, "Cultural Reconversion," this volume, 31–32.

9. Ibid., 30–31.

Postmodernity and Transnational Capitalism in Latin America
George Yúdice

Heterogeneity and Postmodernism *Avant la Lettre?*

There is a curious — and thoroughly understandable — argument that Latin America sets the precedent of postmodernity long before the notion appears in the Euro-North American context.[1] This argument is analogous to others that attempt to endow heterogeneous formations with the cachet of mainstream postmodern rhetoric. Thus, *la raison baroque*, according to Christine Buci-Glucksmann, anticipates a postmodern reluctance to integrate numerous visual spaces into a coherent representation.[2] This idea, in fact, has long had currency in what critics call the Latin American *neobaroque*.[3] Minority writers and intellectuals in the United States have also made similar claims for black and Latino cultures.[4] As regards Latin America, the argument is as follows: the heterogeneous character of Latin American social and cultural formations made it possible for discontinuous, alternative, and hybrid forms to emerge that challenged the hegemony of the *grand récit* of modernity. Even history fragments into a series of discontinuous formations that undermine the synchronicity of the space of the nation:[5] indigenous tribal cultures mix with traditional peasantry, the descendants of slaves, the lumpen of the shanties, and a cosmopolitan elite that would be at home in Paris or New York.

Before we evaluate this contention of Latin America's postmodernity *avant la lettre*, we should explore the question of heterogeneity. The heterogeneity of Latin American cultural formations is not the result of some postmodern simulational sleight of hand; rather, it is produced by the uneven implementation of modernization, leading, on the one hand, to contestatory projects for political, economic, and cultural decolonization, and on the other, to strategies for survival such as informal economies, the legal and illegal activities that elude government recording and control. Hernando de Soto, basing himself on the situation in Peru, argues that it is a top-heavy state — inclined to patronage and other forms of inefficiency and corruption — that causes informality.[6] Samuel Doria Medina, however, attributes the phenomenon to a complex of conditions — unequal distribution of income, tertiarization of the economy, hyperinflation — that are in great measure the result of a state's economic vulnerability within a world economy controlled by nations of the "center":

> The fundamental cause for the formation of an informal economy is the deformation of the economic structure once economic activity has been directed towards extractive industry for export. This creates a sector of the economy that in fact is related to the State, where both are dependent on the center. Consequently, the rest of the economy, which is marginal to the government, develops independently. In other words, having assigned to the country the production of raw materials in order to satisfy the requirements of the central economies, it becomes unnecessary to develop all of society. Since this pattern or structure of accumulation is marginal to society and the rest of the economy, it does not require internal demand or equitable income distribution to generate widespread growth.[7]

Informality, moreover, has grown to enormous proportions since the mid-1970s as a result not only of a weak productive sector and a large concentration of unequally distributed income, which capital flight makes unavailable, but also of extreme vulnerability to the global economic crisis of 1981-82, the external debt crisis, and the increasing importance of coca production.[8] Narcotraffic, the largest sector of the informal economy, in its current transnational cartel form (another recent development that owes something to CIA dealings in the region) is a grotesque (and fitting) parody of capitalist corporate culture. The narratives constructed to account for informality and narcotraffic might seem hardly consistent with the *grand récit* of modernity. And yet they are, in an obverse (if not perverse) relation that deconstructs modernity's collusion with capitalism. This parodic deconstruction is not, of course, restricted to so-called Third

World countries: junk bonds and savings-and-loans fiascos in the United States have had very much the same effect. "Irrationality" is born of the guiding (market) "rationality" of modernity.

Recognition of this "irrationality" is important in devising strategies for overcoming the economic plight of these countries. In contrast to de Soto, who advocates transforming the pathology of "informality" into its own solution by liberating the entrepreneurial spirit of its practitioners from the shackles of state regulation, Doria Medina analyzes its root causes and cautions against entrenching a state of affairs founded on (internal and international) inequality. The institutionalization of informality does nothing to counter the vast accumulation by elites, who elude a more equitable distribution of wealth by resorting to contraband and speculation while the under- and informally employed barely survive. Contraband is particularly pernicious because it induces loss of economic protection, an exaggerated degree of tertiary activities, a loss of income for the National Treasury, and the occupation of active commercial actors in operations (e.g., speculation) that do not generate significant value added.[9] This state of affairs relegates "informals" to the recycling of commodities normally discarded in the "formal" sphere. A "strategy for survival" is thus transformed into a permanent "strategy of life."[10]

Having lost control of the economy, many Latin American countries oscillate between hyperinflation and recession, further strengthening the informal economy and producing a highly stressful way of life for the middle and underclasses.[11]

> It is important to re-emphasize the role of public expectation in the inflationary process, and the importance of its effect on the informal economy. As the public loses confidence in the economic authorities responsible for inflation, their lack of confidence fans inflationary expectations, converting the latter into an engine that drives inflation up even further. Under these circumstances, financial transactions accelerate at a dizzying pace, but they do not involve the formal sector because of the concomitant accelerated depreciation of domestic currency. In short, the national currency no longer serves as a *store of value*, but is replaced by a strong currency such as, in the case of Bolivia, the U.S. dollar.[12]

Hyperinflation is, thus, not only an economic phenomenon; it also cuts deeply into the individual and collective psyche, producing uncertainty, skepticism, criminality, and psychological disorders.

Whether economic or social, "national currency" loses its value; under such circumstances there can be no self-determination. At best, narcotraffic replaces prior national currencies.

It is precisely in the attempt to modernize by "developing" extractive industries for export, under the aegis of "central economies," that modernity takes such ghoulish forms in countries like Bolivia. The *grand récit* of modernity, of course, attributes this ghoulishness to other factors, such as the "backwardness" of peripheral societies, the corruption of their governments, the immaturity of their elites, and so on. Its "rational" self-construal blinds it to its own role as a source of pathology. The critique of modernity-as-development-and-progress put forth by Latin American social scientists, theologians, writers and artists, and grass-roots organizations should be considered an important ingredient of postmodernity, understood as the set of challenges to modernity's self-understanding. These challenges stem from the different ways in which local formations engage the colonizing tentacles of transnational capitalism,[13] which should not be confused with *one* mode of production. It is, rather, a *series of conditions* under which various modes of production and symbolization hold in differing localities.

My argument as regards Latin America is not that informal economies or narcotraffic *are* postmodern phenomena but, rather, that they are simultaneously responses and propositions that pose alternatives to the *grand récit* of postmodernity as it has been constructed by Lyotard, Jameson, and their predecessors. These conditions require alternative narratives with different configurations of features constitutive of modernity and different trajectories and dénouements. Functional state apparatuses, viable political structures, and effective democratic civil societies must be conceived in relation to the specific circumstances of given Latin American countries and not patterned after the reigning paradigm of Western modernity. To understand, for example, why these desiderata are curtailed in narcotrafficking countries, we must look at the intersection of several modes of production, various cultures, different administrative apparatuses, and the struggle for survival and for hegemony on the part of diverse social strata (peasants, workers, narcotraffickers, military, national bourgeoisie, middle classes, national and international organized crime networks, U.S. military-industrial complex, etc.). Whatever the possibilities for democratization, they must be studied as particular responses and propositions to this set of conditions that comprise the *heterogeneous formation*.

Octavio Paz is, perhaps, the first artist–intellectual to claim that finally Latin America had become contemporaneous with the decentered West—even before the term had been coined. As early as *The Labyrinth of Solitude* (1950), he argues that the contradictory logic of modernity—which he labels a *tradición de ruptura*—came to a grinding halt[14] when the leading nations of imperialist capitalism found themselves decentered and as "marginal" as the periphery:

> We have lived on the periphery of history. Today the center, the nucleus of world society has come apart and we have all become peripheral beings, even the Europeans and the North Americans. We are all on the margin because there is no longer any center.[15]

> Third World revolts and ethnic and national rebellions in industrialized societies are the insurrection of particularisms oppressed by another particularism that wears the mask of universality: Western capitalism.[16]

It should be made clear, however, that Paz homogenizes all those "particularisms" in a *generalized marginality*, whose aesthetic he claims to be rooted in the immediacy of a timeless present. Paz's sense of heterogeneity casts these particularisms only as symptoms of a more unfathomable otherness, which like Heidegger's notion of Being, has nothing to do with specific others. For Heidegger, it is to be *unconcealed*, rather, in the "invisible shadow" or "space withdrawn from representation."[17] Taking his cue from Heidegger, who identifies the *poetic* as the dwelling place of Being,[18] Paz reconciles the aporias of modernity—particularism versus universalism, experience versus history, existence versus representation—in the "transhistorical virtuality" of poetry.

Latin America, savagely torn by the contradictions of capitalism, provides for Paz's thought and poetics a paradigmatic source for a secular "fundamentalist" reconciliation. And Paz is its high priest. As such, it is open to Habermas's critique of neoconservative responses to rationality.[19] It is, essentially, an aesthetic moralism, not unlike religious fundamentalism, which seeks to counteract the excesses and "moral decadence" of historical life.

> I think a new star is rising—it is not yet on the horizon but it is announced in many indirect ways; it is the poetics of the *now*. Soon

men will have to erect a Morals, a Politics, an Erotics, and a Poetics of the present. The road to the present passes through the body but it should not be confused with the mechanical and promiscuous hedonism of modern Western societies. The present is the fruit issued forth by the fusion of life and death.[20]

Paz's apocalyptic, messianic proposition not only purges the political dimension from the practices of the new social movements (women, gays and lesbians, ecology, ethnic and racial minorities) by assimilating their projects to a transhistorical aesthetic; it also aims to transcend the conditions set by modernity in one fell swoop, as if those conditions were nothing but the expression of a single logic. Furthermore, as Nelly Richard observes about "postmodernism in the periphery," the sublation of center and margin that is celebrated in the aesthetic practices of certain elites, Paz among them, actually abolishes the value and significance, the *difference*, of the practices of subaltern and colonized peoples:[21]

Just as it appears that for once the Latin American periphery might have achieved the distinction of being postmodernist *avant la lettre*, no sooner does it attain a synchronicity of forms with the international cultural discourses, than that very same postmodernism abolishes any privilege which such a position might offer. Postmodernism dismantles the distinction between centre and periphery, and in so doing nullifies its significance. There are many instances in postmodernist discourse aimed at convincing one of the obsolescence of the opposition centre/periphery, and of the inappropriateness of continuing to see ourselves as the victims of colonisation.[22]

Ticio Escobar, moreover, cautions us to distinguish between the surface effects of a "postmodern" style — fragmentation, recycling, pastiche, and so on — and the significance of these formal manifestations within their respective sets of conditioning circumstances.[23] Consequently, a theory of postmodern culture cannot rely on the formal techniques and properties of particular works. That is why the myriad primers that attempt to register the features of postmodern phenomena, though they provide easily identifiable markers of style, are so unsatisfying. Linda Hutcheon, for example, under the pretext of identifying postmodernism with a "denaturalizing" politics of representation, lumps together Salman Rushdie, Angela Carter, and Manuel Puig as practitioners of a subversive "postmodern parody."[24] It is not, of course, as if this kind of parody had not existed previously; doesn't

Cervantes's intertextuality have a similar effect? It is easy enough to identify stylistic markers; it is more difficult to pay close attention to how conjunctural circumstances condition the ways in which those markers are to be interpreted. Hutcheon shows indifference or ignorance in this latter respect.

Rather than speak of a postmodernism, then, which runs the risk of identifying the style of one group as emblematic of a condition (Lyotard) or a "cultural dominant" (Jameson),[25] it is preferable to theorize postmodernity as a series of conditions variously holding in different social formations that elicit diverse responses and propositions to the multiple ways in which modernization has been attempted in them. It is not a matter, then, of a different order of things following or replacing modernity, as it has been suggested from Weber to Habermas. If postmodernity has any specificity it is in the rethinking of how modernity has been represented, how alternative sciences, morals, and aesthetics, as well as different sociocultural formations, have all contributed to the constitution of modern life.

How we (re)think modernity and postmodernity has consequences for how we construe the ethicopolitical goals of theory. Paz's poetics of reconciling opposites in the transhistory of the present leads to an antimodern irrationality with little room for accommodating the democratic demands of diverse social movements. Rethinking democracy outside of the terms set by the *grand récit* of modernity is an enterprise many Latin American social movements see as necessary. Up to now the formal apparatuses of representative democracy have failed miserably. This is not to say that they have succeeded in Europe and the United States; their "dysfunctionality" in the Latin American context only makes more patent what is wrong with them in the "democratic West" where their pathologies are partly screened by "viable" consumer economies.

According to Ernesto Laclau and Chantal Mouffe, new ways of constructing democracy have been made possible by the new social movements, whose practices have "weakened" the rationality that undergirds modernity:

> The discourse of radical democracy is no longer the discourse of the universal; the epistemological niche from which "universal" classes and subjects spoke has been eradicated and replaced by a polyphony of voices, each of which constructs its own irreducible discursive identity. The conclusion is decisive: there can be no radical, plural

democracy without renouncing the discourse of the universal and the implied premise that it provides a privileged access to the "truth," attainable only by a limited number of subjects.[26]

Laclau and Mouffe's diagnostic also conceives of politics as a *creative articulation process*. With the pluralization and legitimation of manifold social projects, it is increasingly difficult to establish common meanings across the entire social terrain. How to strike a balance "between a logic of complete identity and another of pure difference" is the goal of "radical democracy." It consists of the

> recognition of the multiplicity of social logics and of the necessity to articulate them. This articulation, however, must constantly be recreated and renegotiated, for there is no final point where a definitive balance will be reached.[27]

According to Bernardo Subercaseaux, this creative articulation is the means by which "one's own," always provisional identity is achieved.[28] He sees this as a process of *appropriation* quite different from the mimetism decried by *ninguneístas* who berate their cultures for being a pale reflection of metropolitan society. The flavor of these self-negating breast-beatings, so typical of elite Latin American intellectuals, is captured in *El arte de la palabra*, Enrique Lihn's self-deconstructive pastiche of poststructuralist erasures of the subject:

> We are nothing: imitations, copies, phantoms; repeaters of what we understand badly, that is, hardly at all; deaf organ grinders; the animated fossils of a prehistory that we have lived neither here nor, consequently, anywhere, for we are aboriginal foreigners, transplanted from birth in our respective countries of origin.[29]

For Subercaseaux, as for Richard, Escobar, and Wisnik, the formation of a national identity is not a matter of authenticity versus mimetism but rather of articulation:

> The model of appropriation contrasts with a dual vision [i.e., native vs. alien — G. Y.] of Latin American culture. By definition, a theory of appropriation rejects the existence of an uncontaminated, endogenous cultural core. It also rejects the myth of cultural pluralism and any essentialism whatsoever, for Latin American identity is not something already constituted and fixed but something always in the process of becoming. Consequently, it cannot be understood by recourse to preconceptual or precategorical approaches. . . . The theory of appropriation offers a model of an ecumenical culture, always open and never endogamous.[30]

Roberto Schwarz has also rejected the Manichaean dichotomy between imitation and original "because it does not permit detecting the alien within the proper, the mimetic component within the original, and also the original component within the imitation."[31] Schwarz rethinks this aporia in terms of articulation, with the proviso that subaltern groups should have the opportunity to "refashion [prevalent forms] in accordance with their own interests, which . . . is a way of defining democracy." This statement is very important for my own argument since, as I noted above, the debates on postmodernity are often about the possibilities for establishing a democratic culture.

In what follows, I give a précis of what Euro-North American theorists understand by postmodernity, but not with the intention of applying their terms to Latin American phenomena. On the contrary, it seems to me that such theories need to be deconstructed and reconstructed in relation to Latin American contexts.

Redemption through Culture?

One criterion that holds for advocates of modernity (Habermas) and postmodernity (Jameson) alike is the *emancipatory potential* of cultural works. In Latin America, few are the artists who are not judged in terms of the social effectivity of their work. The 1960s and 1970s were rife with recriminations shot back and forth between writers who advocated art in the service of social justice and those who held that formal innovations were in and of themselves revolutionary.

The debates around the effectivity of José María Arguedas's work, in fact, hinged on this criterion. One influential study, *El mito de la salvación por la cultura*, critiques the idea that the pathologies wrought by a savage capitalism can be healed by recourse to the non-instrumental cultural practices of indigenous Andean peoples.[32] How to tap this source of personal and collective integration in the face of imminent cultural destruction by modernization was the aporia thematized in Arguedas's fiction and anthropological research. In his last novel, *El zorro de arriba y el zorro de abajo*, the attempt to resolve this aporia reaches its most poignant test.[33] In it, he portrays the ravages wrought by capitalism in a Peruvian factory town as well as the attempts to overcome them by recourse to a rapidly vanishing highland indigenous culture whose values nevertheless continue to be disseminated "transculturally" by mestizos settled in the coastal region.[34] Arguedas alternates this fictional text with diary entries in which he criticizes the professionalization of writers and vents his despair at ever recuperating the kind of unalienated life he experienced as a child among the Andean Indians. The very existence of a Peruvian national culture as well as his own life are in the balance. Culture seems to be the only hope, modern politics and leftist revolution having failed. Ultimately, however, culture does not rise to the task and Arguedas commits suicide, the epilogue to the novel serving as his suicide note.

Arguedas's suicide, his second and successful attempt, may have been the result of a particularly dark moment in his life, a life in which, on the contrary, he held the highest hopes for a cultural resolution to the aporias of modernity in Peru. Given his circumstances — economy, politics, and a very reduced public sphere controlled by oligarchic elites — such possibilities remained symbolic. Angel Rama explains that the social redemption to which he aspired was effected by proxy in his literature:

> Literature was for him a *reduced model of transculturation* that made it possible to portray it and test it out. If it was possible in literature it should also be possible in the culture at large. However, not in charge of a government or a revolution, that is, without power, Arguedas was not free to take the best route to that larger transculturation. Nevertheless, he did what he could with all his resources: portray transculturation by means of literary narrative, make it come to life artistically.[35]

Such a notion of culture, in the Latin American context, shares with modern bourgeois aesthetics the will to (re)construct hegemony. The greater reliance on indigenous and other popular (as opposed to mass-mediated) cultures is, perhaps, a notable distinction between the two traditions. The greatest difference, however, is the ever-present lament over the difficulty of establishing an unalienated modern culture in Latin America. There have been many different projects for cultural hegemony in the twenty-odd Latin American nations, but they all have one feature in common: its yet-unattained status. In the 1960s, the writers of the so-called Boom thought they could achieve not only national cultures but, more important, a global continental culture on a par with that of Europe or the United States. Rather than taking indigenous and popular traditions as its base, however, Boom writers sought to forge a new aesthetic language and, consequently, a new hegemonic consciousness. As in Arguedas's case, however, culture was a *proxy* for revolution or political power. According to Carlos Fuentes:

> If we Hispano-Americans are capable of creating our own model of progress [as compared to Western technocratic models], then our language is the only vehicle that can give form, propose goals, establish priorities, elaborate critiques of a given way of life: of saying everything that cannot be said in any other way. I believe that in Spanish America there are novels being written and to be written that, when such a consciousness is attained, will provide the necessary instruments to drink the water and the fruits of our true identity.[36]

Fuentes is, of course, on the right track in seeking alternative models of progress, but by adopting an autotelic aesthetic he is ultimately endorsing the option of elites in their bid for hegemony. The autotelic here is a symbolic expression of the self-determination that such writers sought vis-à-vis the international cultural market. Notwithstanding their protestations to the contrary, Fuentes and his colleagues (Cortázar, Vargas Llosa, et al.) ironically espoused technological development in the realm of the aesthetic — not only in terms of narrative technique but also as regards the growth of an international and promotion industry — falling in step, then, with the global reach of capitalist rationality into all spheres of life. It seems that the aesthetic fulfills the same function in this context as it had in its inception in England and Germany: it serves as *a proxy for power* enabling a particular group to seek consensus on cultural terrain in order to maintain hegemony. Not only did professionalized, superstar novelists like Fuentes or Vargas Llosa[37] sideline "vocational" writers like Arguedas, they also sought to integrate with the growing consumer culture among elites (the beautiful people of *la onda*) that made popular and indigenous cultures irrelevant unless they too integrated or "transculturated" into consumer society.[38]

Today, with poor prospects for military-revolutionary triumph, with the popular appeal of revolutionary heroism partly displaced toward narcotraffickers, and with the transformation of politics into struggles for interpretive power, the cultural sphere has opened up to all kinds of challenges. Its function as a "proxy for power" — it seems preferable to speak of a mediation of power relations — is openly recognized by groups throughout the political spectrum. At stake is the idea that the cultural or the aesthetic can provide a terrain for establishing consensus; everyone recognizes that consensus works in the interest of the hegemony of some groups. The premise that the aesthetic realm is intrinsically free and disinterested has become difficult to accept.

Is there still, then, an emancipatory potential in the aesthetic or cultural realm? In a different context, although directly addressing postmodern challenges to aesthetic disinterest, Terry Eagleton affirms that "there are meanings and values embedded in the tradition of the aesthetic which are of vital importance" to the political goal of achieving equal rights for self-determination.[39] The critical consensus is, however, that the aesthetic lost its emancipatory potential when the historical (i.e., European) avant-gardes were extinguished, on the one hand, by the double whammy of Nazism and Stalinism, and on the other, by the co-optation of consumer capitalism, which transformed *épater le bourgeois* into a marketing strategy. The second and subsequent avatars of the avant-garde, variously named neoavant-garde and transavant-garde, have only confirmed the exhaustion of the drive to innovate and shock humanity back from instrumental rationality into aestheticized life practices. With this exhaustion, or "twilight of the avant-gardes," we enter an era of skepticism, which Paz equates with postmodernity.[40]

What many call postmodernity, Habermas argues, is really a political and cultural *impasse* awaiting resolution in the transformation of the emancipatory project of modernity such that a democratizing communicative rationality, rather than instrumental reason, becomes its driving force. Following Weber and Durkheim, Habermas sees European modernity emerging out of two interrelated diremptions: on the one hand, the separation of "system" (economy and state apparatus) and "lifeworld" (the concept of *Lebenswelt*, taken from Husserl, refers to culture broadly conceived as the ensemble of beliefs and presuppositions that serve as the medium of intersubjective relations), and, on the other, the emergence of modernity through the rationalization of the lifeworld into three autonomous value spheres: the cognitive, the moral, and the aesthetic.[41] These diremptions lead to the splitting-off of modern from traditional society as rationalization provides rules of validation in each sphere, thus displacing the traditional authority of myth, religion, or the absolute right of monarchy. The reproduction of society depends more and more on human actions than on the dictates of traditional authority. From its very beginning, then, modernity is at odds with tradition as a nonsecular form of belief and transcendence.

Modernity, however, is driven by an inherent contradiction resulting from the increased autonomy and reflexivity of a rationalized society. Automatic behavioral systems driven by instrumental reason override processes of mutual understanding that operate according to communicative rationality. The economy and the state apparatus thus come to colonize the lifeworld. At this point the aesthetic sphere emerges as the principal source of resistances to colonization (although practically ignored by the social sciences) by projecting nonalienated modes of cognition. But according to Peter Bürger, as the bourgeoisie expands its domain even resistances to instrumental reason are increasingly institutionalized, cutting off the aesthetic from other spheres of social life. Nineteenth-century Parnassianism, Symbolism, Pre-Raphaelism, and Art for Art's Sake exemplify the specialization of the aesthetic. Modernity generates its own antimodernity but subjects it to the same rules of specialization, thus constituting its internal contradiction. Eagleton further elucidates this contradiction, noting that the putative unalienated and disinterested cognition provided by the aesthetic is, in fact, a proxy for power, a "kind of prosthesis to reason, extending a reified Enlightenment rationality into vital regions which are otherwise beyond its reach."[42]

An ever-increasing colonization of the lifeworld resulted in a Europe disenchanted with its own elite culture, driving its artists and intellectuals to seek ever new regions of experience to tap. The era that saw the rise of nihilism, the avant-gardes, and Spengler's *The Decline of the West* also saw a new way of appropriating the cultural products of non-Western societies. Primitivism is not just a matter of collecting exotic objects from the outer reaches of the empire, it is a source of "still unalienated" cultural capital that will enable aesthetics, as "prosthesis to reason," to open up heretofore untapped regions of the psyche and facilitate their colonization in the process. This era also saw Latin American literature, as the major expression of (elite) cultural life, "catch up to" or get "up to date with" metropolitan culture. In effect, (elite) aesthetics in Latin America finally went beyond a mere *costumbrismo*, tapping local indigenous cultural forms in search of its own unalienated cultural capital. Examples are Andean and Mesoamerican *indigenismo* (Icaza, Alegría, Asturias, and the Nicaraguan *Vanguardia*), Caribbean *negrismo* (Palés Matos and Guillén), and Brazilian *Modernismo* (Tarsila do Amaral, Mário and Oswald de Andrade).

All of the preceding are expressions of the avant-garde will to abolish the institutionalized separation between autonomous art and bourgeois everyday life, seeking to establish a new practice of everyday life patterned after art.

> The avant-gardistes proposed the sublation of art — sublation in the Hegelian sense of the term: art was not to be simply destroyed, but transferred to the praxis of life where it would be preserved, albeit in changed form. The avant-gardistes thus adopted an essential element of Aestheticism [that] had made the distance from the praxis of life the content of works. The praxis of life to which Aestheticism refers and which it negates is the means-ends rationality of the bourgeois everyday. Now, it is not the aim of the avant-gardistes to integrate art into *this* praxis. On the contrary, they assent to the aestheticists' rejection of the world and its means-ends rationality. What distinguished them from the latter is the attempt to organize a new life praxis from a basis in art.[43]

It may be argued that the difference between metropolitan European and Latin American/peripheral avant-gardes revolves around how the aesthetic practice that serves as a model for a new everyday practice is construed. In Latin America, many of the avant-gardes sought to reactualize indigenous traditions, thus projecting new imaginaries with strong ethical *contents*. If we rethink peripheral avant-gardes as the endeavor to create new life praxes by rearticulating local traditions,[44] as in testimonial literature, it may prove too hasty to have declared the death of the avant-garde. Evidently, avant-garde would mean something else if thus construed. It would not, for example, be the sole domain of elites but would require, as in testimonial literature, the collaboration of elites and subalterns rather than the self-serving representation, incorporation, or co-optation of the latter by the former.

From the perspective of elite metropolitcan culture, and its enclaves in peripheral societies, the avant-gardes petered out:

> Today we witness the twilight of the aesthetics of rupture; the art and literature of our turn of the century have gradually lost their powers of negation. For a long time now their negations have been ritualistic

repetitions, their rebellions formulas, their transgressions ceremonies.[45]

But this is because they did not really change the framework of their aesthetic rationality. For thinkers like Paz, autonomous aesthetics continues to set the tenor of cultural practice; any collaboration with the subaltern is considered populist demagoguery, and any experimentation involving elite, popular, and mass culture a commodification. Consequently the entire problem of the avant-garde is left behind as the world enters a new *episteme*, according to Paz:

> Critics, somewhat belatedly, have noticed that for the past quarter-century we have been entering a new historical period and another form of art. Talk of the avant-garde has become popular as a new label has emerged for our time: the "postmodern era," a term just as dubious and contradictory as the idea of modernity. What comes after the modern cannot but be ultramodern: a modernity even more modern than yesterday's.[46]

Paz, it seems to me, has got it wrong. His account is a willful misrecognition that the postmodern does not necessarily seek to innovate, as does the modern, but rather to rearticulate alternative traditions in order to disalienate contemporary life. Even a mainstream account, like Lyotard's, situates postmodernity "not after nor in opposition to the modern which includes it, however much it may remain concealed within it."[47] Before considering in what ways postmodernity can be construed as continuous with modernity, I should like to review briefly Lyotard's checklist of postmodern features, which Jameson extends to the entire field of culture.

What defines postmodernity for Lyotard is the loss of credibility in the *grand récits* that legitimize knowledge in the name of any mode of unification, whether Christianity, revolution, the Hegelian Absolute Spirit, Marxism, or even the idea that "the people reign over history."[48] There is no longer faith in global or totalizing explanations. Jameson, in turn, sees postmodernity as a "cultural dominant" disseminated globally by the third or "late" stage of capitalism. Its cultural landscape is no longer the mechanical reproduction of the nineteenth and early twentieth centuries but rather the semiotic reproduction (a mode of symbolization or articulation of signs and not a mode of reproduction proper) that becomes dominant after World War II.[49]

Jameson's keenest insight is his explanation of why there has been a loss of faith in totalizing explanations. He derives his account from those works infused by the aesthetic of simulation, "whose power or authenticity is documented by [their] success . . . in evoking a whole new postmodern space in emergence around us." This evocation is powerful, according to Jameson, because it makes palpable what we can no longer understand without the prosthesis of simulation:

> Our faulty representations of some immense communicational and computer network are themselves but a distorted figuration of something even deeper, namely the whole world system of present-day multinational capitalism. The technology of contemporary society is therefore mesmerizing and fascinating, not so much in its own right, but because *it seems to offer some privileged representational shorthand* for grasping a network of power and control even more difficult for our minds and imaginations to grasp—namely the whole new decentred global network of the third stage of capital itself.[50]

Jameson's argument relies on an allegorical reading of the works he refers to, inasmuch as he treats them as simulacra of an unrepresentable, sublime referent. Such works no longer refer to the problem of power, "the physical incommensurability of the human organism with Nature, but also [to] the limits of figuration and the incapacity of the human mind to give representation to such enormous forces."[51] Consequently, for Jameson, the postmodern sublime can only be adequately theorized "in terms of that enormous and threatening, yet only dimly perceivable, other reality of economic and social institutions."[52]

Contrary to theorists of the avant-garde, Jameson does not propose how these works resist the colonization of the lifeworld. For Jameson, our everyday life is totally colonized, so much so that it is impossible to achieve any direct cognition of the world. Hence the sublime experience of failing to represent the reality to which the simulacra and the fragments might allude.[53] Rather than resistance, Jameson, following Kevin Lynch in *The Image of the City*, advocates an "aesthetics of cognitive mapping" so as to compensate for that unrepresentability that impedes the subject from recognizing its "*Imaginary* relationship to his or her *Real* conditions of existence."[54]

One of these conditions is the obsolescence of a "semiautonomous" cultural or aesthetic sphere with a corresponding critical distance. But it isn't that culture has disappeared; it has, rather, exploded and expanded

> throughout the social realm, to the point at which everything in our social life — from economic value and state power to practices and to the very structure of the psyche itself — can be said to have become 'cultural' in some original and yet untheorized sense.[55]

All of this entails that the "Left" must redefine its strategies for offense and resistance. The writing on the wall suggests that such time-honored notions as negativity, opposition, subversion, critical distance, and so on have been made irrelevant in the new postmodern landscape.

> The short-hand language of 'cooptation' . . . offers a most inadequate theoretical basis for understanding a situation in which we all, in one way or another, dimly feel that not only punctual and local countercultural forms of cultural resistance and guerrilla warfare, but also even overtly political interventions like those of the *Clash*, are all somehow secretly disarmed by a system of which they themselves might well be considered a part, since they can achieve no distance from it.[56]

I have quoted Jameson at length, not only because his essays provide the most detailed descriptions of the kinds of works that can be considered to constitute mainstream postmodernism but also to serve as a backdrop against which we can gauge other, nonmainstream contemporary expressions. On the basis of the latter, it seems to me that Jameson's conclusions are unacceptable. He has argued that every "Third World" text is necessarily a national allegory that is easily discerned.[57] How does this statement reflect on cultural texts from peripheral societies? Are they less interesting because their subtexts are not as unfathomable as those of "postmodern" texts? Is it true that the allegorized referent is more complex in "First World" contexts? If we accept Jameson's premise that late capitalism is the transcendental referent that infuses postmodern textuality and eludes cognition, and if peripheral societies are also part of the global network of transnational capital, why then are their texts not as complex? Or does he mean to imply that "Third World" readers are more astute in cognitive mapping? That is hardly the case, since Jameson has already argued that it is the cultural landscape of "First World" societies that makes the referent elusive. We can only infer, then, that Jameson looks either nostalgically or condescendingly at those writers and readers who go on about their interpretations as if the "Real" of late capitalism were a simple matter of national conflicts figured according to long-outdated cognitive maps from a postmodern perspective.

These objections to Jameson's diagnostic can be extended to almost all the theorists of modernity and postmodernity who privilege a Euro-North American model of cultural evolution: at some point bourgeois society attains an autonomous aesthetic sphere harboring unalienated experience that is eventually reified through institutionalized specialization; the avant-gardes recuperate the critical potential of the aesthetic but either capitulate under fascist and authoritarian regimes or are commodified in consumer societies; finally, rather than the collapse of the aesthetic, postmodernity is the implosion of the social and the political such that the aesthetic permeates all experience. The lifeworld has become simulation, a black hole.

This evolutionary model relegates non-Western societies to a perennial lag, even in those cases, as in Latin American *ninguneísmo*, in which subjects see themselves as copies. But they are copies — dissimulations and not simulations — of referents that have ceased to exist, much like the supernovas whose light we continue to see millions of years after they collapsed. Lihn, whose parody of the death of the subject I referred to above, sardonically casts Latin America as the mirror image of a black hole. Mainstream theories of postmodernity leave little room for an alternative.

If we dispense with this evolutionary model, however, and seek other premises, it is possible to construe a positive account of Latin American cultural practices that does not lapse into knee-jerk affirmations of authenticity or despairing laments over an ersatz ontology. A new generation of cultural critics has put forth such concepts as "transculturation,"[58] "cultural rearticulation,"[59] and "cultural reconversion"[60] to account for the ways in which the diverse groups that constitute Latin America negotiate their cultural capital.

The Rearticulation of Tradition

In contrast to Paz, who understood modernity in relation to the "tradición de ruptura y ruptura de la tradición," the new Latin American cultural critics emphasize how groups *recycle* their traditions in national and international markets. Theirs is no longer a nostalgic aspiration for a return to unalienated modes of life. By focusing on consumption and other means of cultural mediation, they are in a better position — vis-à-vis nationalist ideologues — to gauge how and to what extent the diverse groups of Latin America's cultural heterogeneity interact with one another and what the prospects are for subaltern groups to gain a greater participation in the distribution of goods and services. Increased restructuring of the economy and of state administration by neoconservatives (facilitated by international capital's imposition of austerity programs) has certainly made it more difficult to achieve an egalitarian distribution of wealth. Nevertheless, restructuring has created new possibilities for interaction and maneuver, as traditional cultures are faced with "segmented and differentiated participation in the global market . . . according to local codes of reception."[61]

The result of restructuring and the responses and propositions in relation to it are

something similar to what certain representatives of postmodernism claim: the decentering and deconstruction of western culture as it is depicted in primers; of its rationality, key institutions and cognitive habits and styles, which we are led to believe are imposed uniformly. [Cultural heterogeneity resembles] the implosion of consumed, produced, and reproduced meanings and the concomitant destructuring of collective representations, the problems in and desire for identity, a confusion of temporal demarcations, paralysis of the creative imagination, the loss of utopias, the atomization of local memory, the obsolescence of traditions.[62]

It *resembles* these "First World" cultural phenomena but only superficially. Not only, as explained above, are the causes different, the ways in which different localities respond to the conditions imposed by transnational capitalism are also different: for example, the hyperinflationary situation in Latin American countries is not the same as the hyperinflationary circulation of signs — the "obscene obesity of information" — which Baudrillard sees as the culture of the United States.[63]

Hyperinflation in Latin America, on the contrary, is the result not of consumerism but of external debt, speculation, narcotraffic, and, most important for the point being made, the struggle for consumption that informal economies represent. Jameson is, therefore, wrong to attribute "postmodern cognitive mappings" only to "First World" cultural production. It is just that in Latin America the mappings are different; they correlate to different sets of conditions imposed by transnational capitalism.

According to García Canclini, consumption, understood as an "appropriation of products," should not be reduced to consumerism, passive reception, useless waste, and depoliticization or to habits targeted by market research. It is, rather, the terrain of struggle between classes and other group formations over the distribution of goods, and as such it also serves as the medium in which needs and other cultural categories, such as identity, are constituted. Consumption is a particularly apt space of cultural mediation in which hegemony can be challenged:

> We know that struggle by means of cultural mediations offers neither immediate nor spectacular results. But it is the only guarantee that we are not passing from the simulacrum of hegemony to the simulacrum of democracy — a way of avoiding the resurgence of a defeated hegemony in the complicitous habits that hegemony has installed in our ways of thinking and interacting. The political uncertainties of the cultural struggle seem preferable to a revolutionary epic that repudiates culture.[64]

García Canclini's research on the rearticulation within transnational capital of popular or folk traditions as a means to expand possibilities of consumption, in its narrow and wider senses, demonstrates that modernization does not require the elimination of economic and cultural forces that do not directly serve the growth of capitalism so long as these forces "cohere into a significant sector, which satisfies its needs or those of a balanced reproduction of the system."[65] Consequently, modernity does not have to be theorized in the traditional avant-gardist terms of a *tradición de ruptura*. Rather than a *still* unfinished project, as Habermas understands it, modernity in Latin America is a series of necessarily unfinished projects. In the case of Brazil, for example, Renato Ortiz finds no break:

> The *ruptura* never occurred as it did in European countries because the idea that dominated our imaginary was always connected to the need to construct a modern Brazilian nation.[66]

In Latin America, in effect, the kind of institutionalization that guaranteed the autonomy of the three value spheres did not take place in any rigorous fashion. Knowledge, politics, and aesthetics, above all, continually cross-fertilize each other. Thus, Brazilian avant-gardes — in contrast to the European avant-gardes, which, according to Peter Bürger, sought to reintegrate art and the "praxis of life" by dismantling institutionalization — were not so much a break with the (indigenous, Afro-Brazilian and Luso-colonial) past as a rearticulation of it in their attempts to establish a national culture. Mário de Andrade, one of the leaders of *Modernismo* in the 1920s, confessed that this movement "anticipated and prepared the way for the creation of a new state of national being," alluding to Getúlio Vargas's Estado Novo, which centralized the economy and all state apparatuses under one directorate.[67]

Paradoxically, modernity in Latin America is more a question of establishing new relationships with tradition than of surpassing it. Among the many ways in which this can be done, cultural critics have emphasized the role of pastiche, that *appropriative* form of stylization that neither rejects nor celebrates the past but, in the words of Silviano Santiago, "assumes it."[68] In a very insightful essay, Santiago not only explains how the Brazilian avant-garde can be rethought in relation to tradition; he even suggests that the avant-garde may itself be rearticulated for present cultural circumstances, although it will be necessary to deemphasize the transgressive poetics of *ruptura* that does not hold in many Latin American cases. Santiago illustrates his premise with the *Modernistas'* interest in recuperating Brazil's baroque colonial heritage:

> The most interesting case . . . of the relationship of Modernismo to tradition, which also permits us to disengage Modernismo from any neoconservative appropriations, is the trip taken by Mário and Oswald de Andrade and Blaise Cendrars to Minas Gerais in 1924. Those poets were totally steeped in futurist principles, they had an absolute belief in the civilization of machines and progress. But suddenly they decided to travel in search of colonial Brazil. There they encountered our national history and — more important to the point we're making — the primitivism of Minas's eighteenth-century baroque.[69]

Santiago goes on to explain that this rearticulation and recuperation of tradition is achieved by means of *supplementation*, the process by which the excluded is reincorporated into the status quo. Santiago, however, uses Derrida's notion — as laid out in *Of Grammatology* — somewhat against the grain. Derrida invokes the term according to the rhetoric of marginality such that whatever is excluded is a *threat* to the status quo. Metaphors of violence and danger abound in his exposition of it.[70] It is because modernity continued to privilege tradition — as it did Nature — that innovation could be construed as a supplement. The radical avant-gardes exposed modernity's ideological strategies of "naturalization" and inverted the paradigm, transforming innovation — *ruptura* — into a continually self-supplementing process. By doing this, however, they obviated any role for tradition. Subsequently, poststructuralists fetishized the inversion as *écriture* (Derrida), *le sémiotique* (Kristeva), and *jouissance* (Barthes); they attempted to exorcise the straw man of modernity — and its demon, Cartesian subjectivity — and mine the foundational lack left in its place. By doing so, however, they lapsed into a negative theology that revered the signifier hovering over the abyss of absence.

Many Latin American writers and critics — especially Paz, Sarduy, Rodríguez Monegal, and Haroldo de Campos — were seduced into thinking they could more easily occupy this privileged place, since Latin American culture had always been defined as a form of lack (by elite intellectuals). This is the point of Lihn's parody of *ninguneísmo*, quoted above. But this rhetoric of marginality can also be quite hubristic; Latin American intellectuals declare themselves superior because from their marginal place they cannibalize everything, suck all values into the black hole. In an essay in which he puts his own literary movement — *concretismo* — at the pinnacle of this "anthropophagic rationality," Haroldo de Campos proclaims that

> writers of a supposedly peripheral literature suddenly appropriated the entirety of the code, claiming it as their own patrimony, like a hollow prize awaiting a new historical subject. They thus restored a more universal and radical function to poetics. The Brazilian [concrete poetry movement] was its condition of possibility.[71]

A rethinking of the avant-garde, however, makes it possible to rearticulate tradition as a supplement that does not subordinate the other elements of the articulation. According to Santiago:

> Pastiche does not reject the past in a gesture of mockery, contempt, or irony. Pastiche accepts the past as it is and the work of art is nothing but a supplement. . . . The supplement is something you add to something already complete. I would not say that pastiche is reverence toward the past, but I would say that it assumes [*endossa*] the past, contrary to parody, which always ridicules it.[72]

Santiago, in fact, envisions cultural articulations that include avant-garde practices that can take their place next to elements from other traditions.

Universalizing modes of democratization have not been the most successful in Latin America. This is due not only to their encounter with economic underdevelopment or authoritarian and charismatic forms of state power. It is also due, in great part, to the tendency to understand democratization in terms of modernization, that is, the eradication of traditions whose "enchanted" or "auratic" modes of life may prove inimical to coexistence with others or to the projects of elites and their allies. The problem is, of course, that modernization has severely handicapped many groups who hold to these traditions. And the problems have only gotten worse with the turn to the right under the aegis of neoconservatism. Facile proclamations of Latin America's cannibalizing subversiveness at best mask the problem. Marginality is not transformed willy-nilly into a share of the common wealth. Habermas is certainly correct when he contends that neoconservative and "anarchistic" postmoderns are not at odds but, rather, serve the same purpose. To celebrate "parasitism" (whose Latin American correlate is the problem of informal economies) or the hyperreal (which in Latin America is wrought by the hyperinflationary effects of the external debt and narcotraffic) is like cheerleading on the sidelines as neoconservatives sell out the citizenry.

The rearticulation of the traditions of Latin America's cultural heterogeneity, on the other hand, provides one of the most significant ways for furthering democratization. Liberation theology and the Christian base communities, with their emphasis on *conscientización* achieved through rewriting the Gospels in light of everyday experiences, have paved the way for other social movements to seek recognition and enfranchisement. In the past, the representation of the interests of the array of groups that make up this cultural heterogeneity was either absent from the public sphere or projected by elites who sought to maintain their own hegemony. Pastiche, as Santiago defines it, is the literary counterpart of those rearticulatory practices that seek to assume alternative traditions within modernity. These involve the struggles for interpretive power on the part of peasants, women, and ethnic, racial, and religious groups. For interpretive power enables them to justify their needs and on that basis demand satisfaction. The criteria, forms, and terms of these rearticulatory practices are both old and new: old because they draw from their traditions; new because they no longer operate solely within the framework of class or nation. Jameson could not be more wrong with respect to the significance of Latin American cultural practices. They are not "national allegories." They are not allegories at all. They are, on the contrary, practices for or against democratization, for or against the recognition, representation, and enfranchisement of all as citizens.

NOTES

1. See José Joaquín Brunner, "Notas sobre la modernidad y lo postmoderno en la cultura latinoamericana," *David y Goliat*, 17 (Sept. 1987); Nelly Richard, "Postmodernism and Periphery," *Third Text*, 2 (Winter 1987/88); José Miguel Wisnik, "The Interpretation of Postmodernism in the Aesthetics of Brazilian Cultural Productions," conference paper delivered at "The Debate on Postmodernism in Latin America: Brazil, Mexico and Peru," University of Texas, Austin (April 29-30, 1988); Ticio Escobar, "Postmodernismo/precapitalismo," *Casa de las Américas*, 168 (1988): 13-19.

2. Christine Buci-Glucksmann, *La raison baroque: De Baudelaire à Benjamin* (Paris: Galilée, 1984) and *La folie du voir: De l'esthétique baroque* (Paris: Galilée, 1986).

3 See, e.g., Severo Sarduy, "El barroco y el neobarroco," in *América Latina en su literatura*, ed. César Fernández Moreno (México: Siglo XXI, 1972), *Barroco* (Buenos Aires: Sudamericana, 1974), and *La simulación* (Caracas: Monte Avila, 1982).

4. See Henry Louis Gates, Jr., *The Signifying Monkey: A Theory of African-American Literary Criticism* (New York: Oxford University Press, 1988); Guillermo Gómez-Peña, "Documented/Undocumented," in *Multi-Cultural Literacy*, ed. Rick Simonson and Scott Walker (St. Paul, Minn.: Graywolf Press, 1988); Cornel West, "Postmodernism and Black America," in *Remaking History*, ed. Barbara Kruger and Phil Mariani (Seattle: Bay Press: Dia Art Foundation Discussions in Contemporary Culture, no. 4, 1989): 131-48.

5. See Antonio Cornejo-Polar, "Indigenist and Heterogeneous Literatures: Their Dual Sociocultural Status," trans. Susan Casal-Sánchez, *Latin American Perspectives*, 16 (Spring 1989), 12-28.

6. Hernando de Soto, *The Other Path: The Invisible Revolution in the Third World* (London: Tauris, 1989).

7. Samuel Doria Medina, *La economía informal en Bolivia* (La Paz, 1986). I quote from the English translation: Naomi Robbins, "Bolivia's Informal Economy," (Master's thesis, CUNY, 1990), 28.

8. Ibid., 48 and 72.

9. Ibid., 83-85.

10. Ibid., 29.

11. Ibid., 37.

12. Ibid., 40; emphasis added.

13. Hugo Achugar has written an excellent study of Uruguayan *Modernismo* precisely by taking into account the "aesthetico-ideological responses and propositions" by different classes and class sectors to late nineteenth- and early twentieth-century modernization. Achugar explains that his usage of "response/proposition" bears a "distant relation to the notion of 'semantic gesture' put forth by the Prague School. . . . It attempts to capture the interaction of literary product and society, how the latter

conditions signic structure. Thus, a book of poems, a novel, or a painting [is] considered in its historical concreteness, both ideologically and as the double movement of response to a given historical situation and proposition of a (utopian) future. All of this, of course, is realized or conveyed aesthetically." See Hugo Achugar, *Poesía y sociedad (Uruguay 1880-1911)* (Montevideo: Arca, 1985), 22, note 2.

14. See also Octavio Paz, "El romanticismo y la poesía contemporánea," *Vuelta,* 11 (June 1987). In the same issue of *Vuelta,* Paz introduces a special section entitled "¿Postmodernidad?" that includes essays by Jean Clair and Cornelius Castoriadis.

15. Octavio Paz, *The Labyrinth of Solitude* (México: Fondo de Cultura Económica, 1959), 152.

16. Octavio Paz, "El ocaso de las vanguardias," in *Los hijos del limo* (Barcelona: Seix Barral, 1974), 201.

17. Martin Heidegger, "The Age of the World Picture," in *The Question Concerning Technology and Other Essays,* trans. William Lovitt (New York: Garland, 1977), 135 and 154.

18. Martin Heidegger, "... Poetically Man Dwells ... ," in *Poetry, Language, Thought,* trans. Albert Hofstadter (New York: Harper & Row, 1975), 222.

19. See Jürgen Habermas, *The Philosophical Discourse of Modernity* (Cambridge, Mass.: MIT Press, 1987).

20. Paz, "El romanticismo y la poesía contemporánea," 27.

21. Elsewhere I have offered a critique of the adoption by elites of a rhetoric of marginality. See "Marginality and the Ethics of Survival," in *Universal Abandon? The Politics of Postmodernism,* ed. Andrew Ross (Minneapolis: University of Minnesota Press, 1988).

22. Richard, "Postmodernism and Periphery," 10.

23. Escobar, "Postmodernismo/precapitalismo," 15.

24. Linda Hutcheon, *The Politics of Postmodernism* (New York: Routledge, 1989), 3 and 8. See also Hutcheon, *A Poetics of Postmodernism: History, Theory, Fiction* (New York: Routledge, 1988).

25. I do not agree with Fredric Jameson's characterization of postmodern culture as those local tactics and practices of "first world" elites that, he contends, come to embody symbolically the global logic of the system. According to Jameson, the cultural production of a particular class fraction (call it "new petty bourgeoisie," "professional-managerial," "baby boom," or "yuppy") of "First World" elites "articulate[s] the world in the most useful way functionally, or in ways that can be functionally reappropriated." Fredric Jameson, "Marxism and Postmodernism," *New Left Review,* 176 (July-Aug. 1989), 41.

Jameson seems to be making a category error here. Transnational capital may or may not have a global logic, but it does not translate *tout court* into the cultural practices of a given group. That would be tantamount to declaring a particular group the chosen people of the transcendent Being (whether God or Capital). If, on the other hand, diverse social formations, and the groups that comprise them, manage — by response and proposition — the forms that the conditions of postmodernity take in their localities, then there are as many different cultures of postmodernity as there are social formations and particular struggles for hegemony within them.

26. Ernesto Laclau and Chantal Mouffe, *Hegemony and Socialist Strategy: Towards a Radical Democratic Politics* (London: Verso, 1985), 191-92. See also Ernesto Laclau, "The Politics and Limits of Modernity," trans. George Yúdice, in *Universal Abandon?* ed. Ross.

27. Laclau and Mouffe, *Hegemony*, 188.

28. Bernardo Subercaseaux, "La apropiación cultural en el pensamiento latino-americano," *Mundo*, 1 (Summer 1987).

29. Enrique Lihn, *El arte de la palabra* (Barcelona: Pomaire, 1980), 82. I translated into English and published an excerpt of this novel in *Review*, 29 (May/Aug. 1981), 55-61. Wisnik, "Interpretation of Postmodernism," also alludes to the self-erasure of Latin American postmodernists who "consume imported stereotypes," especially current stereotypes concerning simulation. See also Richard, "Postmodernism and Periphery," 7.

30. Subercaseaux, "La apropiación cultural," 34-35.

31. Roberto Schwarz, "Nacional por substracción," *Punto de vista*, 9 (Nov. 1986), 22. This essay was published in English translation by Linda Briggs in *New Left Review*, 167 (Jan.-Feb. 1988), 77-90.

32. Silverio Muñoz, *José María Argüedas y El mito de la salvación por la cultura* (Minneapolis: Instituto para Estudios de Ideologias y Literatura, 1980).

33. José María Arguedas, *El zorro de arriba y el zorro de abajo* (Buenos Aires: Losada, 1971).

34. Angel Rama elaborates on the phenomenon of "transculturation" in *Transculturación narrativa en América Latina* (México: Siglo XXI, 1982).

35. Ibid., 202-3.

36. Carlos Fuentes, *La nueva novela hispanoamericana* (México: Joaquín Mortiz, 1969), 98.

37. See William Rowe, "Liberalism and Authority: The Case of Mario Vargas Llosa," chapter 3, this volume.

38. See Jean Franco, "Narrador, autor, superestrella: la narrativa latinoamericana en la época de cultura de masas," *Revista Iberoamericana*, 47 (1981), 129-48.

39. Terry Eagleton, *The Ideology of the Aesthetic* (Oxford: Basil Blackwell, 1990), 415.

40. Paz, *Los hijos del limo* and "El romanticismo y la poesía contemporánea."

41. Jürgen Habermas, *The Theory of Communicative Action*. Vol. 2: *Lifeworld and System: A Critique of Functionalist Reason* (Boston: Beacon Press, 1987), especially "The Uncoupling of System and Lifeworld," 153-97.

The classic account of the rationalization of Western culture is Max Weber, *The Protestant Ethic and the Spirit of Capitalism* (New York: Scribner's, 1958). It should be pointed out that Weber grounds this rationalization solely in the West. He concedes that other cultures evince different modes of rationalization, but they do not produce the kind of rational moral conduct (conditioned by the Protestant ethic) that leads to the development of capitalism (25-26). See also Wolfgang Schluchter, *The Rise of Western Rationalism: Max Weber's Developmental History* (Berkeley: University of California Press, 1981), 19.

42. Eagleton, *Ideology of the Aesthetic*, 16.

43. Peter Bürger, *Theory of the Avant-Garde* (Minneapolis: University of Minnesota Press, 1984), 49.

44. I have attempted such a rethinking in "Repensando a vanguárdia desde a periferia," forthcoming in the working papers series (*Papéis avulsos*) of the Centro Interdisciplinar de Estudos Contemporâneos (Rio de Janeiro, 1991).

45. Paz, "El romanticismo y la poesía contemporánea," 26.

46. Ibid.

47. Jean-François Lyotard, *La postmodernidad (explicada a los niños)* (Barcelona: Gedisa, 1987), back cover.

48. Ibid., 31.

49. Fredric Jameson, "Postmodernism, or the Logic of Late Capitalism," *New Left Review*, 146 (July-Aug. 1984), 79.

50. Ibid., 79-80; emphasis added.

51. Ibid., 77.

52. Ibid., 80.

53. Among the simulacra and fragments of the postmodern, Jameson lists the following: (1) the rise of aesthetic populism, tolerant of mass culture and kitsch; (2) the destruction of the expression of Being (represented by Van Gogh's *Peasant Shoes*), replaced by simulations (as in Warhol's *Diamond Dust Shoes*; (3) the waning of affect, with its corresponding reference to human depth (e.g., Freud's drives), and the emergence of *jouissance*, the euphoric experience of the death of the subject (Lacan); (4) the substitution of parody (transgression) by pastiche (conformity); (5) the replacement of History by historicism, the *mise en spectacle* of all past styles; (6) the *mode rétro* minus any feeling of nostalgia (e.g., *The Big Chill*); (7) the loss of a radical past; (8) social narcissism and schizophrenia resulting from deoedipalization (Lasch); (9) the transformation of work and subject into *textuality* constituted by differences; (10) hysterical or camp sublime, no longer resulting from the incapacity to figure or represent incommensurability but from the terror of simulated existence; (11) the apotheosis of the machinism of the third, or cybernetic, industrial revolution; (12) the abolition of critical distance; and (13) the loss of coordinates in urban space.

54. Jameson, "Postmodernism," 90. Jameson is quoting Althusser here.

55. Ibid., 87.

56. Ibid.

57. See Jameson, "Third World Literature in the Era of Multinational Capitalism," *Social Text*, 15 (Fall 1986), 69, 79-80. See also the eloquent critique by Aijaz Ahmad, "Jameson's Rhetoric of Otherness and the 'National Allegory,'" *Social Text*, 17 (Fall 1987), 3-25.

58. See Rama, *Transculturación narrativa en América Latina*.

59. José Joaquín Brunner, "Notas sobre la modernidad y lo postmoderno en la cultura latinoamericana."

60. Néstor García Canclini, *Culturas híbridas: Estrategias para entrar y salir de la modernidad* (México: Grijalbo, 1990). See also García Canclini, "Cultural Reconversion," chapter 2, this volume.

61. Brunner, "Notas sobre la modernidad y lo postmoderno en la cultura latinoamericana," 33.

62. Ibid., 34.

63. Jean Baudrillard, *Fatal Strategies*, trans. Philip Beitchman (New York: Semiotext(e)/Pluto, 1990).

64. Néstor García Canclini, "Culture and Power: The State of Research," *Media, Culture and Society*, 10 (1988), 495.

65. Ibid., 485.

66. Renato Ortiz, *A Moderna Tradição Brasileira. Cultura Brasileira e Indústria Cultural* (São Paulo: Brasiliense, 1988), 209.

67. Mário de Andrade, "O Movimento Modernista," in *Aspectos da Literatura Brasileira* (São Paulo, n.d.).

68. Silviano Santiago, "Permanência do discurso da tradição no modernismo," in

Gerd Bornheim et al., *Cultura Brasileira: Tradição/Contradição* (Rio de Janeiro: Jorge Zahar/Funarte, 1987), 136.

69. Ibid., 124.

70. Jacques Derrida, *Of Grammatology*, intro. and trans. Gayatri Chakravorty Spivak (Baltimore: Johns Hopkins University Press, 1976).

71. Haroldo de Campos, "Da razão antropofágica: A Europa sob o signo da devoração," *Colóquio Letras*, 62 (June 1981), 19.

72. Ibid., 136.

Cultural Reconversion
Néstor García Canclini
Translated by Holly Staver

How can we speak of a modern city, which is often neither modern nor a city? How do we study the crafty way it reorganizes everything that enters and tries to contain that disorder? The social sciences contribute their own abundance and dispersion to this difficulty. The anthropologist arrives on foot, the sociologist by car on the main highway, and the media analyst by plane. Each observes whatever he or she can and constructs a different and therefore partial vision. There is a fourth perspective, the historian's, which is acquired not by entering but by leaving the city, moving from its oldest center to its contemporary outskirts. But the center of the present-day city is no longer located in the past.

The traditional humanities and social sciences identified repertoires that people had to master in order to count as cultured members of the modern world. On the other hand, anthropology and folklore reclaimed traditional knowledge and practices that had been devalued by the Enlightenment and reconstituted the popular. Both traditionalists and modernizers wanted to construct pure objects of knowledge. The former imagined "authentic" national and popular cultures. In their studies and policies, they sought to preserve these cultures from industrialization, urbanization, and foreign influence. Modernizers conceived of art for art's sake, knowledge for the sake of knowledge, without regard for territorial boundaries, and they entrusted their fantasies of progress to autonomous experimentation and innovation.

Cultural products and institutions were divided into two camps. Artworks went to museums of modern art and to biennial exhibitions;

crafts went to traditional museums and popular fairs. This bifurcation was both the raison d'être and the result of the academic disciplines that studied these works: art history and aesthetics concerned themselves with high art, anthropology, and folklore with popular art. When electronic media came on the scene, both sides thought their objects of study would be destroyed since culture was conceived by them solely within the purview of their respective disciplines.

With *desarrollismo* (the ideology of progress through industrial development) this ingenuous way of separating tradition from modernity no longer worked. Never before had so many millions of books been produced, nor so many thousands of copies of each edition published. Toward the end of 1986, before the film appeared, *The Name of the Rose* had sold five million copies in twenty-five languages. The books of García Márquez and Vargas Llosa reach a greater mass audience than the films on which those writers have collaborated. Mass media do not replace schools because they do not offer the kind of information and work qualifications that only formal education continues to provide. Higher education has grown exponentially over the last few decades.

There have never been so many artisans and popular musicians, nor such diffusion of folklore. These products continue to have both traditional functions (they provide work and supplementary income to indigenous groups and *campesinos*) and new functions (they attract tourists and provide signs of symbolic differentiation in urban consumption) that industrially produced goods cannot fulfill.

As recent changes in the symbolic market have made clearer, modernization is not a matter of replacing traditional high and popular forms but of reformulating their function and meaning. Communication between writers, publishers, critics, and readers is being reshaped by increased sales of literature in supermarkets and newsstands. Schools and universities are finding their traditional methods of transmitting knowledge inadequate because of the entry of the masses into their classrooms and the use of new technologies in the production and dissemination of knowledge. Crafts are growing in number and changing in purpose as they are distributed farther away from the groups that produce them, in urban markets and tourist centers.

High, popular, and mass are no longer to be found in their familiar places. The traditional and the modern are mixed together all the time, even in cities where the disposition of neighborhoods and institutions has been governed by criteria of social strata. Artisans sell weavings and native pottery in front of art museums. Painters who might once have been classified as elite incorporate quotes from comic strips in their works, or work in industrial design. Designers of commercials borrow images from popular artisans and painters of high art. In London and New York, rock music is being transformed by the melodic structures of African, Asian, and Latin American music. In these new settings, our cultural capital is reconverted. Through cultural exchange, we are making the most of what we have and are trying to say something more or different.

Reconversion

Economic reconversion and other neoconservative reforms have had powerful repercussions on cultural policies, and these are even greater in the countries of the periphery. These countries are in the process of decreasing state investment in education, science, and art: salaries have fallen and unemployment has increased, widening the scientific and cultural gap between the metropolis and dependent societies. But they have also aggravated a long-standing cultural crisis. For this reason the recent decrease in the production and consumption of the classical culture of elites (film, theater, magazines) and of popular sectors (higher education, spectacles) should not be attributed only to the economic recession of the 1980s. The exhaustion of certain cultural resources and relationships becomes more intelligible when seen as part of a global restructuring of society and politics.

Not all traditions or all forms of modernization are in crisis. Old and new symbolic products still offer attractive investment opportunities. At the same time, there is the growth of electronic cultures and also of museums and their publics; artisans and popular singers prosper and expand their audience. Instead of the death of traditional cultural forms, we now discover that tradition is in transition, and articulated to modern processes. Reconversion prolongs their existence.

Briefly, to reconvert cultural capital means to transfer symbolic patrimony from one site to another in order to conserve it, increase its yield, and better the position of those who practice it. These strategies are basic to many modern institutions. One of the examples described in this study is that of the national museums of anthropology—like the one in Mexico, which concentrates the traditional assets of ethnic groups dispersed throughout its territory in a central building where their value is increased in the form of modern national patrimony. Something similar occurs with complex technologies—television and video—that synthesize the visual, literary, and auditory capital developed by a number of disciplines, reinvesting them in a new system of symbolic production and communication.

Under these circumstances certain groups whose knowledges become obsolete or devalued are able to recycle their skills by transferring them to another area. For example, some artists abandon obsolete avant-garde movements in favor of the postmodern. Neoartisans may use their skill in weaving and woodwork in modern decoration.

But cultural reconversions, in addition to being strategies for social mobility, or for following the movement from the traditional to the modern, are hybrid transformations generated by the horizontal coexistence of a number of symbolic systems. This is characteristic of any complex society. It enables the conservatory musician to use knowledge of classical or contemporary harmony to produce erudite experiments in rock, jazz, or salsa. It allows a painter to use what she or he has learned not just from the history of painting, but also from graphic design, cinema, and video clips. In Latin American countries, where numerous traditions coexist with varying degrees of modernity, and where sociocultural heterogeneity presents a multiplicity of simultaneous patrimonies, this process of interchange and reutilization is even more intense. High, popular, and mass art nourish each other reciprocally.

Reconversion thus challenges the assumption that cultural identity is based on a patrimony, and that this patrimony is constituted by the occupation of a territory and by collections of works and monuments. It further undermines the belief that the secularization of cultural spheres—their autonomy and autonomous development—contributes to the expansion, experimental innovation, and democratization of societies. It questions the notion that popular sectors achieve emancipation and are integrated into modernity by means of the socialization of hegemonic cultural assets through education and mass dissemination. Finally, reconversion casts into doubt the idea that localistic or nationalistic fundamentalisms can be overcome by new global technologies of communication that also encourage cultural creativity.

What is now happening, however, is entirely different. Urbanization and industrialization not only generate new cultural forms but contribute to the reorganization of all symbolic processes. The fact that 60 to 70 percent of the population is now concentrated in big cities and is connected to national and transnational networks means that the contents, practices, and rites of the past — including those of migrant *campesinos* — are reordered according to a different logic. Radio, TV, and video generate specific formats and messages, but above all they imply the passage from direct, microsocial interactions to the distant consumption of serially produced goods within a centralized system.

The basic processes, organization, and agents of cultural production and dissemination are changing. Simpler crafts and industry are being displaced by advanced technologies; the direct producers (artisans, artists, designers) are no longer the principal creators and administrators of the processes of social signification. The role of traditional promoters of cultural activity (states, the agricultural sector of the oligarchy, and social movements) has diminished, while that of organisms linked to the expanding modes of capitalist development (financial institutions, cultural foundations, and chains of art galleries related to finance capital or high-tech industries) is on the rise.

A corresponding modification is taking place in the constitution of political culture and the valuation of the aesthetic. Traditional opinion shapers (political, union, and community organization leaders) and those who determine artistic value (artisans, artists, critics, teachers) are relinquishing some of their functions to those who control the new structure of the symbolic market: information networks, *marchands*, entrepreneurial-minded galleries and publishing houses, radio and television producers, and video and record producers. Local forms of opinion and taste that preserve any differences are incorporated into the national and transnational market. Consequently, many spaces that have represented regional cultures (theaters, magazines, cultural centers) are becoming attuned to transterritorial systems for the production and circulation of messages.

Contemporary hybrid cultures respond to an oblique organization of power and social differentiation. Big business competes with state cultural administration, artistic movements, and traditional entrepreneurs and sponsoring organizations (such as schools, churches, and amateur associations). Instead of eliminating them, commercial culture tends to absorb these agents. Similar effects can be observed in habits of audience perception and reception. The mass media have been accused of homogenizing audiences, but, in fact, they encourage new techniques of segmentation by broadcasting diversified information and programs that appeal to varied consumers. The old distinction between high and popular coexists with other ways of dividing up the social spectrum: children, youth, adults; national differences reconfigured through transnational interaction; and newly legitimized sexual identities. To study inequalities and differences today is not simply to see mechanisms of exclusion and opposition; it is also necessary to identify the processes that unequally articulate social positions, cognitive systems, and the tastes of diverse sectors.

The dense web of cultural and economic decisions leads to asymmetries between producers and consumers and between diverse publics. But these inequalities are almost never imposed from the top down, as is assumed by those who establish Manichaean oppositions between dominating and dominated classes, or between central and peripheral countries. The survival of popular culture is often attributed to simple resistance based on tradition. A more nuanced understanding of the process by which popular culture negotiates its position leads to a more decentered and complex vision of how hegemony is allied to subalternity in the practices of power.

Strategies and Rituals of Modernization

Where should we reinvest our traditional cultures in the present reorganization of the symbolic marketplace? To what extent do new technologies, and the current constitution of what is public and what is private, outdate or reorder the learning and tastes of the popular and elite classes? What reorganization of the teaching and dissemination of culture and of paradigms do these changes require in institutions that make cultural policy?

While traditional patrimony remains the responsibility of the state, the promotion of modern culture is increasingly the task of private enterprises and organizations. While governments understand their policy in terms of the protection and preservation of historical patrimony, innovative initiatives remain under the control of those who enjoy enough economic power to take financial risks. Both look for symbolic revenue in art. The state seeks legitimacy and consensus by appearing to represent national history; private enterprise hopes to gain profit and to construct by means of avant-garde culture a disinterested image of its economic expansion.

Innovation in the visual arts has for thirty years greatly depended on big businesses, because of their role as patrons and also because they are responsible for the mass dissemination of innovation through industrial and graphic design. The 1970s inaugurated a type of patronage different from any in the past. The industrial bourgeoisie modernized production and introduced new patterns of consumption. Foundations and centers dedicated to artistic experiment were intended to give the private sector a leading role in the reorganization of the cultural market. Some of these actions were promoted by transnational enterprises and reflected the aesthetic trends of the metropolis, especially the United States. Thus, Shifra Goldman, using North American sources, demonstrates how large consortia (Esso, Standard Oil, Shell, General Motors) allied with museums, reviews, artists, and North and Latin American critics to disseminate throughout the continent a formal, "depoliticized" kind of experimentation that replaced social realism.[1] Nevertheless, historical interpretations that put all the emphasis on the conspiratorial intentions and Machiavellian alliances of dominant groups impoverish the complexity and conflicts of modernity.

One aspect of this complexity was the introduction of new materials (acrylics, plastics, polyesters) and new processes of construction (electronic and lighting techniques, mass-produced works). This was not a simple imitation of the art of the metropolis, for those materials and technologies had already been incorporated into industrial production, and therefore into the everyday life and taste of Latin American countries. The same could be said of the new mass culture incorporated into the plastic arts: television monitors, fashion wear, and media celebrities.

The privatization and commercialization of art did not follow the same path in all countries. In Argentina the Instituto de Tella, the Fundación Matarazzo, and publications like *Primera Plana* rapidly created spaces for the circulation and valorization of experimental art. In Mexico the revolution created a different situation since art was sponsored by the postrevolutionary state. In the 1950s and 1960s, the conflict came to a head because of the stagnation of muralism and the technical quality of a group of new painters (Tamayo, Cuevas, Gironella, Vlady). These painters gained recognition in private galleries and cultural spaces, although the state also began to encourage them. For instance, in 1964 the Museo de Arte Moderno was founded; and in 1968 the Ruta de la Amistad, a series of eighteen geometric sculptures on the outskirts of Mexico City, was inaugurated during the Olympic Games. This group won prizes and was featured in government-sponsored shows both at home and abroad.

By the late 1980s, the situation in Mexico began to resemble that in most other Latin American countries. Cultural competition between private enterprise and the state became centralized in a huge entrepreneurial complex, Televisa, which has four national television channels as well as many subsidiaries in Mexico and the United States that act as producers and distributors for video, publishing, radio, and museums. The Centro Cultural Contemporáneo, formerly the Museo de Arte Contemporáneo Rufino Tamayo, was founded by Televisa. This diversified activity under a monopolistic administration structures relations between cultural markets. Something similar has occurred in Brazil with the Globo network, owner of television channels, radio stations, and soap operas for export, which created a new entrepreneurial attitude toward culture that changed relations between artists, technicians, producers, and their respective publics. The fact that these enterprises also own large exhibition and advertising spaces, as well as TV and radio networks and magazines and other institutions, allows them to program expensive and highly influential cultural activities. They thus control communication and critical response and, therefore, up to a point, the way in which diverse publics decode their messages.

The scope of contemporary private patronage can be grasped best perhaps by studying the Centro de Arte y Comunicación (CAYC) de Buenos Aires, practically a one-man institution headed by Jorge Glusberg. Glusberg, owner of Modulor, one of the largest electric lighting firms in Argentina, finances the activities of the center, brings together artists (Grupo de los 13, Grupo CAYC), and pays for their foreign exhibitions. Glusberg also covers the cost of catalogues, advertising, transportation of the works, and, when necessary, artistic materials. He has thus established a network of loyal connections among artists, architects, urban planners, and critics.

In addition, CAYC acts as an interdisciplinary center and brings together the art world and communications experts, semioticians, sociologists, technical experts, and politicians. This gives Glusberg great influence in different areas of cultural and scientific production and has allowed him to form ties with international institutions. For two decades he has organized annual exhibitions in Europe and the United States by Argentinean artists. He also organizes exhibitions of foreign artists and sponsors colloquia featuring prominent critics (such as Umberto Eco, Giulio Carlo Argán, and Pierre Restany). Glusberg is also active as a critic; he writes most of the catalogues, edits the art and architecture pages of the principal newspapers (*La Opinión* and *Clarín*), and contributes to international journal articles that publicize the work of the center. Glusberg also exercises control as president of the Asociación Argentina de Críticos de Arte and vice president of the Asociación Internacional de Críticos. The continuity of his influence, extending over four decades, is all the more surprising given Argentina's chronic political instability and the fact that only one government has completed its term during this period. This continuity, however, can also be seen as an extreme form of opportunism. In the 1960s and early 1970s, Glusberg both drew in conceptual artists and attempted to seek a broader public. When the military government came to power in 1976, they officially promoted his exhibitions. Glusberg's company, Modulor, received a contract to install stadium lighting for the World Soccer Cup in Argentina in 1978. In December 1983, a week after the dictatorship came to an end and the Alfonsín government took power, Glusberg organized "Democracy Week." Clearly, this patronage tends to dilute the critical force of art. We interviewed a number of Argentinean and Mexican plastic artists, asking them what an artist had to do to sell and gain recognition. In their answers they insistently referred to market factors and to the depression of the Latin American market in the 1980s, and they attributed the "instability" of art as much to a continual process of obsolescence as to the fluctuations of demand. Under these conditions, pressure is very strong to go along with the noncritical, playful style of the art of the end of this century, devoid of social concerns and aesthetic risk.

Reconversion and Popular Culture

Just as there is reconversion by hegemonic groups, popular classes also adapt their knowledge and traditional practices to the new circumstances. In most cases, the difficulties of survival reduce this adaptation to a pragmatic and commercial apprenticeship, although younger generations increasingly redraw the boundaries between traditional and modern, local and foreign, popular and elite. One has only to look at folk designs to see the impact of the imagery of contemporary art and the mass media.

When I first studied these changes I could only deplore the influence that the taste of urban consumers and tourists had on crafts. However, on a field trip eight years ago to a weaving pueblo in Teotilán del Valle, I entered a shop in which a fifty-year-old man and his father were watching television and conversing in Zapotec. When I asked about the wall hangings with images from the work of Picasso, Klee, and Miró, the artisan told me that he began to weave the new designs in 1968 on the suggestion of a group of tourists who worked for the Museum of Modern Art in New York. He then took out an album of clippings of newspaper reviews and analyses, in English, of his exhibitions in California. In the half hour I spoke to him I saw him move comfortably from Zapotec to Spanish and English, from art to craft, from his ethnic culture to mass culture, and from practical knowledge of his craft to cosmopolitan criticism. I had to admit that my worry over the loss of tradition was not shared by this man who easily negotiated three cultural systems.

Deterritorialization

Migration today is not limited to writers, artists, and political exiles as in the past; it now includes people of all social strata and moves in many different directions. The new cultural flows set into motion by displacements of Latin Americans to the United States and Europe, from the less developed to the more prosperous countries of our own continent, and from poor regions to urban centers, can no longer be attributed to imperialist domination alone. According to the most conservative estimates, two million Argentines, Chileans, Brazilians, and Uruguayans emigrated for political or economic reasons during the 1970s.

It is fitting, then, that the most insightful reflections on deterritorialization should emerge from the busiest crossing point in the hemisphere: the border between Mexico and the United States. Although uprooted and unemployed peasants and Indians who left their lands seeking survival predominate, this area is also the scene of a new and powerful creativity. The 250 Spanish-language radio and television stations, the 1,500 periodicals in Spanish, and the great interest in Latin American literature and music in the United States are evidence of a vast "Hispanic" market of nearly thirty million (12 percent of the population; 38 percent in New Mexico, 25 percent in Texas, and 23 percent in California). Films like *Zoot Suit* and *La Bamba*, the music of Rubén Blades and Los Lobos, experimental theater like that of Luis Valdez, and visual artists who combine popular culture with modern and postmodern media all demonstrate an increasing integration into the North American "mainstream."[2]

Deterritorialization thus cuts across class lines, as Roger Rouse, for instance, has shown in his migration study of Aguililla, a small farming town in southwestern Michoacán that is connected to the rest of Mexico by a single dirt road. The main economic activities of this town are subsistence farming and cattle raising. However, emigration dating from the 1940s has provided another source of income: dollars from relatives in California, especially Redwood City, on the margins of an important center of microelectronics and postindustrial culture in Silicon Valley. The emigrants from Michoacán work there mainly in the service sector. Most spend brief periods in the United States; those who stay longer are in constant touch with their hometown. As a result, the two communities have become inextricably intertwined:

> By their constant back-and-forth migration and their increasing use of the telephone, Aguilillenses reinforce their cultural identity with people who live two thousand miles away as easily as with their next-door neighbors. The continual circulation of people, money, commodities, and information, as well as the intermingling of the two localities, leads us to understand them as a single community dispersed in several places.[3]

These "intertwined economies, intersecting social systems, and fragmented personalities" pose a challenge to two conventional categories of social theory. The first, the idea of community, refers to isolated peasant villages and also to the abstraction of a cohesive national state, both of which are defined by a circumscribed territory. The premise is that the community functions as the organizing dynamic because of struggles among its members. The second category, the opposition between center and periphery, is the "abstract expression of an idealized imperial system" in which power is distributed in concentrically organized hierarchies that are concentrated at the center and diminishing toward the margins. Neither of these models is adequate today. According to Rouse, social space is more accurately mapped in terms of "circuits" and "borders."

A similar dislocation holds in the United States, where national capital is increasingly being displaced by foreign capital and the population is increasingly of mixed origin. In downtown Los Angeles, for example, 75 percent of the real estate belongs to foreign capital and 40 percent of the population of the greater metropolitan area is composed of Asians and Latinos. By the year 2010, this percentage is expected to rise to 60 percent.[4] According to Renato Rosaldo, the "Third World is imploding into the First", and

> the idea of an authentic culture as an internally cohesive and autonomous space is untenable except, perhaps, as a useful fiction or a revealing distortion.[5]

The mix of groups in California—immigrants from Mexico, Colombia, Norway, Russia, Italy, and the East Coast of the United States—once led Michel de Certeau to observe that "life in the United States is a constant crossing of borders."[6]

During my two research trips (1985 and 1988) to study intercultural conflicts on the Mexican side of the border, it often occurred to me that, along with New York, Tijuana is one of the major laboratories of postmodernity.[7] In 1950 it had no more than sixty thousand inhabitants; today it tops one million, with emigrants from every region of Mexico, especially Oaxaca, Puebla, Michoacán, and Mexico City. Large numbers cross the border from Tijuana into the United States, some every day and migrant workers during planting and harvest seasons. Even many of those who remain in Tijuana are also involved in commercial transactions between the two countries; they work either in *maquiladoras* (assembly plants) set up by U.S. companies on Mexican soil or in the tourist industry, serving the three or four million U.S. citizens who visit Tijuana every year.

Historically, Tijuana was known primarily as a casino town. With new factories, modern hotels, cultural centers, and access to international networks of information, Tijuana has become a city of contradictions, with both cosmopolitan and strong regional characteristics. Border markers may be rigidly fixed in place or torn down. Buildings may be evoked in different sites than where they are or were. Every day the city reinvents itself and offers new spectacles.

The artists and writers of the border experiment with these hybrid phenomena. Guillermo Gómez-Peña, editor of the Tijuana–San Diego bilingual journal *La Línea Quebrada/The Broken Line*, for example, emphasized the protean character of cultural identity in a recent radio interview:

REPORTER: If you love our country as much as you claim, why do you live in California?

GÓMEZ-PEÑA: I'm demexicanizing myself in order to mexiunderstand myself better.

REPORTER: And what do you consider yourself?

GÓMEZ-PEÑA: Post-Mexican, Pre-Chicano, Pan-Latino, Trans-Territorial, Art-American . . . It all depends on the day of the week or the project I'm working on.[8]

Many Tijuana journals have as their main project the redefinition of identity and culture based on the border experience. *La Línea Quebrada*, the most radical, is aimed at a generation who grew up "watching cowboy [*charro*] movies and science fiction flicks, listening to *cumbias* and the Moody Blues, building altars and making super-8 movies, reading *El Corno Emplumado* and *Artforum*." Falling into the "crack between two worlds," "not being what [they] might have been because [they] don't fit in, never going home because [they] don't know where it is," these border artists opt for all available identities. Gómez-Peña declares that

when I'm asked about my nationality or ethnic identity, I can't give a one word answer, since my identity now has multiple repertoires: I'm Mexican, but also Chicano and Latin American. On the border they call me *chilango* or *mexiquillo*; in Mexico City I'm a *pocho* or *norteño*; and in Europe I'm a *sudaca*. Anglos call me "Hispanic" or "Latino," and Germans have at times taken me for a Turk or an Italian.

Expressing feelings equally valid for a migrant worker and a young rocker, Gómez-Peña says "the deepest emotion of our generation is the loss we feel on picking up and leaving." But, in exchange, the experience has gained them "a more experimental, that is, a more tolerant and multifocal culture."[9]

Other Tijuana artists and writers challenge the euphemistic treatment of the contradictions and uprooting that they discern in the work of *La Línea Quebrada*. They reject the celebration of migrations caused by poverty in the homeland and in the United States. Native Tijuanos or those who have resided there for fifteen years or longer are outraged by the insolence of these artists' unconcerned parodies: "These are people who have just arrived and immediately tell us who we are, they dictate how we should discover ourselves."[10]

Those who celebrate the city for its openness and cosmopolitan character are also quick to fix its rituals and marks of identity and to distinguish themselves from passing tourists and anthropologists.

The editors of the Tijuana journal *Esquina Baja* stressed the importance of "creating a reading public" and having "a local journal of high quality design, layout, and so on in order to counter the centralizing tendency that prevails in our country. There is a prejudice against what we do in the provinces; if it doesn't make it in Mexico City it's not worth much, so they say."[11]

"Missionary" cultural activities promoted by the central government meet with objections. Baja Californians, for example, counter programs of national affirmation with their own expressions of Mexicanness. Given their experience at the margin of U.S. culture they are not as susceptible to its glamour as Mexicans of the more distant capital. The contact between traditional symbolic systems and international information networks, cultural industries, and migrant populations does not diminish the importance of identity, national sovereignty, and the unequal access to knowledge and cultural capital. Conflict does not disappear, as postmodern neoconservatives would have it, but becomes less polarized and intransigent. This more flexible cultural affirmation is less subject to fundamentalist backlash.

NOTES

1. Shifra M. Goldman, *Contemporary Mexican Painting in a Time of Change* (Austin and London: University of Texas, 1977), especially chapters 2 and 3.

2. Two historians of Chicano art, Shifra M. Goldman and Tomás Ybarra Frausto,

have documented this cultural production and offered highly original analyses. See the introductions to their book, *Arte Chicano: A Comprehensive Annotated Bibliography of Chicano Art, 1965-1981* (Berkeley: Chicano Studies Library Publications Unit—University of California, 1985). See also their articles in Ida Rodríguez Prampolini, ed., *A través de la frontera* (México: UNAM-CEESTEM, 1983).

3. Roger Rouse, "Mexicano, Chicano, Pocho: La migración mexicana y el espacio social del posmodernismo," *Página Uno* (literary supplement of *Unomasuno*), Dec. 31, 1988, 1-2.

4. Ibid., 2.

5. Renato Rosaldo, *Culture and Truth: The Remaking of Social Analysis* (Boston: Beacon Press, 1989), 217.

6. Michel de Certeau, "Californie, un théatre de passants," *Autrement*, 31 (April 1981), 10-18. It goes without saying that Michel de Certeau's conception of life as a constant border-crossing is not wholly adequate in the case of "second-class" United States citizens, such as blacks, Puerto Ricans, and Chicanos.

7. For the research report, see Néstor García Canclini and Patricia Safa, *Tijuana: La casa de toda la gente* (México: ENAH-UAM-Programa Cultural de la Frontera, 1989). The authors were assisted by Jennifer Metcalfe, Federico Rosas, and Ernesto Bermejillo.

8. [Many of the same topics discussed in this interview are covered, almost verbatim, in Guillermo Gómez-Peña, "Documented/Undocumented," in *Multi-Cultural Literacy: Opening the American Mind*, ed. Rick Simonson and Scott Walker (St. Paul, Minn.: Graywolf Press, 1988), 127-34.—Trans.]

9. Guillermo Gómez-Peña, "Wacha ese border, son," *La Jornada Semanal*, 162 (Oct. 25, 1987), 3-5. [See also "Documented/Undocumented," 129—Trans.]

10. Personal testimony recorded in García Canclini and Safa, *Tijuana*.

11. Ibid.

Liberalism and Authority:
The Case of Mario Vargas Llosa
William Rowe

When asked in a recent questionnaire for their response to Vargas Llosa's campaign against the nationalization of banks in Peru, Latin American intellectuals revealed in their answers a tacit assumption that the only positions available were attack or defense.[1] In this, they were colluding with Vargas Llosa's chosen mode: the style of his discourse is polemics, a style that includes an invitation of *ad hominem* argument in order to advance its claim to superior moral capital. A further difficulty in addressing the issues at stake is the need to disengage from a debate whose terms have become fossilized, preventing comprehension of changing historical circumstances. New historical contexts have become obscured by old political languages, as if the political map itself had not changed since the 1960s, only that some intellectuals had moved rightward. To construe Vargas Llosa's current position as an evolution or a betrayal, or to play him off against himself, is to remain uncritically inside the polemics.

The position for which he is now notorious began to emerge around the early 1970s, after the Padilla affair, though its sources— historical, intellectual, and literary—form a convergence of which Padilla is merely one symptom. One of the places where the characteristics of Vargas Llosa's polemical language begin to be revealed is in the series of articles by Angel Rama and Vargas Llosa on the subject of the latter's book about García Márquez, *History of a Deicide* (Historia de un deicidio).[2] Rama, in his review of the book, asserts that the notion of "demons" (*demonios*) — Vargas Llosa's term for creativity — carries an archaic and theological burden that individualizes the process of fiction writing and removes it from the sphere of social acts.[3] Vargas Llosa's reply is marked by a Christian vocabulary: Rama's "terrorism" is an act of "excommunion" and "anathema," not far from "the ideological blackmail of a new Inquisition that has arisen at the heart of the left."[4] The dogmatic judgmentalism attributed to the interlocutor also establishes the terms of engagement with him. In an article on Camus published in 1975, Vargas Llosa attributes "dogma," "idolatry," and "edict" to those with whom he disagrees;[5] beyond its immediate condemnatory function, this vocabulary produces a language that judges the opponent and in the same act justifies itself as a necessary response to the latter—from object of criticism, religious language shifts to become a mode of judgment. When the enemy is condemned by the same type of thinking he is condemned for, we are in Manichaean territory, where possessing the correct ideas matters more than truth, and attacker and attacked come to resemble each other. Thus, to take a further example, Vargas Llosa expresses his disagreement with Frantz Fanon and Che Guevara by calling them apocalyptic prophets who turned their ideas into a religion.[6] Although he would have us think of him as a pragmatist, the tone of these condemnations of "fanaticism" is far from pragmatic. Polemicism resorts to religious, judiciary, and political models, whose objective is not the search for truth but permission for the polemicist to tell "the truth in the form of his judgment and by virtue of the authority he has conferred on himself."[7]

The chief butt of Vargas Llosa's judgment has been those he labels "cheap intellectuals." Their "fanaticism," "narrow dogmatism," and "Marxist catechism" are instances of "revolutionary ideology made into a weapon for the purposes of excreting the enemy and stealing his positions, of satanizing those who got in the way and promoting one's pals."[8] The category can be expanded to include all who can be called "progressive intellectuals," disqualifying them from dialogue; the game of polemics, as Foucault suggests, consists not of recognizing the other person "as a subject having the right to speak, but of abolishing him, as interlocutor, from any possible dialogue."[9]

But merely to fault Vargas Llosa's language would be to reinforce the polemic. It is important to note that in the 1970s certain left-wing intellectuals, such as the Cuban Roberto Fernández Retamar, were equally involved in the deployment of religious language. The crucial point is to consider his political aims. He is not simply seeking to destroy his adversaries, nor does the hypothesis of some personal bad-temperedness explain his conduct.[10] The issues are the competition for public legitimacy and the difficulty of advocating liberalism in a society where the conditions for liberal debate do not pertain and both dependency and internal structural violence impede democratic political processes. This, of course, is a key problem for Latin American political discourse, from Bolívar to the present day, reaching its sharpest contradictions in the work of the nineteenth-century Argentinian writer Domingo F. Sarmiento. For Sarmiento, liberalism required the full incorporation of Argentina into the orbit of Western capitalism and a social modernization that could be achieved only by authoritarian social discipline. The aspect that has particularly engaged Vargas Llosa is liberal individualism, the project of a society based upon the idea of individual autonomy. In his first four novels (if we include *Los cachorros*), the failure of liberal individualism in Peru is charted mercilessly. He disengaged from this territory precisely when the Velasco military government carried out what were probably the most important social reforms of the century, reforms that made extensive modernization possible, which previous democratically elected governments had failed to achieve. It was precisely the failure of the Santiago Zavalas, representing the narrow base of the political class in Peru, that meant overdue reforms had to be implemented by a military regime. But after *Conversation in the Cathedral* (Conversación en la Cathedral), Vargas Llosa's concern shifted from exposing the structural weaknesses of Peruvian society to an increasing impatience with the lack of liberal democratic institutions and behavior, a lack that is blamed more and more upon immoral conduct attributed to the left rather than upon any failure of the ruling sectors of the society. His novels in the 1970s cease to explore the structural violence of Peruvian society and turn instead to the comedy of manners, where the failure of liberalism can be compensated by a superior consensual irony emanating from middle-class cultural values, inside which the frustrated individualism of the earlier novels can now (with the increased modernization of the society) function more confidently as an ideology.

The contradictory phenomenon of a polemically imposed liberalism can be traced back retrospectively to the early novels, which reveal the collisions between liberal forms and an undemocratic society.[11] *Time of the Hero* (La ciudad y los perros) is a democratic novel in that all parties are allowed to speak, appealing to whatever moral terms they choose. Nevertheless, a covert omniscience operates, generating pathos within a tragic pattern. The limitations of pity as a dramatic instrument can be verified, by contrast, in the work of the playwright Howard Barker, for whom pity is a barrier that must be passed through if knowledge is to be gained.[12] Knowledge, which the boys direly lack, merely brings about conformity to the hierarchies of violence and produces loss of innocence (the only resource for change), rather than inventing new possibilities of being. Innocence, the only cultural capital the middle class has thus far accumulated, adumbrates an imaginary historical space similar to that mythical original contract from which liberal individualist ideology derives society. *The Green House* (La casa verde) is, as critics have concurred, the most open of the earlier novels, the one with the greatest variety of voices and social experience, which are placed in unfinished conjunction within exuberant formal shifts that explore the plurality of Peruvian society and culture. *Conversation in the Cathedral*, likewise, is dialogical, to the extent that an analysis of power is produced through the exposure of all its voices. But there is also a nondialogical place, a situation of voyeuristic impotence, almost a fascination with the smell of power, that overrides differences and becomes the single place of the reader, particularly on second and subsequent readings, when the factor of suspense ceases to operate. Coming between the latter two novels, in more than a chronological sense, is *The Cubs* (Los cachorros), the most radical of the earlier works and an underrated text. The absence of dialogue in this text signals, critically and with great effectiveness, the castrating effect of social membership: the individual, divested of innocence, is decomposed into a rhetorical space constituted by the social marking of gender, the molding of sexual identity of machismo, and the training of the self in the values of family and work in a conformist urban environment. Here power operates as a direct penetration by a voice, the castrating voice by which the person must be invaded in order to become an individual, given that individualization is homogenization, in line with the needs of the liberal state.[13] The voice, moreover, is the vehicle for the introduction of modernity, here stripped of all liberal democratic alibis and aligned with the acculturative penetration of U.S. mass culture.

With *Captain Pantoja and the Special Service* (Pantaleón y las visitadoras) and *Aunt Julia and the Scriptwriter* (La tía Julia y el escribidor),

Vargas Llosa's literary writing shifted away from the passionate critique of social destructiveness. His moral seriousness now moves to the political essays, which advocate the primacy of ethics over politics. The place where this priority is most fully set out is the long essay on Albert Camus published in *Plural* in 1975, when Octavio Paz was the editor. Here he fully reverses his previous preference for Sartre over Camus (many of the essays of *Against All Odds* (Contra viento y marea) were first published under the title "Between Sartre and Camus"), and, with an attack on anything that can be placed within the category of "ideology" or "totalitarianism," renders definitive his break with previous advocacy of socialist values. Camus's moral critique of ideology as a form of permission is used to place together "all ideological dictatorships of left and right."[14] Along with the globalizing attitude that flattens out historical differences, the language tends to solidify into imperviousness, losing referential accuracy and analytical precision: "Modern experience shows that separating the fight against hunger, exploitation, and colonialism from the struggle for the freedom and dignity of the individual is as suicidal and absurd as separating the idea of liberty from genuine justice."[15] Here those emotional intensifiers ("suicidal," "absurd"), which had always been characteristic of Vargas Llosa's style, cease to be risks taken and instead reinforce with black-and-white polarization phrases that since Camus's time have lost their moral edge and become propagandistic.

The main limitation of Vargas Llosa's claim to a moral stance is that most of his nonfictional writing since 1975 has been politically pragmatic. The morality remains unelaborated as an ethics, a behavior, a relationship with beauty. Yet his own moral authority is an indispensable support of his political discourse, allowing him to write as both significant witness and authoritative judge of events, in El Salvador and Nicaragua, for instance. Instead of a morality capable of cutting across political positioning and formulas, a set of principles that derive their authority not from a person but from their power of conviction, he establishes his own person as the site of authority, in opposition, for instance, to allegedly unprincipled intellectuals — which is the mode of a politician, not an intellectual, and undermines that intellectual legitimacy he has sought to preserve. Do these *ad personam* arguments amount perhaps to a rhetoric of self as untainted, a transposition of the literary rhetoric of innocence now satirized in *Aunt Julia and the Scriptwriter*? Certainly, there is a connection between the establishment of moral authority and the strategy of the Uchuraccay report, with its shifting between the ethical and the pragmatic. The three-man commission, whose most important member was Vargas Llosa, was appointed by President Belaúnde in 1983 to investigate the murder of eight journalists in the highlands of Ayacucho. It places its conclusions upon the authority of three degrees of certainty: "total," "relative," and "dubious conviction."[16] No reference is made to the process of verification, nor is there any clarification of the epistemological status of this "conviction," criticized by the Peruvian historian Pablo Macera as a "quasi-theological" term.[17] That the subjectivity that informs the "conviction" might be permeated to a greater or lesser degree by the needs of the state is something that cannot be thought within the terms of the report.[18]

Vargas Llosa uses Camus's "morality of limits" to legitimate a two-tier strategy, where the appeal to a morality above politics is combined with pragmatic accommodation. This, of course, is very different from the main discourse of the social sciences in Latin America, characterized by the demand for structural change, which by the 1970s had gained a major purchase on the political process. He places social scientists under global censure, alleging their uncreative repetition of Marxist clichés and opportunistic conduct. Such total disqualifications of opponents are a feature of the strategy of ethical privilege, which is no doubt also sanctioned by the imperative to clear a liberal space. The latter is exemplified by the relativizing of ideas of both the left and the right, for the sake of a middle way. The result, however, is not pluralism but accommodation; the criticism, for instance, of developmentalism (*desarrollismo*), in terms such as "mutilation," "injustice," "leveling tendency," and "development reduces to uniformity," is neutralized by a simultaneous vocabulary of "civilization," "progress," and "cultural integration," and by such statements as that Andean culture "never developed."[19] As a result, the differences between cultural pluralism and acculturation simply dissolve into the status quo.

Perhaps the most extreme case of the abandonment of pluralism on a practical level is the second of two articles written about the invasion of Grenada and published in 1984. There, it is argued that national sovereignty is not a principle that can be upheld, given that the two superpowers inevitably intervene in their "own" spheres of influence; it is, the argument continues, the only positive principle that can be appealed to as being "the democratic morality and ideology which the North American system represents"[20] — values which are not, of course, necessarily practiced. The only basis left for criticizing the invasion is that it was not necessary, on the grounds that although there was increasing influence from Cuba and the USSR there was no actual aggression. Plurality is swallowed by accommodation to dependency, ethics by pragmatics.

Mirko Lauer has made the point that Vargas Llosa, while adopting a liberal posture, has not kept to the rules of the game, both because of his partiality (his unwillingness, for example, to look critically at capitalism) and of his failure to uphold a set of positive principles: "The essence of liberalism is not denunciation, but the formulation of those social, and indeed philosophical principles capable of upholding that individual freedom for all which this doctrine proposes."[21] When, in the 1970s, Vargas Llosa constantly referred to the need to defend freedom against ideology and totalitarianism, it sounded like the continuation of a familiar and traditional liberal debate (Camus, Popper, Berlin), but the historical realities were changing, with monetarism, the southern-cone dictatorships, IMF policies toward Latin America, the explosion of national debt, and the collapse of commodity prices, and in the 1980s with the domination of Western policies by Thatcherism and the Reagan administration. By 1980, Vargas Llosa was aligned with Belaundismo and beginning to mix the language of classical liberalism with that of neoliberalism. From the Camusian principle of ethical constraint, freedom had become an instrument of ideological legitimation.

Julio Ortega has usefully mapped the changes in the position of Latin American writers between the 1960s and the 1980s, when the role of the novelist in the period of the "Boom" was predicated on both social modernization and political liberation. But the two elements entered into historical contradictions: with writers moving from critical independence to dependence on "public opinion." The new circuit of communication relied on a middle class bound by the rules of a game controlled by the "developmentalist bourgeoisie" (*burguesía desarrollista*),[22] whose authoritarianism, briefly interrupted or disguised, was again and again reestablished. Moving from "spokesmen of dissidence" to "spokesmen of the status quo," as the liberal spaces opened in the 1960s closed again, writers also began to be affected by the need for an easily consumable product. In Chile in

1973, Peru in 1975, and shortly thereafter in Argentina and Uruguay, projects for change were dismantled, and the history of the whole period showed the incompatibility between *desarrollista* modernization and social justice.

In the 1960s, before becoming internationally famous, Vargas Llosa invoked two Peruvian writers, Sebastián Salazar Bondy and Carlos Oquendo de Amat, as indicators of the social marginalization of the writer in Peru. It is clear, in retrospect, that their situation was not strictly parallel to Vargas Llosa's. His complaint that writing has no prestige in Peru is accurate in relation to the pre-1968 oligarchy; but what he himself was seeking and obtained was a mass middle-class readership and, through that, a legitimate place in the dominant circuits of social communication. Social changes in the 1960s created a context in which this became possible. In his acceptance speech for the Rómulo Gallegos prize in 1967, a key step toward international success, in addition to speaking about Oquendo de Amat he introduced the concept of "personal demons," cutting the personal motivations of the writer adrift from any historical context through the notion of an absolute nonconformity. A decade later, in the 1970s, he cast José María Arguedas in the role of victim of the politicization of the writer.[23] In retrospect, once again, it is clear that the later works of Arguedas, the ones Vargas Llosa was referring to, address the broadest issues of Peruvian culture, something that Vargas Llosa's novels of the 1970s did not do. The latter's own break with any liberating project is legitimated by the condemnation of Arguedas. The various stages of his position could be charted briefly as follows: from local reporter and commentator on cultural issues to protagonist in the arena of Peruvian and Latin American public opinion (beginning in approximately 1967 with the Rómulo Gallegos prize), to polemicist against the left with increasing implications of the need for center-right government; and finally to a figure whose views and authority can be syndicated internationally. By then, his models of order and security had become "the northern democracies" (particularly Thatcherite England). For Lauer, part of the explanation for this trajectory is to be found in the fact that in looking for a social role for the intellectual, he found himself in a political one, given that the structure of power in Peru does not allow other roles,[24] and the culmination of this involvement with power was the invitation he received from Belaúnde to assume the premiership. His recent championing of a campaign against the nationalization of Peruvian banks, his leadership of the *Libertad* movement, and his becoming the presidential candidate of the right are another matter, a deliberate option for political power. It is important to emphasize the choices and responsibilities, and one way to do so is to point to the contrasting decisions made by García Márquez, for whom the experience of fame as power and isolation led to a need to analyze the historical forms of power in Latin America, resulting in the writing of his novel *The Autumn of the Patriarch* (El otoño del patriarca). Whereas Vargas Llosa, when asked in a recent interview if he wanted to be president, replied that "participating in politics had become a 'moral imperative' for [me], forcing him to put aside other 'vocations.'"[25]

The ideas Vargas Llosa is currently committed to are principally those of Hernando de Soto, the Peruvian economist, for whose book *The Other Path* he wrote a prologue in 1986. It marks the irruption of neoliberalism into Peruvian politics, advocating the reduction of the state and the establishment of the free market as remedies for underdevelopment. Not surprisingly, it received an accolade from President Reagan. Its most significant step is the identification of the "informal economy" as the response of the poor to their historical condition of marginalization. De Soto proclaims that there are two insurrections in contemporary Peru: that of the Partido Comunista del Perú (Sendero Luminoso) and that of the "informal economic sector."[26] Neoliberal populism enables Vargas Llosa to overcome the previous major problem for his liberal program, the existence of structural violence; now the victims of injustice can become the protagonists of its solution through popular capitalism. Freedom now means freedom from the state, Marxist criticisms of which can be absorbed and superseded; the de Soto book, claims Vargas Llosa, "reduces to sheer rhetoric a large proportion of current radical or Marxist criticisms of the situation of the underdeveloped world."[27] Neither de Soto nor Vargas Llosa examine what might be the practical consequences of this type of program — that the popular organizations that arose in response to capitalist development (e.g., worker and peasant unions or family food cooperatives [*comedores populares*]) would have to be destroyed, as would those state services for which the majority have fought over many years in order to obtain their basic needs. State controls over multinationals presumably would be removed. The social destructiveness of neoliberalism would be much greater in Peru than in the United Kingdom or the United States. Julio Cotler commented recently that "90 percent of the population, when they need a doctor don't go to the San Borja Clinic; they go to a [state] medical post. . . . What they are demanding is that the state should be theirs and for them."[28] The question of who rules whom and how, and of the forms of state power and state control, is left unanswered by Vargas Llosa and de Soto, an ambiguity reminiscent of Thatcherism (for which Vargas Llosa has often expressed his admiration), with its double-talking combination of Lockean and Hobbesian models of society.[29] As Franz Hinkelammert has suggested, there is a sense in which the new antistatism merely updates the ideology of the absolute state;[30] and when social controls break down, the old forms of state violence then begin to be wheeled out.[31] To summarize: just as economic liberalism so far has not produced democracy in Latin America (the history of England cannot be repeated in this way), so there is no reason to believe that the basic conditions for consensual democracy (health, education, law, material security) will be achieved by neoliberalism.

De Soto is quite clear about his goal: "to escape from backwardness and go forward to modernity."[32] That liberal nationhood the Latin American bourgeoisies had been unable to achieve for more than one and a half centuries since emancipation will now be realized apocalyptically by the poor. Vargas Llosa writes, in his introduction: "The option of freedom was never seriously applied in our countries nor all its implications explored. It is only now, in the most unexpected way, through the spontaneous action of the poor in their struggle for survival, that freedom has begun to gain ground, imposing itself as a more sensible and efficient answer to underdevelopment than those which conservatives and progressives have applied over the years."[33] Despite its claim to have abandoned utopianism, this position leaves intact the metaphysic of progress, deploying freedom as yet another permissive utopia, an imposition justified and masked by the historical goal of the autonomous individual. One of the results of this new discourse is that the 1960s, as a historical period when crucial actions of resistance and liberation begin to occur, disappear behind the horizon of individualism as the goal of history. For Vargas Llosa the sovereignty of the individual is the ethical culmination of human history, an achievement to be placed on a par with the great scientific discoveries of the modern period.[34] Macpherson's critique of liberal individualism can be used to reveal the political consequences of this stance in Peruvian and Latin American terms. Macpherson points out that an individuality that "can only fully be realized in accumulating property . . . is necessarily collectivism," in that it requires a "wholesale transfer of individual rights to get sufficient collective force for the protection of property." In other words, individualism is a mode of organization based on state protection for property ownership, arising historically in Renaissance Italy.[35] If we look more closely at "the poor," whose providential march toward liberty is the basis of this new populism, the term can be translated as those whom successive liberal projects have failed to hammer into conformity since the 1820s (Indian and mestizo peasantry, urban proletariat, and more recently, rural immigrants to the cities). Their mode of organization has never been individualism. De Soto and Vargas Llosa's strategy is to disarm them. Macpherson's other main criticism is that "full individuality for some . . . [is] produced by consuming the individuality of others,"[36] a feature that is caused magically to disappear in Vargas Llosa's new discourse through a recycling of the originary myths of capitalism. The advantage of the new posture is that it makes "the poor" protagonists of their own oppression in an act of self-disappearance, while disguising the program of cultural uniformity implied,[37] given that one of the aims of *The Other Path* is to generate an antidote to a possible cultural revolution — on the part of the marginalized majority — that might reject the distorted modernization dependent on the United States, which had begun to gather momentum during the first Belaúnde government in the 1960s; that is, its purpose is to counteract the type of cultural revolution explored by Arguedas in *The Fox from Above and the Fox from Below* (El zorro de arriba y el zorro de abajo).

This new solution requires not just the desocialization of the state and the economy, but also the homogenization of the plurality of cultures that make up Peru. If we take the Peruvian context once again as a test for the practical dimensions of Vargas Llosa's political discourse, the following would need to be emphasized as the chief factors in approximately the last decade: the acculturative thrust of the market as it penetrates new areas; the failure of the right to resolve economic problems or to achieve cultural or political legitimacy; the failure of the left to produce a coherent political project; the failure of the state to represent the nation; and the challenge issued by Sendero Luminoso from its Andean base to the legitimacy of the state. Vargas

Llosa's discourse of freedom is in complete alliance with the rein-
forcement of the "free" market as a solution to the failure of the state
and the rise of Shining Path, and it seeks to restore the right to legitimacy. One of President García's responses was to emphasize that "the
Andean values, the skin colour, the culture, all were trampled by
Lima,"[38] acknowledging, albeit with a populist gesture, the historical
bearing of Andean culture upon the question of hegemony.

While other major Peruvian writers such as Inca Garcilaso, Guamán
Poma, Mariátegui, Haya de la Torre, Vallejo, and Arguedas have taken
the nonoccidental cultures of Peru to be vital to the making of a national culture, Vargas Llosa has allied himself with the homogenizing
drive of the metropolis to absorb the hinterlands, arguing that nationalism has no validity and that there is no such thing as cultural dependency, thus accepting the inevitability of *Reader's Digest* culture.[39] The
various essays he has published on Arguedas, whose work, especially
The Fox, shows an opposite Andeanization of the nation, can be taken
as indicators of the changes in his positioning of himself vis-à-vis Peruvian cultural identity. In 1964 he commended Arguedas's social accuracy, his achievement of "true literary realism."[40] However, in an essay
first published in Cuba in 1966, he calls *The Deep Rivers* (Los ríos
profundos) "an alienated testimony about the Andes," cleverly playing
off the Cuban idea of the literature of "testimony," as social relevance
and responsibility, against "animism," as personal and social aliena-
tion.[41] Andean culture is here diminished to the "animism" of the
protagonist, whose imputed irrationality disqualifies the text from being a valid paradigm of national culture. In a preface to Gerald Martin's edition of M. A. Asturias's *Men of Maize* (Hombres de maíz),
Vargas Llosa is ready to grant the richness of native culture insofar as it
belongs to the past. Otherwise, though, it is kept inside the categories
of "primitive mentality" or Jungian archetypes, incapable of constituting a contemporary rationality.[42] In a longer essay, originally his
speech on being incorporated into the Peruvian Academy, he places
Arguedas inside the *demons* conception, thus reducing his condition
of a man "half way between two cultures," a condition that characterizes the greater part of the population, to a personal ill-adjustment
that supposedly drove him to write fiction—an instance of how the
demons notion, by making the personal nonpolitical, has no historical
content.[43] In another essay written in the same year and entitled "The
Archaic Utopia," Arguedas is taken as the victim of ideological pres-

sure upon the writer, within an argument for the separation of literature and politics. He is found guilty of bad faith in his "attempt . . . to
hand down to posterity the image of a writer driven to sacrifice himself for the problems of his country."[44] Animism is, surprisingly, vindi-
cated, but only because it is antipolitical: "In his best work, magic
killed socialism."[45] Globally, in terms of any contribution to the nation, the cultural forms of the Andes are claimed to have nothing to
offer beyond an archaic utopia. The dismissal of Arguedas reaches its
extreme when *All Bloods* (Todas las sangres) is labeled "a great literary failure" or when, in an article from 1980, he is included in a list of
writers condemned as folkloric, superficial, and Manichaean.[46]

Vargas Llosa's concern with models for the integration of Peruvian
culture dates from the time he was working on *The War of the End of
the World* (La guerra del fin del mundo). In comments on his experiences in northeastern Brazil, he decontextualizes the Canudos conflict by transposing it into an allegory of the dangers of utopianism. It
is not seen as part of the historical resistance of the modern state on
the part of the traditional society of the hinterlands.[47] The destruction
of "archaic" societies by modernization is placed within a tragic structure as "fated."[48] The novel itself, which exemplifies these views,
seems finally to exhaust the *demons* of creativity in a switching of
roles and values between politics and literature that reaches comple-
tion in *The Real Life of Alejandro Mayta* (Historia de Mayta). Of the
two sides in the conflict, Conselheiro and the rebels are closest to the
personal obsessions, the rebellion against reality, and the idea of creativity as arising from marginalization that Vargas Llosa had taken to be
the sources of the novel as a radical literary form; shown now as politically dangerous, those sources seem to be written off by this text as
legitimate creative energies. All this is perhaps a consequence of his
earlier hitching of his theory of literature as rebellion to the political
program of preserving liberal freedom.[49] *The War of the End of the
World* universalizes the dangers that Vargas Llosa attributes to a lack of
liberal structures in Latin America.

Critics have pointed to the paralysis that prevents the two factions in
the novel from interacting historically, bound as they are within an
allegory of the dangers of fanaticism,[50] and to a relativism that is altogether different from the process of dialogue.[51] A further and significant limitation of Vargas Llosa's handling of history is brought out by
James Dunkerley, in his review of *The Real Life of Alejandro Mayta*:

the fact that he has not chosen to write about the Túpac Amaru rebellion of 1781 or the struggles of the 1820s for the establishment of the republic—key episodes in Peruvian history that offer the same ingredients as the Canudos rebellion. "One suspects," Dunkerley comments, "that they have not emerged as themes precisely because, however partially and temporarily, they transcended the limits that Vargas Llosa would have as the incarnation of order, successfully transforming history. The obvious irony is that both Indian rebellion and militarism established the republic of Peru."[52] There is also the fact that the Canudos of *The War of the End of the World* is more pathetic than threatening, and that its culture is something far less disturbing in Vargas Llosa's book than in da Cunha's, where the chaotic and elastic space of Canudos threatens to fatally entangle the rationality of the Brazilian republic and of the author himself. It seems valid here to draw a parallel between Vargas Llosa's sense of historical meaning and his confession in *The Perpetual Orgy* (La orgía perpetua) of what has governed his literary preferences: his "feeling of repugnance toward chaos" and "that propensity which has made me prefer from childhood works constructed according to a rigorous and symmetrical order, with a beginning and an end, which are closed in upon themselves and give the impression of sovereignty and completeness, as opposed to those open ones which deliberately suggest indeterminacy."[53]

Just as in the essays he takes up Camus's criticism of ideology without offering any basis for social cohesiveness, so in the fiction, beginning with *Los jefes* (in *The Cubs and Other Stories*), structures of conflict constitute the basis of sociality. Unlike the writing of Alfredo Bryce, where desire moves across social division and threatens the stability of hierarchies, mutual attraction to Vargas Llosa's work tends either to follow the lines of social hierarchy or to become a site of manipulative power; while the fraternal love among Antonio Conselheiro's people occurs, tragically, inside unlimited conflict. Nevertheless, the earlier novels, and especially *The Green House*, explored the making of connections across the lines of power and cultural division, with the multiple interweaving of conversations across time and space being a main technical device for such exploration. The result was the making of a liberal space through the (temporary) subversion of hierarchy. With *The Real Life of Alejandro Mayta*, however, the technique of communicating vessels becomes subsumed into a political program. The connections do not traverse the political ordering of reality, they simply confirm it.

Let us finally consider the two novels where the conflict between politics and creativity reaches its extreme: *Mayta* and *The Storyteller* (El hablador). The author of *Mayta*, that is, the person adopted by Vargas Llosa, tells how Ernesto Cardenal's communism has become for him an impediment to reading his poetry, "like an acid that degrades it,"[54] and this link joins the chain of Manichaean contaminations that imprison the protagonist in his personal and political failure. Such connections have the logic of obsession, of the *demons* that should nourish literature but not politics. But in this novel obsessions are underwritten by the credentials of the author as liberal,[55] since just as Mayta is contaminated by Ernesto Cardenal so is the author saturated by the "real" (the recognizable) Vargas Llosa, such openness of reference to actual historical events being part of the novel's strategy. The result is a short circuit between the literary and the political, previously kept separate as the irrational and the rational, respectively. Irrationality invades politics, where it becomes destructive, and rationality (as authoritarian liberalism) controls writing. The attributions of homosexuality and psychic repression, made by the author, purport to explain Mayta's deviant politics—that is, if we take them interpretatively. But their symbolism functions to reinforce a normalizing ideology that takes upon itself the task of defining the limits, where aberrance begins. The novel's literary procedure makes Mayta open to any contamination the author may choose to direct toward him. If we analyze the process, it is one of projection disguised as invention and interpreted as deviation, with the abnormal now no longer an object of exorcism, pathos, or even irony. When it turns out that Mayta is not a homosexual, we then find ourselves in another layer of invention: the author deciphers the "real" Mayta, degraded and disillusioned and associated with Hugo Blanco (with the contaminating acid spreading). Mayta fails, both because he does not fit with Vargas Llosa's political version of Peru and because of the corroding fatality of marginalization, where he joins the protagonists of *The Time of the Hero* and *Conversation in the Cathedral*. It might be argued that everything that Mayta is, is acknowledged as invention. But as in certain types of journalism, the mud sticks. The invented denotations were always an excuse for political connotations, drawing on a predetermined political symbolism. It is this symbolic code that dominates the novel, despite virtuosities in the narrative order, and meshes with the persona of the author, now no longer the "vulture" figure drawing energy from marginalization, but a self-legitimating authority, and enunciator of doxology, in contrast with the unstable and marginalized Mayta. This novel can be seen as a skillful transposition of the drama of the essays, of their contrasting of correct and incorrect opinion. Like *The War of the End of the World* and the Uchuraccay report, it displays a political law that abhors extremes and punishes them sacrificially. It should be added that the need for apocalyptic scenarios, first explored in the novels, became a major rhetorical ploy of his political campaign for the presidency.[56]

Vargas Llosa's most recent novel, *The Storyteller*, uses the same methods as *Mayta*, although the defictionalizing of the author is taken further. This formal device, which merges the voice of the essayist and public figure with that of the novelist, does not generate a moral stance but seeks instead the legitimation of opinion as literature. Saúl Zuratas, a type of fallen alter ego of the author, is a culturally and physically marginalized intellectual who takes the romantic option of integrating with the Machiguenga, one of the least acculturated tribes in the eastern jungles of Peru. This action produces a reductive equivalence of marginalities, which corrodes ethnology as recognition of the irreducible plurality of Peruvian culture and mocks *indigenismo* as recognition of the cultural difference of native populations. The result is a vindication of national integration by other means; the obvious impossibility of integrating with the Machiguenga is used to lend weight to the idea that they can only integrate with us, the central and stable implicit *nosotros* of the text. Fiction has ceased to be a complex figuration of multiplicities in conversational space–time, to become administration of opinion.

Zuratas's adventure is specifically compared with "the fanatical indigenism of the nineteen thirties in San Marcos University," a phenomenon that "comes periodically, like a cold."[57] One person who was in that place in the 1930s is José María Arguedas, and this novel is a further addition to the series of replies to Arguedas that Vargas Llosa has been producing since the 1960s. For instance, the author reuses the "archaic utopia" phrase and refers to the difficulty of finding a literary form adequate to "a primitive man's way of narrating," and to his own failure to solve the problem. Those parts of the text that present the voice of Zuratas as a Machiguenga "storyteller" read like a bad *indigenista* novel, where the voice of the native culture is obviously and awkwardly constructed from the acculturating culture. These passages, which occasionally mimic the sentence structures of Arguedas's *Yawar Fiesta*, have virtually no intellectual content. Is it the intention that we should read the latter as illustrative of that failure the linguistic awkwardness is meant to represent? The doubt arises from the fact that the text vacillates between parody and imitation, and that the parodic effect, which worked well in *Aunt Julia and the Scriptwriter*, here tends to be subordinated to the desire to prove the failure of the enterprise. What is clearly shown by this text, whose author is placed in Florence, symbol of the perfection of European high culture and center from which the marginalities look the same, is that Vargas Llosa cannot conceive of simultaneous and opposing sets of signs, that is, of a heterogeneous culture, but only of an alienated discourse as the sole way in which the Other can speak within the nation, leaving us the only option an eventual integration or disappearance of the Other into a single national discourse—an apologetics for acculturation. History is a question of "backward" or "forward,"[58] or destruction or integration.

It has been suggested that because Vargas Llosa was more of a "realist" than other novelists of the 1960s, he was bound to encounter greater contradictions than they did.[59] But the issue is one not of closeness to some pregiven notion of history, but of the possibilities that are opened and those that are closed. In the early work, Boa and Cuéllar are the two extremes at which liberalism cannot function: Boa repels social homogenization, Cuéllar is castrated by it. In the 1970s, Vargas Llosa's works attempted to preserve a middle ground by satirizing the distorted social rationality of the peripheral modernity of Latin America. With *The War of the End of the World*, he opts for the destruction of the two extremes; what remains, however, is not an open society but a program of exclusions and enforced integrations. The "liberal imagination" becomes finally the author's authority.

Postscript

In the Peruvian elections of 1990, Vargas Llosa stood as candidate for a coalition of right-wing parties. He was defeated in the second round by Alberto Fujimori, an independent. His neoliberal economic package emphasized "popular capitalism" as a "revolutionary" solution and included the privatization of state enterprises. Particular stress was laid on a three-year period of economic "shock," during which Peruvians would be asked for "sacrifices" in order to rescue the economy. The campaign was characterized by Vargas Llosa's unprecedentedly high spending on publicity and by racist sentiment against Fujimori, who is of Japanese descent (a racism from which Vargas Llosa disassociated himself). Two main theories about the results have emerged. The first holds that the population had reached a state of gut rejection of all politics and politicians. The second ascribes the popular rejection of Vargas Llosa to consciousness of the deep and unresolved divisions of Peruvian society: "The second round has revealed the bankruptcy of créole Peru, descended from the Spanish conquistadors. The results confirm the existence . . . of another Peru, to a great extent impermeable to the values, style, and even the aesthetics of créole Peru."[60]

NOTES

1. *La República* (Lima), Sept 5, 1987, 16.
2. Angel Rama and Mario Vargas Llosa, *García Márquez y la problemática de la novela* (Buenos Aires: Corregidor, 1973).
3. Rama and Vargas Llosa, *García Márquez*, 8-11, 35-36.
4. Mario Vargas Llosa, *Contra viento y marea* (Barcelona: Seix Barral, 1986), 1:282. Vargas Llosa's reply also appears in Rama and Vargas Llosa, *García Márquez*, 53-54.
5. Vargas Llosa, *Contra viento y marea*, 1:324.
6. Ibid., 1:341.
7. Paul Rabinow, ed., *The Foucault Reader* (London: Penguin Books, 1986), 382.
8. Vargas Llosa, *Contra viento y marea*, 2:150.
9. Rabinow, *Foucault Reader*, 382.
10. James Dunkerley, "Mario Vargas Llosa: Parables and Deceits," *New Left Review*, 162 (April-March 1987), 112-23, sees a connection with Vargas Llosa's provincial mestizo background (see 113, 116, 118).
11. See Jean Franco, "From Modernization to Resistance: Latin-American Literature 1959-1976," *Latin American Perspectives*, 5, (1978).
12. Howard Barker, Lecture at the University of London, Oct. 12, 1988. See Barker, *Pity in History*, in *Gambit*, 11 (1984).
13. See Philip Corrigan and Derek Sayer, *The Great Arch* (Oxford: Blackwell, 1985), 141; David Musselwhite, *Partings Welded Together* (London: Metheun, 1987), 11.
14. Vargas Llosa, *Contra viento y marea*, 1:335-36.
15. Ibid., 1:341.
16. Informe de la comisión investigadora de los sucesos de Uchuraccay (Lima, 1983).
17. *La República* (Lima), Jan. 21, 1984, 11.
18. I am grateful to Peter Gose for this point.

19. Vargas Llosa, *Contra viento y marea*, 2:212.

20. Ibid., 2:389.

21. Mirko Lauer, "Vargas Llosa: Los límites de la imaginación no liberal," *La República* (Lima), April 15, 1984, 30.

22. Julio Ortega, "La literatura latinoamericana en la década del 80," *Eco*, 215 (1979), 7-8.

23. Mario Vargas Llosa, "La utopía arcaica," *Co-textes* (Montpellier, n.d.), 4:24-63.

24. Lauer, "Vargas Llosa," 27.

25. *Latinamerica Press*, March 24, 1988, 1.

26. Hernando de Soto, *El otro sendero* (Lima, 1986), 286.

27. Ibid., xviii.

28. Julio Cotler, "Nueva derecha busca aplastar al Apra y la IV," *La República* (Lima), Sept. 2, 1987, 13.

29. I am grateful to Tony Dunn for the point about Thatcherism.

30. Franz Hinkelammert, "Frente a la cultura de la post-modernidad: Proyecto político y utopía," *David y Goliath*, 17 (Sept. 1987), 21–29, 23.

31. See Julio Ortega, "Sobre el discurso político de Octavio Paz," *Socialismo y Participación*, 33 (March 1986), 89-95, 94-95.

32. De Soto, *El otro sendero*, 317.

33. Ibid., xxvi.

34. Vargas Llosa, *Contra viento y marea*, 2:434-35.

35. C. B. Macpherson, *Political Theory of Possessive Individualism* (Oxford: Oxford University Press, 1962), 255-56. See also T. C. Heller, ed., *Reconstructing Individualism* (Stanford, Calif.: Stanford University Press, 1986), 8, 211, 212.

36. Macpherson, *Possessive Individualism*, 261. To set against Vargas Llosa's individualism, it is worth quoting Oscar Wilde's expression of a different tradition: "The recognition of private property has really harmed individualism, and obscured it, by confusing a man with what he possesses." Wilde, *The Soul of Man under Socialism* (London: Journeyman, 1988), 11-12).

37. In a speech given at Miranda House, London, 1987, Vargas Llosa spoke of the incapacity of Quechua culture for individualism.

38. *Financial Times*, Sept. 9, 1987.

39. Vargas Llosa, *Contra viento y marea*, 2:314-15, 320-21.

40. Mario Vargas Llosa, "José María Arguedas descubre al indio auténtico," *Visión del Perú*, 1 (August 1964), 3-7.

41. Mario Vargas Llosa, "Los ríos profundos," *Casa de las Américas*, 6 (March-April 1966), 105-9. Subsequently reprinted with the title "Ensoñación y magia en José María Arguedas," as a preface to various editions of *Los ríos profundos*.

42. Miguel Angel Asturias, *Hombres de maíz* (México: Edición Crítica, 1981), xvii-xx. I draw here on a point made by Gordon Brotherston in a seminar given at the Institute of Latin American Studies, London, in June 1987.

43. Mario Vargas Llosa, *José María Arguedas, entre sapos y halcones* (Madrid: Ediciones Cultura Hispánica, 1978), 26, 34.

44. Vargas Llosa, "La utopía arcaica," 26.

45. Ibid., 52.

46. Ibid., 54; Vargas Llosa, *Contra viento y marea*, 2:230.

47. Vargas Llosa, *Contra viento y marea*, 2:181-83.

48. Ibid., 2:219.

49. Ibid., 1:341.

50. See Gerald Martin, "Mario Vargas Llosa: Errant Knight of the Liberal Imagination," in John King, Ed., *Modern Latin American Fiction: A Survey* (London: Faber & Faber, 1987), 205-33, 223; Antonio Cornejo Polar, "Mario Vargas Llosa: *La guerra del fin del mundo*," *Revista de Crítica Literaria Latinoamericana*, 15 (1982), 219-21.

51. See Mikhail Bakhtin, *Problems of Dostoevsky's Poetics* (Manchester: Manchester University Press, 1984), 69.

52. Dunkerley, "Mario Vargas Llosa," 118-19.

53. Mario Vargas Llosa, *La orgía perpetua* (Madrid: Taurus, 1975), 18.

54. Mario Vargas Llosa, *Historia de Mayta* (Barcelona: Seix Barral, 1984), 92.

55. See Vargas Llosa, *Historia de Mayta*, 91.

56. Elizabeth Farnsworth, "The Temptation of Mario," *Mother Jones*, 14 (January 1989), 22-47.

57. Mario Vargas Llosa, *El hablador* (Barcelona: Seix Barral, 1987), 34.

58. Ibid., 75.

59. See Martin, "Mario Vargas Llosa," 209. Martin's position is based on a Lukacsian privileging of realism.

60. *Resumen Semanal* (Lima: Desco), 564, 2 and 573, 1.

Going Public: Reinhabiting the Private
Jean Franco

Women's Movements and the Social Imaginary

During the last decade, Latin American women have emerged as protagonists in a number of grass-roots movements — the Mothers' movements of the southern cone, peasant movements, Catholic base communities, union movements, and local struggles around basic needs
such as child nutrition, homes, soup kitchens, and water supply.
These "new social movements" have given a significantly original dimension to contemporary political life,[1] precisely at a time when feminist groups have also grown rapidly in numbers and influence[2] and
when an unprecedented number of women writers have emerged on
the scene. If any generalized observation holds over the vast spectrum
of struggles, local movements, nomadic cultures, and literary productions, it is perhaps their timeliness, their opportune emergence at a
moment when the separation of the private from the public sphere —
which had been the basis for the subordination of women by historic
capitalism — has never seemed so arbitrary or fragile.[3] And this moment itself is, as Nancy Fraser points out, one of "emergence into
visibility and contestability of problems and possibilities that cannot
be solved or realized within the established framework of gendered
roles and institutions."[4] One of those "problems" that could only become visible with the emergence of women's movements was the
position of the intellectual. Do the new social movements represent,
for the 1990s, the terrain of practice and political conscience that formerly had been occupied by the left? Between the 1920s and the

1960s, the male intelligentsia, confronting mass political and social movements (ranging from left political parties to the guerrilla movements), were again and again obliged to define their commitment, their responsibility, and art's relationship to the social. Women writers now find themselves in a similar position as they confront the reality of the new social movements. Yet they cannot simply repeat the discourse of responsibility, commitment, and representation, for literature itself no longer occupies the same position in the cultural spectrum as it did in the past.

The New Social Movements

In Latin America two factors contributed to women's participation in the new social movements—the authoritarian regimes of the 1970s and the extreme hardship caused by debt crisis and neoconservative policies that have been put into effect without the protective shield of the welfare state. Despite "redemocratization," the threat of authoritarianism and its consequences still cast shadows on national politics; and despite promises of economic miracles, the majority of Latin Americans have no access to the consumer society that is celebrated daily on television screens and billboards. Furthermore, as states become less and less inclined to take responsibility for the breakdown and collapse of services, people are often cast on their own resources, as was evident in Mexico after the earthquake disaster.[5] It is in these situations that women have increasingly acted as citizens, a position that had been difficult for them to assume as long as the public sphere was assumed to be a masculine domain.

Although it is easy to see that both military governments and redemocratization under the aegis of free-market capitalism alter the relation of the citizen to the state, it should also be emphasized that even in "welfare" states (Chile, Uruguay, and Mexico in the 1960s), the social contract rode on the inequalities of the sexual contract, which subordinated women to a reproductive rather than a citizen's role. Though women's participation in politics was not impossible, existing social arrangements did not encourage participation.[6] Under military regimes, this situation worsened since political activity in the public sphere was banned. Thus, in Argentina between 1976 and 1982 only those who unquestioningly supported the military regime were defined as citizens, and large sectors of the population found themselves in the shadowy realm of the subversive.

Yet, although the culture of fear—the use of torture and disappearance, and death-camp executions—was intended not only to deter the militant opposition but also to freeze all public activity, it was ineffective as a deterrent against the mothers of disappeared children. These women, known as the Mothers of Plaza de Mayo, not only gathered together in a public place but used their marginalized position to reclaim the *polis*. They created an Antigone space in which the rights (and rites) of kinship were given precedence over the discourse of the state. For though the military were secretly torturing and killing women and children, as well as male militants, in their public rhetoric they represented themselves as protectors of the family of the nation and ridiculed the demonstrating mothers as "locas" (madwomen) who were outside the family of the nation. A few old women raving about their children in the name of motherhood hardly seemed much of a threat.[7]

Many scholars, particularly outside Latin America, have essentialized the Mothers' movements, arguing that the women exemplified "maternal thinking" by acting within their traditional roles.[8] Others regard the Mothers' movements as purely conjunctural and unable to generate a more lasting political movement.[9] But such arguments overlook the fact that the Mothers did not merely act within a traditional role but substantially altered tradition by casting themselves as a new kind of citizen and also by appealing beyond the state to international organizations. Their use of symbols was particularly eloquent and effective. They wore white kerchiefs and silently carried blown-up snapshots of their children, often taken at family gatherings. In this way, "private life"—as an image frozen in time—was represented publicly as a contrast to the present, highlighting the destruction of that very family life that the military publicly professed to protect. The women turned the city into a theater in which the entire population was obliged to become spectators,[10] making public both their children's disappearance and the disappearance of the public sphere itself. In doing so, they drew attention to the very anomaly of women's presence in the symbolic center of the nation, Plaza de Mayo.

The Chilean feminist Julieta Kirkwood argued that paradoxical as it seemed, authoritarian governments often forced women to make connections between state repression and oppression in the home:

> People have begun to say that the family is authoritarian; that the socialization of children is authoritarian and rigid in its assignment of gender roles; that education, factory work, social organizations, and political parties have been constituted in an authoritarian manner.[11]

Certainly, authoritarian regimes had the effect of enhancing the ethical value of private life, religion, literature, and art as regions of refuge from the brutal reality of an oppressive state. The church, especially in Chile, courageously sheltered and defended human-rights movements. Yet as the case of Sandinista Nicaragua would show, the church could also prove to be a barrier that prevented women from debating sensitive issues such as reproductive rights.[12] This is why, despite Julieta Kirkwood's belief that authoritarian governments awakened women to the domestic oppression, human-rights movements, particularly those dominated by the church, did not necessarily induct women into feminism.

Survival movements are a different matter. These movements come into being when the state can no longer deal with the day-to-day survival of its citizens. Women who must feed their families, find shelter, and protect their children in areas where policing is nonexistent or ineffective or in the hands of drug lords, have been forced to take matters into their own hands, organizing soup kitchens and glass-of-milk programs and occupying land for housing. It is in these movements that awareness of women's oppression has strengthened, although their activists often repudiate the label of feminism, which has been tainted by associations with man-hating puritans or with middle-class women whose interests do not coincide with those of the subaltern classes.[13] Nevertheless, some grass-roots movements, especially in Brazil and Mexico, have had an extraordinary political impact, forcing governments to respond to issues such as housing and violence against women. In Mexico, for example, women participated actively in the neighborhood groups formed to help in the work of reconstruction after the 1985 earthquake, sometimes because they were heads of households, sometimes because their men were away or working.

The power of such grass-roots movements has had an impact on the feminist movement in which, more and more, their presence, their questioning, and their politics have become an issue.[14] In any event, these social movements cannot be ignored. They exist all over the continent; they have produced their own organic intellectuals. And in many ways, as I shall now go on to argue, they have a direct and an indirect impact on culture.

Women Intellectuals between Commercialization and Grass-Roots Movements

Is there any connection between the new social movements and the emergence of a substantial corpus of writing by women? The answer seems to be a qualified no, qualified because there is a literature and art that springs directly from disappearance, poverty, and survival.[15] This exception merely underscores the deep-rooted class privilege that had traditionally been associated with literature.[16] At the same time, it is no coincidence that women's writing and new social movements have emerged at a time when the nation has ceased to be the necessary framework either of political action or of writing and when a dominant ideology of pluralism seems to undermine oppositional stances that rest on marginality.

One of the ironies of pluralism is that even commitment becomes marketable. There is now an unprecedented demand for literary works by women, particularly works that, in some way or other, seem to reflect women's "experience." Traditional genres such as lyric poetry and the novel compete with biographies, autobiographies, testimonials, and chronicles. Similarly, nearly all styles now appear equally valid. Women write best-sellers and hermetic avant-garde fiction. They are realists, magical realists, writers of fantasy, defenders of aesthetic space, destroyers of the aesthetic. Women's writing is neither a school nor a style. Indeed, the genre and mode in which women write constitute their positionality within a debate whose terms are seldom explicitly articulated. The separation of the intellectual from the popular classes, the gulf between different class positions on sexuality, are transposed into questions of narrative voice, genre, and style.

The class privilege of the intelligentsia has always posed a problem for Latin Americans, but in women's writing it becomes particularly acute since women writers are privileged and marginalized at one and the same time. Further, on questions of sexuality there is a considerable cultural gap between the middle classes and working classes. This may explain why some women writers feel obliged to separate the political from the aesthetic. Consider, for example, the case of the Chilean writer Diamela Eltit. She actively collaborated with the *Por la vida* movement, which stages demonstrations to publicize disappearance; she wrote novels that are so hermetic they seem to baffle critics, and she staged public performances such as kissing a homeless man or reading her novel in a brothel in a poor sector of Santiago. In this one author, we find a tangle of conflicting intentions: to act against the authoritarian state, to take literature symbolically into the most marginal of spaces, to work against the easy readability of the commercial text, to foreground the woman's body as a site of contention, to increase or exaggerate the marginality of art, and juxtapose literature's marginality to that of prostitutes, vagabonds, and the homeless. Or consider the very different example of Elena Poniatowska, whose chronicles and testimonials "give voice" to the subordinate classes and set the everyday language of survival against official history but who also writes an autobiographical novel, *La "Flor de lis,"* in which she powerfully affirms her identity with her snobbish and aristocratic mother from whom she cannot separate herself, except by transposing her desire onto the heterogeneous "mother country," Mexico, which her biological mother had always rejected. It is not that we should see these writers as contradictory but, rather, that they both confront the problem of class stratification, which can no longer be overcome simply by proclaiming oneself the voice of the subaltern.[17] It is the very intractability of this situation, the impossibility of the grand maternalist or avant-garde gesture, that accounts for the importance of testimonial literature, a genre that seems to cross the breach of class and racial stratification.

Appropriating the Public Sphere

The testimonial is a life story usually related by a member of the subaltern classes to a transcriber who is a member of the intelligentsia. It is this genre that uses the "referential" to authenticate the collective memory of the uprooted, the homeless, and the tortured, and that most clearly registers the emergence of a new class of participants in the public sphere. The testimonial covers a spectrum between autobiography and oral history, but the word *testimony* has both legal and religious connotations and implies a subject as witness to and participant in public events. Clearly, it is not exclusively a woman's genre, although it lends itself effectively to the story of conversion and *conscientización* that occurs once women transgress the boundaries of domestic space. The momentous nature of this move can only be appreciated when we recall that, within the traditional left, a woman knew "that she could never take power which is the workers' and peasants' prerogative. It was recognized, though, that she possessed another kind of power, power within the home, affective power, emotional blackmail (as queen, angel, or demon of the home) either because of her biological nature or because of the fact that she took pleasure in submission. And being so well trained in the private sphere, she abhors the public sphere."[18] Many testimonials by women thus bear witness to the breaking of the taboo on "going public" and their initial fears. A Mexican woman, for instance, states,

> Of course I was afraid. Many of us were confronting something new, others had some experience from before the foundation of the Union of Neighborhoods. Now we understand that the Union is a political and civic education, a link between Mexican women and their own reality.[19]

But if these women acquire a political education through their activities, they do not necessarily subscribe to a feminist agenda or at least to a feminist agenda that separates women's problems from those of society as a whole. As a Mexican woman from a neighborhood organization states, "If we understand our own problems to be rape, abortion, violence, our aim should not be to make our men the prime enemy but to situate these as social problems that affect both men and women and make these demands those of the entire social movement."[20]

Because of its exemplary nature, testimonial literature has become an important genre for empowering subaltern women. It is important, however, to stress that the term *testimonial* embraces a corpus of texts that range from fragments embedded in other texts to full-length life stories like those of the Guatemalan Indian woman Rigoberta Menchú and the Bolivian Domitila. The common feature of these stories is generally an abnormal event that activates the subject, the appropriation of public space, and the successful acquisition of a new public identity. In the most powerful of these narratives, for instance, that of Rigoberta Menchú, the narrator is able to exercise some control over the information, thus constituting her own subaltern narrative.[21]

On the other hand, for the woman intellectual who records and edits the testimony the process is of an altogether different nature. For very often the intellectual virtually disappears from the text in order to let "the subaltern speak," thus raising the question of her relationship to the political struggles she records. Is it that of a bystander? An impartial observer? Is she creating on the basis of somebody else's raw material? Or is it possible by means of double-voicing to bridge the gulf between the intelligentsia and the popular classes?

The chronicles and testimonial novels of Elena Poniatowska, though not simply focused on women, are interesting in this respect. Poniatowska has consistently amplified the testimonial genre by converting it into fiction and by incorporating many testimonials into a chronicle of a single event. This corresponds to a recurrent theme of "popular agency," that is, the potentiality of ordinary people (the young people of *La noche de Tlatelolco*, the earthquake survivors of *Nada, nadie*) to act on their own behalf. Lurking under the surface is a certain utopian belief in popular power that becomes quite explicit in her essay "The Women of Juchitán," which in the guise of a description of a collection of photographs celebrates the eroticization of the social.

"The Women of Juchitán" was written as an introduction to a book of photographs by Graciela Iturbide. Juchitán is the rebellious town in the province of Oaxaca, which has been the scene of a running war against the central government and the domination of its party, the PRI (Partido Revolucionario Institucional). "The Women of Juchitán" is, indeed, frankly utopian and even contrasts with other more sober chronicles of Juchitán, notably those of Carlos Monsiváis.[22] But the essay is not to be judged as a piece of exposé journalism; rather, it is an imaginative vision of a society structured around women's sexuality. She describes the Juchitec women thus:

> You should see them arriving like walking towers, their window open, their hearts like windows, their ample breadth a moonlit night. You should see them come, they are already the government, they, the

people, guardians of men, givers of food, their children riding their hips or swinging in the hammock of their breasts, the wind in their skirts, flowery vessels, the honeycomb of their sex overflowing with men. Here they come, bellies swaying, their machos in tow, their machos who, in contrast, are wearing colorless pants, shirts, leather sandals, and straw hats which they lift high into the air as they shout, "Long live the women of Juchitán."[23]

This celebration of excess is an antidote to the sober and often pedestrian accounts of women's movements that prevail in academic literature. Poniatowska's view is not that of the participant observer of a single event but a lyrical essay on the possibilities of nonpatriarchal sexuality and politics. In the writing of Poniatowska (and perhaps that of Rosario Ferré), we find the utopian dimension of women's writing in the fusion of sexual and political liberation. At the same time, this particular bridging of class difference is not common. For most women writers, it is the family romance itself that first must be undermined from within.

Reinhabiting the Private

The international marketing of Latin American literature under the brand name of "magic realism"; the seductive example of television, where melodrama and romance reach vast audiences; and the unabashed marketing of writers such as García Márquez and Vargas Llosa have given commercialization a good name, at least in certain circles. There is no reason to begrudge Isabel Allende the same translation rights as García Márquez or those of progressive writers such as Ariel Dorfman and Eduardo Galeano. The proliferation of women's studies courses and the incorporation of Third World women writers into the curriculum have suddenly provided them with the kind of international readership that the writers of the "Boom" have long enjoyed. Why then do I, unreasonably and with the temerity of an outsider, want something *more* than the merely marketable? Perhaps because the global reach of a novelist like Allende seems to put "quality" writing too readily at the service of the formulas that have always acted as female pacifiers — heterosexual romance combined with seigneurial goodwill toward the subaltern classes. The texts that most interest me are neither those in which the subaltern speaks while hiding the intellectual agent of that speech, nor those that refuse to acknowledge the privilege on which the "lettered city" has always depended. Yet in order to challenge that privilege women writers have been forced to reexamine that hidden sphere of the public/private dichotomy—the private itself, which traditionally has been so closely linked to the subjective and to the aesthetic.

The *private* is, in fact, a slippery term, used by economists to define private enterprise as opposed to the state and by social scientists to refer to the family or the household. But it also refers to the individual and the particular as opposed to the social. Even for male writers, however, the private was necessarily riddled with conflict; while seemingly the space for freedom and creativity, insofar as it was the space of the individual, the private revealed the limitation of death and mortality. In Vallejo's *Trilce* and Neruda's *Residencia en la tierra*, the private is the space of death, of futility, and redemption is only achieved through a new configuration of the social. In other writers, the limitations of male individuation can only be overcome by some incorporation or union with the feminine—in the poetry of Octavio Paz, for example, or the compensatory fictions of Puig and Rulfo—though this feminine is an ideal construct with little relationship to women's bodily experience.

The "ideology of the aesthetic" which, as Terry Eagleton claims, came into being with the bourgeois state's separation of the ethical, the political, and the aesthetic, bridged the frontiers between private and public.[24] Yet this aesthetic was also coded in a way that excluded the domestic, the banal, and the routine—in other words, those aspects of private life that were thought of as "feminine" and that reflected its colonization by the state.[25] The aesthetic allowed men to have their cake and eat it too, to separate the private from the (masculine) public sphere of citizenship so that eventually it could serve as a negative dialectic, while at the same time they relegated women to domestic space that was too crudely material to enter into the aesthetic. The contribution of French feminism, beginning with Simone de Beauvoir, was precisely to signal that scandalous move which had sublimated male sexuality while erasing the body and particularly the female body from consideration.[26]

Like French feminists, many Latin American women writers understand their position to be not so much one of confronting a dominant patriarchy with a new feminine position but rather one of unsettling the stance that supports gender power/knowledge as masculine. This "unsettling" is accomplished in a variety of ways, through parody and pastiche, by mixing genres, and by constituting subversive mythologies. The writing of Rosario Ferré, Luisa Valenzuela, Cristina Peri Rossi, Griselda Gambaro, Reina Roffe, Ana Lydia Vega, Albalucía del Angel, Carmen Boullosa, Isabel Allende — for example — corresponds to this project of displacing the male-centered national allegory and exposes the dubious stereotyping that was always inherent in the epics of nationhood that constitute the Latin American canon.[27] But there is also a reverse strategy, for if the sexual contract excluded women from the public sphere it also allowed middle-class women a particularly privileged and leisured existence, thanks to the class division between mistress and servant. The ambiguous overlapping of privilege and the aesthetic was indeed the central concern of Latin America's leading woman modernist, Clarice Lispector.

Known outside Brazil, thanks in part to the writings of the French feminist Hélène Cixous, Lispector seems a modernist par excellence, one of the few women to have gained acceptance in that exclusive male club.[28] The scandal of Lispector's writing, however, is not so much her "mastering" of modernist aesthetics as the inescapable and often quite naked intrusion of class difference and gender subordination that only serves to highlight the ugly scaffolding on which the temple of beauty has been erected. In her novels and short stories, sheltered women who have accepted the "sexual contract" without difficulty suddenly find themselves exposed by a simple breakdown of everyday life — the chauffeur hasn't turned up or the maid has just left. In one of her short stories, "Beauty and the Beast; or, The Wound That Was Too Big," a woman emerges from a beauty salon to find that her chauffeur has mistaken the time and there is no way to get home. She has money with her, but the bill is of such a large denomination that no taxi driver would take it. In the midst of this farcical dilemma, she is confronted by a wounded beggar who asks her for money. Lispector turns this raw encounter into an implacable demonstration of all the ethical, political, and aesthetic discourses that render dialogue between these two marginalized members of society impossible. The two are incommensurable. "Do you speak English?" the woman absurdly asks the beggar who, believing her to be mad or deaf, shouts at the top of his voice, "FALO" (a word play on "I speak" and phallus). Is the wounded beggar, whose name she forgets to ask, necessary for beauty, for conspicuous consumption, for the aesthetic? Lispector's writing is always on the edge of this disturbing possibility. Lispector's last novel, *The Hour of the Star*, is a powerful exploration not only of subaltern silence, but of authorial power. A plain, poor, and not very intelligent girl from the Northeast becomes the subject of the narrative written by a sophisticated male writer who, of course, appears to have absolute control over the material. The story is deliberately banal. The girl finds a boyfriend who leaves her for someone else. A fortune teller promises that she will meet her true love, and as she rushes across the street in happy anticipation she is run down by a speeding car. Despite the narrator's condescending attitude toward his material, the novel raises the disturbing question of whether aesthetic pleasure is in any way superior to or different from the poor girl's self-deception. In one of her most powerful novels, *The Passion According to G. H.*, a woman tidying up the room of a maid who has just left her service finds a cockroach (metonymically linked to the servant class), tries to kill it, and then when it is dying, she is driven to ingest the liquid it exudes in a parody of Christian communion. In all these texts, the idea that all forms of life are equal shockingly foregrounds arbitrary inequalities.

The epiphany that critics inevitably underscore in Lispector's writing is achieved in full awareness of the savage heart that gives life to the aesthetic; that savagery is represented not by the cockroach or the beggar or the working girl, but by those who occupy the center thanks to the marginalization of the Other.[29] While it is true that Othering is a feature of modernist writing, Lispector, epiphany and all, allows the roughness and the violence of the operation to surface.

Lispector's position has been an isolated one, however. Her modernist aesthetic was seen as apolitical, especially in the 1960s when literary and political commitment found their ideal representations in the guerrilla fighter. The guerrilla movement became not only the logical extension of cultural politics, but also a test of heroism. It was precisely in the aftermath of guerrilla politics that women's writing acquires special significance since it is precisely women's marginalization that seems to provide a critical standpoint, especially for those women who were caught in the contradictions of a vanguard movement that allowed them equality only in death.

The generation of women formed in the oppositional politics of the 1970s and 1980s is understandably engaged with problems of exile, marginality, and the nomadic—problems, in other words, that emerged with full force at the end of the 1970s.[30] The genres at their disposal, however—poetry and narrative—come to them loaded with the freight of history. Poetry, once widely practiced and appreciated, has receded in importance: "committed poetry" is more likely to be transmitted through the lyrics of popular songs than in published collections. And narrative, too, is far more widely diffused through television genres than through the printed word. In consequence, to write poetry or narrative that refuses to fall into the category of romance inevitably means addressing a restricted public, although this is not necessarily a disadvantage, as I hope to show in my discussion of two writers, the Peruvian Carmen Ollé and the Argentine Tununa Mercado.

Noches de Adrenalina[31] by Carmen Ollé can be regarded as a form of "testimonial." The poems in the collection monitor her long march through the political movements of the 1960s to self-exile in Paris. The poetic subject thus repeats the itinerary of a famous predecessor, César Vallejo, for whom the body was simultaneously the source of individuation and its negation. For Ollé, there is no escaping the body:

> fat / small / beardless / hairy / transparent /
> rickety / big ass / dark circles under her eyes.

Yet she is not simply determined by this destiny, for the body in all its gross and universal materiality is both the support and the object of sexual fantasy that seeks satisfaction in guilty adolescent masturbation, painful and pleasurable orgasm, adult narcissism. She pictures the women of her generation sobbing in front of the bathroom mirror, "before *The Death of the Family* caught up with us." At San Marcos, the heroes are the militant leftists: "By day they interrupted our metaphysics classes with rage / and we would applaud that sweaty black hair on / their backs." Her very identity is, at this stage of her life, mediated by the male orgasm. "I opt for nudity. / I can't contemplate it but for the mirror or in his eyes / in his aroused look that marks a curve / veering from the waist toward the butt / and erect loin and I am she who turns on his axis / while the reflection he offers me doesn't belong to me / he authors the instant in which my body is his pleasure / and barely lit up by the lamp this is nudity of nothing / other than desire." As in the poetry of César Vallejo, the harsh and sometimes pleasurable bodily sensations form a sort of rabble that constantly disturbs the more sedate progress of intellectual history—Marxism, existentialism, the counterculture. The poet-narrator is constantly on the alert, monitoring the emissions of the body—pissing, menstruation, lubrication—as well as its gradual degeneration, from the lost tooth to the last period. And yet the poems chart not only the body's aging and the intellect's disillusionment, but a process of transformation. This does not involve, as in the testimonial, an appropriation of the public sphere, but a transcendence of the social limitations imposed by gender division.

> I love her
> as I would a fickle woman
> and not knowing how to love her makes me sick
> our desire is rigid and hardly
> fired by a feminine body
> maturity has obstructed what in adolescence
> was transparent
> he/she

Given Ollé's subsequent development,[32] *Nights of Adrenaline* can perhaps be considered a kind of exorcism of Leiris and Bataille, holding out the possibility of self-love that the devaluation of the feminine has obstructed. But more than this, it suggests that there can be no "public sphere of debate" that does not include the hitherto "private" body.

Exile with its politically charged pathos has, perhaps predictably, provided many women writers with a correlative for their own marginality. In Tununa Mercado's novel *En estado de memoria*,[33] the narrator is a nomad who wanders between Mexico, Europe, and Argentina. But this novel is less a description of exile than a series of off-center meditations that allow the author to question "literature," the politics of exile (and of marginality), the seduction of memory, and the possibility of the aesthetic.

What is original about Mercado's text is indeed its questioning of marginality. The position of Mercado's narrator is essentially one of vicariousness. She is employed as a ghostwriter and editor, someone who has never pursued writing as a vocation and yet earns her living as a writer; but vicariousness is also the condition of her entire life down to the clothes that she wears, which are castoffs that had belonged to other people, and her different "homes," which never seem to belong to her and where "everything was provisional." The narrator's political activity is also vicarious. In Mexico, she demonstrates outside the Argentine embassy to protest events that have happened to people far away, knowing that the demonstration is only a shadow of "real" politics elsewhere. On a visit to Spain she offers to visit the native soil of one of her friends, a Spanish exile, thus vicariously searching for somebody else's past. In Mexico, she spends her weekends visiting the house of another exile—Leon Trotsky—and obsessively going over the last days of his life. On a visit to Argentina, she finds herself one day walking into her old primary school and trying to recapture, as an adult, the sensations of childhood. But such experiences are not of recovery, but rather of loss and absence, of death and disappearance. Returning home definitively to "redemocratized" Argentina, she still feels homeless. Even the Thursday ritual of the Mothers in the Plaza de Mayo cannot give her any sense of belonging since, after the first euphoria of return, after the expressions of solidarity, she recognizes that the energy of the antiauthoritarian movement has drained away in the new pluralistic yet strangely depoliticized environment.

Mercado's novel thus confronts one of the major issues of our time—the issue of a pluralism that permits and even encourages difference. The narrator's obsession with a tramp, a "linyera" she meets in the park, may, in fact, reflect a certain nostalgia for a marginality that has, however, no longer any possible social significance. For the marginal is merely an individual rebellion while, on the other hand, the social text has become unreadable except individually.

This dilemma is illustrated by the experience of an exile reading group in which the narrator participates. The reading group embarks on a thirty-year reading of Hegel's *Phenomenology of Mind*. This experience does not open up universal knowledge for the narrator and her friends, but rather becomes a teasing process in which the readers are sometimes absorbed by the reading, sometimes completely baffled, but never in control of it. What the reading produces is a revelation, a feeling and a cooperation, but not knowledge/power. This "distracted" relation to a text, chosen almost at random, is matched by her attitude to writing, which she never accepts as a life project or in a spirit of professionalism. The narrator compares writing to weaving, though the two processes are not exactly analogous.

Absorbed in weaving, she can attain a felicitous state of self-forgetfulness. Writing, on the other hand, is essentially a negative revelation: "not knowing, not being able to fill the vacuum, not comprehending the universal."

Who better, then, than such a narrator to register the irrevocable absences; the sense of loss, of time wasted; the fragility of justifications that sum up the purely negative state of exile? In its refusal of rhetorical and institutional certainties, the novel confronts the reader with an aesthetic that is also ascetic, an absolute state of nonpossession, an anarchy. At the novel's end, the narrator is writing on a wall that gradually slips out of view, "like paper through a crack." When the wall of gender difference comes down, it is not simply the center that is destroyed but also marginal positions, including that of "woman" and "woman writing as woman." The "writing on the wall" both heralds a destruction and performs that destruction.

The imperative for Latin American women is thus not only the occupation and transformation of public space, the seizure of citizenship, but also the recognition that speaking as a woman within a pluralistic society may actually reinstitute, in a disguised form, the same relationship of privilege that has separated the intelligentsia from the subaltern classes. The woman intellectual must witness not only the destruction of the wall, but that of her own anonymous inscription on that very wall.

In the documentary film *Double Day*, an Argentine schoolteacher was asked why girls lined up on one side of the classroom and boys on another. "Because this is the girl's side and that's the boy's side," the teacher replied without even the slightest inkling that his answer might seem absurd. This is the natural (and the ideological), the way things seemed to be. But the ways things seem to be now are not the way they were when the film was made. Girls sit on the boys' side. Women have broadened the public sphere of debate, not only as members of social movements but as intellectuals. In Mexico, for example, women act both as intellectuals in MUSIAL, "Mujeres por la soberanía y la integración de América Latina" (Women in support of Latin American sovereignty and integration) and also as mediators for marginalized women.[34] The woman intellectual cannot claim unproblematically to represent women and be their voice, but she can broaden the terms of political debate by redefining sovereignty and by using privilege to destroy privilege. I have myself shamelessly privileged a few texts that unsettle the idea that women now occupy unproblematically "their" space, for this is one way of striking a path through the forest of pluralism.

NOTES

1. See Jane S. Jaquette, ed., *The Women's Movements in Latin America: Feminism and the Transition to Democracy* (Boston: Unwin Hyman, 1989). See also "The Homeless Organize," *Nacla Report on the Americas* 23 (Nov.–Dec. 1989); Ilse Scherer-Warren and Paulo J. Krischke, eds., *Uma revolucão no cotidiano? Os novos movimentos sociais na America do Sul* (São Paulo: Editora Brasiliense, 1987); and Elizabeth Jelin, ed., *Women and Social Change in Latin America*, trans. J. Ann Zammit and Marilyn Thomson (London: Zed Books, 1990). See also Giovanni Arrighi, Terence K. Hopkins, and Immanuel Wallerstein, *Antisystemic Movements* (London: Verso, 1989).

2. Nancy Saporta Sternbach, Marysa Navarro Aranguren, Patricia Chuchryk, and Sonia Alvarez, in "Feminisms in Latin America" (unpublished essay), have given a detailed analysis of the various "encuentros de mujeres."

3. We have to distinguish between the critique of theories that are based on the notion of the public sphere (for instance, those of Habermas) and the real effect of this imaginary separation. For a critique, see Nancy Fraser, *Unruly Practices: Power, Discourse, and Gender in Contemporary Social Theory* (Minneapolis: University of Minnesota Press, 1989).

4. Fraser, *Unruly Practices*, 134.

5. Alejandra Massolo and Martha Schteingart, (eds., "Participación social, reconstrucción y mujer: El sismo de 1985," *Documentos de trabajo* 1 (UNICEF, Colegio de México). On women and the new social movements, see Elizabeth Jelin, "Citizenship and Identity: Final Reflections," which is the concluding essay in Jelin, *Women and Social Change in Latin America*, 187.

6. One of the best discussions is to be found in Carole Pateman, *The Sexual Contract* (Oxford: Basil Blackwell, 1988).

7. See, for instance, J. P. Bousquet, *Los locas de la Plaza de Mayo* (Buenos Aires: El Cid, 1983); and Elizabeth Jelin, ed., *Ciudadanía y participación*.

8. See, for example, Sara Ruddick, "Maternal Peace Politics and Women's Resistance: The Example of Argentina and Chile," *The Barnard Occasional Papers on Women's Issues* 4 (Winter, 1989), 34-55.

9. For instance, María del Carmen Feijóo, "The Challenge of Constructing Civilian Peace: Women and Democracy in Argentina," in Jaquette, *Women's Movements in Latin America*, 72-94, recognizes the contribution of the Mothers' movements but also sees possible limitations.

10. For instance, they circulated money with messages written on the notes, thus implicating random members of the public in the struggle. See Hebe Bonafini, *Historias de vida* (Buenos Aires: Fraterna, 1985), 162.

11. Julieta Kirkwood, *Ser política en Chile: las feministas y los partidos* (Santiago: FLASCO, 1986), 180

12. Maxine Molyneux, "Mobilization without Emancipation? Women's Interests, the State and Revolution in Nicaragua," *Feminist Studies* 11 (1985). See also Joel Kovacs, *In Nicaragua* (London: Free Association Books, 1988), which has some interesting things

to say about everyday life in Nicaragua and the relations between women. See especially chapter 4, "La mujer."

13. See, for instance the testimonies in Massolo and Schteingart, "Participación social, reconstrucción y mujer."

14. For a detailed discussion of some of the tensions, see Saporta Sternbach et al., "Feminisms in Latin America." On Brazil, see Sonia Alvarez, "Brazil"; and for Chile, Patricia M. Chuchryk, "Feminist Anti-Authoritarian Politics: The Role of Women's Organizations in the Chilean Transition to Democracy." Both articles are included in Jaquette, *Women's Movements in Latin America.*

15. See, for example, Ruth Molina de Cuevas, *Y me vistieron de luto* (San José, Costa Rica: Editorial Universitaria Centroamericana, 1990). The poems are dedicated to her sons who disappeared and "to the mothers who like myself are waiting."

16. Angel Rama, *La ciudad letrada* (Hanover, N.H.: Ediciones del Norte, 1984).

17. Eltit discusses her performances on the BBC film "Love and Power," which was part of the series *Made in Latin America.* It must be remembered, however, that highly codified avant-garde writing and performance have been particular features of literature under authoritarian regimes. For Elena Poniatowska, see *La "Flor de Lis"* (México, D.F.: Era, 1988).

18. Julieta Kirkwood, *Ser política*, 191.

19. Massolo and Schteingart, "Participación social, reconstrucción y mujer," 76.

20. Ibid., 78.

21. Elizabeth Burgos-Debray, ed., *I . . . Rigoberta Menchú: An Indian Woman in Guatemala*, trans. Ann Wright (London: Verso, 1984). There have many articles on Rigoberta Menchú. See, for example, George Yúdice, "Marginality and the Ethics of Survival," in Andrew Ross, ed., *Universal Abandon?: The Politics of Postmodernism* (Minneapolis: University of Minnesota Press, 1988). See also Moema Viezzer, ed., *Si me permiten hablar": Testimonio de Domitila, Una mujer de las minas de Bolivia* (México: Siglo XXI, 1977). See also David Acebey, ed., *Aquí también Domitila* (México: Siglo XXI, 1985).

22. Carlos Monsiváis, *Entrada libre: Crónicas de una sociedad que se organiza* (México: Era, 1987).

23. Graciela Iturbide and Elena Poniatowska, *Juchitán de las mujeres* (México, D.F.: Ediciones Toledo, 1989), 13-14. See also Poniatowska's chronicle of the 1985 earthquake, *Nada, nadie: Las voces del temblor* (México: Era, 1988).

24. Terry Eagleton, *The Ideology of the Aesthetic*, (Oxford: Basil Blackwell, 1990).

25. As Nancy Fraser points out, in *Unruly Practices*, even in classic capitalism the family was never totally private.

26. For a discussion of French feminism in relation to Hispanic culture, see Paul Julian Smith, *The Body Hispanic* (Oxford: Oxford University Press, 1989).

27. Among writers whose work has been translated, we might mention Rosario Ferré's *Sweet Diamond Dust* (New York: Ballantine, 1988); Isabel Allende's first novel, *The House of the Spirits*, trans. Magda Bogin (New York: Knopf, 1985); and Luisa Valenzuela, *The Lizard's Tail*, trans. Gregory Rabassa (New York: Farrar, Straus & Giroux, 1983). Some interesting attempts to change the "subject" include Cristina Peri Rossi, *La nave de los locos* (Barcelona: Seix Barral, 1984), and *El campo*, by Griselda Gambaro, a theater piece that acts out the savagery of the death camp and male-female relationships. Albalucía del Angel, in *Estaba la pájara pinta sentada en el verde limón* (Barcelona: Argos Vergara, 1984), rewrites the story of Colombian *violencia.*

28. See Hélène Cixous, *Reading with Clarice Lispector*, trans. Verena Andermatt Conley (Minneapolis: University of Minnesota Press, 1990). For a critique of Lispector as exemplary woman writer, see Daphne Patai, "El esencialismo de Clarice Lispector," *Nuevo Texto Crítico* 3 (1990), 21-35.

29. "A Bela e a Fera ou a ferida grande demais" (Beauty and the Beast; or, The Wound That Was Too Big) is included in Benedito Nunes, ed., *Paixão Segundo G.H.* (Campus Universitário, Trinidad; Florianópolis SC, Brazil: UNESCO, Coleção Arquivos, 1988), 151-57. The novel has been translated as *The Passion according to G.H.*, trans. Ronald W. Sousa (Minneapolis: University of Minnesota Press, 1988). Also translated by Giovanni Pontiero is *The Hour of the Star* (New York: Carcaner, 1986).

30. In general, the left position has been that socialism will bring about women's liberation. See, for example, Latin American and Caribbean Women's Collective, *Slaves of Slaves: The Challenge of Latin American Women*, trans. Michael Pallis (London: Zed Press, 1977); Isabel Larguía and John Dumoulin, *Hacia una ciencia de la liberación de la mujer* (Caracas: Universidad Central de Venezuela, 1975); Heleieth Saffioti, *Women in Class Society*, trans. Michael Vale (New York and London: Monthly Review Press, 1978).

31. Carmen Ollé, *Noches de Adrenalina* (Lima: Cuadernos de Hipocampo, 1981). Translations by Ann Archer.

32. She has since published in a nonconfessional mode, *Todo orgullo humea la noche* (Lima: Lluvia, 1988).

33. Tununa Mercado, *En estado de memoria* (Buenos Aires: Ada Korn, 1990). For these last paragraphs — especially the questioning of "marginality" — I wish to express my debt to Josefina Ludmer, especially in the light of her recent work on delinquency, the state, and the counterstate. For a different but powerful discussion of marginality, see also Diamela Eltit's conversations with the man known as "El Padre Mío," Diamela Eltit, *El Padre Mío* (Santiago: Francisco Zegers, 1989).

34. MUSIAL, which includes some of Mexico's most prominent women intellectuals, began as a discussion group. The women now issue declarations as women and intellectuals on particular problems concerned with sovereignty — on Panama and Nicaragua, for example.

"The Other Side of the Process":
Racial Formation in Contemporary Brazil
Howard Winant

*A história oficial, como se sabe, tem-se preocupado em retratar a
sociedade branca-européia, omitindo o outro lado do processo.
[Official history, as is well known, has been preoccupied with
portraying white European society, omitting the other side of the
process.]*

Benedita Souza da Silva

In the centennial year of the abolition of slavery in Brazil, the country's enormous black[1] population has been restive. There were manifestos and demonstrations; notable efforts were made to invigorate dormant and divided political organizations. Incidents of racial discrimination, and black protest against it, appeared more often on the television news. Strong guarantees of minority rights and racial equality were at one point included in the draft of the new Brazilian constitution, although, with the important exception of Indian rights, these provisions survive only in diluted fashion in the final document.[2]

To be sure, the new racial activism was tentative and uncertain. There have been several unsuccessful attempts in the past to sustain a national black movement. The unique capacity of Brazilian society to combine political repression and co-optation with a culturally sophisticated denial of racial conflict has always made the development of black oppositional currents very difficult. Brazilian elites, both right and left, continue to dismiss the significance of the racial variable in political and cultural life. The long-standing tendency to subordinate racial dynamics to those of class is still easily observed across the entire political spectrum. This *class reductionism* retains many adherents, especially among whites.

Yet there is today an unmistakable willingness, greater than ever before, to acknowledge the profound racial inequalities in Brazil. Using recent census data, sophisticated studies of racial stratification have demonstrated the unchanging stratification patterns of Brazilian society; black mobility is extremely limited (Hasenbalg, 1979; do Valle Silva, 1980, 1985).

The permanent concentration of blacks and mulattoes in the lowest socioeconomic strata and the bankruptcy of much existing racial theory raise several intriguing questions. Are concepts of race changing in Brazil? Why has a modicum of black activism and organization come into being over the last decade or so? What current political possibilities (and continuing obstacles) confront racial movements, in particular the black movement? What is the impact on blacks of the "transition to democracy" that began in the 1970s with the *abertura* (the "opening" to democracy) and finally achieved a civilian government in 1985? The current moment is particularly propitious for a reexamination of the potential of racial politics in Brazil.

In this essay I suggest that contemporary Brazilian racial dynamics are indeed being transformed. This shift is not something happening in isolation, but is deeply intertwined with the political process that is commonly if somewhat inaccurately called the "transition to democracy." For this reason, party politics, the drafting of a new constitution, social policy in many different spheres (agrarian reform, education, health), and even foreign policy are now to be seen as racial issues. This, in itself, is an unprecedented development. Furthermore, the legacy of twenty years of military dictatorship has profoundly transformed the Brazilian political terrain, with important consequences for racial mobilization. The proliferation of social movements that appeared under the dictatorship—*comunidades eclesiais de base* (CEBs, Christian base communities), neighborhood and favela organizations, women's groups, as well as cultural and community-based entities of various kinds—has made new forms of politics possible, offering a potential challenge to traditional paternalism and clientelism. All of this has manifested itself within the black movement, and has important implications for that movement's future.

Changing racial dynamics are linked as well to the ever-deepening Brazilian economic crisis, as the traditional articulation (or reduction) of race in terms of class is problematized. In the trade unions and left political parties—PT and PDT, especially—black activity is noticeable, and in some areas there are now black caucuses and new levels of debate about the particular situation of black workers. Black women's voices are being raised, and attention is being drawn to the implacable racial logic of malnutrition, illiteracy, and landlessness.

Last but far from least, the racially defined foundations of Brazilian culture are becoming more pronounced. This is taking place in two ways: first, the racial history of Brazil is receiving renewed attention, not least because of the 1988 centenary of *abolição*, abolition; second, racial identities and racial signification processes are being *politicized*, albeit slowly. The history of racial oppression is difficult to confine to the remote past when evidence of its persistence is manifest, and when the cultural constructs that formerly explained racial dynamics have been steadily eroded. Today, blacks are beginning to challenge the racial "common sense," both mainstream and radical, that race and racism are of limited political significance in the Brazilian context.

This transformation points toward a reinterpretation not only of Brazilian politics, but also of Brazilian culture. As in other societies such as the United States, racial dynamics in Brazil potentially challenge formidable cultural systems: those of identity formation and social signification.

Given the immediacy of many of these developments, there is a necessarily speculative aspect to the questions I ask. What political forms has the black movement taken thus far? How does it compare with racial movements in the postwar United States? What challenges does it pose for racial theory in Brazil? What are the linkages between racial politics and democratic transition in Brazil?

Such questions derive in part from a comparative frame of reference. In recent decades there have been many comparisons of Brazilian and U.S. racial dynamics (Skidmore, 1974; Harris, 1964; Van den Berghe, 1967; Degler, 1971; Hasenbalg, 1979). What could a new effort possibly contribute to this illustrious list? The answer lies in the uniqueness of the *racial-formation perspective*. Racial-formation theory permits a more nuanced examination of racial dynamics than other perspectives have allowed. It squarely opposes reductionism — the tendency to understand race as a manifestation of some other, supposedly more fundamental or "objective" social relationship. Finally, the racial-formation perspective, unlike other racial theories, understands race as a complex of social meanings and relationships that is always changing. Since in this account racial meanings, racial identities, and racial inequalities have no fixed significance, but are constantly being rearticulated by both political and cultural processes, the racial-formation perspective is useful in comparative analysis, where cultural themes and political logics may be combined in quite different ways. It also encourages us to ask whether Brazilian racial dynamics might not be shifting in a more epochal sense, as they did in the postwar United States.

A final cautionary note: large-scale racial conflict, indeed large-scale racial consciousness (in the political sense of that term), has not yet emerged in Brazil. The transformation to which I am pointing is an accumulation of forces, an intensification of contradictions, not a movement eruption. We must not expect the kind of ruptural events that came to characterize the black movement in the United States: I am thinking of the Montgomery bus boycott, the Birmingham and Selma events, Watts, and other historical moments. Brazilian conditions are different, as many writers have correctly argued.

Contemporary Racial Theory and Brazil

Until quite recently Brazil was seen as a country with a comparatively benign pattern of race relations.[3] Only in the 1950s, when UNESCO sponsored a series of studies of racial dynamics — looking particularly at Bahía and São Paulo — did the traditional theoretical approaches, which focused on the concept of "racial democracy," come under sustained attack.[4] The work of such UNESCO researchers as Thales de Azevedo, Roger Bastide, Florestan Fernandes, and Marvin Harris documented as never before the prevalence of racial discrimination and the persistence of the supposedly discredited ideology of "whitening." This research set new terms for debate, constituting (not without some disagreements) a new racial "revisionism."

Racial revisionism was full of insights into Brazilian racial dynamics, but it also had significant limitations. Chief among these was a tendency to reduce race to class, depriving racial dynamics of their own, autonomous significance.

Florestan Fernandes's work probably remains the most comprehensive sociology of race relations in Brazil. In terms of racial *theory*, however, his perspective had great limitations. In Fernandes's view,

Brazil's "racial dilemma" is a result of survivals from the days of slavery, which came into conflict with capitalist development, and would be liquidated by modernity. "The Brazilian racial dilemma," Fernandes writes, "constitutes a pathological social phenomenon, which can only be corrected by processes that would remove the obstruction of racial inequality from the competitive social order" (1978, vol. 2, 460).

The importance of Fernandes's work is his recognition of the centrality of racial dynamics in Brazil's development, not only in the past and even the present, but also in the future. Race, however, remains a "dilemma" whose "resolution" will signify sociopolitical maturity. In other words, Fernandes still understands race as a problem whose solution is integration. Implicitly, there is a new stage to be achieved in Brazilian development, in which racial conflict will no longer present an obstacle or diversion from class conflict.

Fernandes at least recognized the continuing presence and significance of race; other revisionists tended to dismiss or minimize it. While Fernandes's basic optimism was tempered by the question of whether the full modernization of class society could be achieved, Thales de Azevedo saw evidence that the process was already far advanced: according to him, class conflict was *replacing* racial conflict in Bahía (Azevedo, 1966, 30-43). Marvin Harris, who worked closely with Azevedo, suggested that the Brazilian system of racial identification necessarily subordinated race to class.[5] Comparing Brazilian and U.S. racial dynamics, Harris argued that the absence of a "descent rule" by which racial identity could be inherited, and the flexibility of racial meanings, led to a situation in which "racial identity is a mild and wavering thing in Brazil, while in the United States it is for millions of people a passport to hell" (Harris, 1964, 64).

Actually, there are several versions of the dynamic in which race is subordinated to class. For the original revisionists, the question was whether this process was a social fact, already in progress and perhaps even well advanced, or a mere possibility. For Azevedo, the process was already well under way; for Fernandes, it was a tendency that might—tragically—never come to pass unless the Brazilian people exhibited enough political will to transcend the racial dilemma and modernize their social order.

Later work, such as that of Carl Degler (1971) and Amaury de Souza (1971; see also Bastide, 1965) suggested various ways in which racial dynamics could *persist* while still remaining subordinated to class conflicts. Degler, comparing Brazil and the United States, concluded that because Brazil distinguished mulattoes from blacks and afforded them greater social mobility—the so-called mulatto escape hatch—racial polarization had been avoided there. If the "escape hatch" were there, then the United States pattern of growing racial solidarity would not occur; thus, at least for some blacks (that is, mulattoes) questions of class would automatically take precedence over those of race. Other blacks, recognizing that mobility was available to the lighter skinned, would seek this possibility, if not for themselves then for their children. De Souza made a similar argument that had less recourse to historical data and focused instead on "whitening" as a sort of rational-choice model, in which blacks had to weigh the costs of individual mobility against those of racial solidarity; consequently, a type of "prisoner's dilemma" confronted any effort to organize black political opposition. Such views tended to confirm the traditional wisdom about "whitening" as the preferred solution to Brazil's racial problems; they also stressed economic mobility (and, thus, integration in class society) as the key question in Brazilian racial dynamics.

The Critique of Reductionism. These analyses consistently practiced racial *reductionism*; that is, they understood race epiphenomenally, as a manifestation of some other, supposedly more fundamental, social process or relationship. In the vast majority of studies, race was interpreted in terms of class.

While it is certainly not illegitimate to examine the linkage between race and class, reductionism goes one step further: it fails to recognize the independence and depth of race. As a consequence of centuries of inscription in the social order, racial dynamics inevitably acquire their own autonomous logic, penetrating the fabric of social life and the cultural system at every level. Thus they cannot be fully understood, in the manner of Fernandes, as "survivals" of a plantation slavocracy in which capitalist social relationships had not yet developed. Such a perspective ultimately denies the linkages between racial phenomena and postslavery society. There can be little doubt that since abolition the meaning of race has transformed tremendously; it has been "modernized" and reinterpreted quite regularly (Skidmore, 1974).

Nor is it tenable to suggest that in Brazil racial distinctions are ephemeral, mere adjuncts to class categories, as do Harris and Azevedo. Substantial racial inequality may be observed in levels of income, employment, and returns to schooling; in access to education and literacy rates, in health care, in housing, and importantly, by region (Costa, 1983; do Valle Silva, 1985; Hasenbalg, 1979, 1983).[6] In order to substantiate the thesis of "transition from race to class," it would be necessary to demonstrate that inequality levels were tending to equalize *across* racial lines; the fact that one hundred years after the end of slavery blacks are still overwhelmingly concentrated in the bottom strata certainly suggests that race is still a salient determinant of life-chances.

Degler's and de Souza's emphasis on the distinction between blacks and mulattoes — and the consequences of mobility for mulattoes — also is not borne out by careful analysis of patterns of racial inequality in Brazil. Nelson do Valle Silva's detailed study of racial stratification reveals no significant difference between black and mulatto mobility. Looking at a variety of indicators (income, returns to schooling, and so forth), and using 1960 and 1976 census data that distinguish between blacks and mulattoes, do Valle Silva finds that "blacks and mulattoes seem to display unexpectedly familiar profiles." Further,

> these results lead us to reject the two hypotheses advanced by the Brazilian sociological literature. Mulattoes do not behave differently from Blacks, nor does race play a negligible role in the process of income attainment. In fact it was found that Blacks and mulattoes are almost equally discriminated against. . . . This clearly contradicts the idea of a "mulatto escape-hatch" being the essence of Brazilian race relations. (do Valle Silva, 1985, 54-55; see also do Valle Silva, 1980)

Perhaps the most striking limitation of the revisionist literature is its nearly exclusive focus on racial inequality. This is not to deny the importance of the economic dimensions of race. However, the preoccupation with inequality to the near total exclusion of any other aspect of race is a logical feature of approaches that treat racial dynamics as manifestations of more fundamental class relationships. These approaches tend to take the meaning of race for granted, and to see racial identities as relatively rigid and unchanging.

In revisionist approaches then, there are two notable difficulties, both of which flow from reductionism: first, there is the apparent fact that previous explanations of racial inequality are eroding; second, there is an unwillingness or inability to see race as a theoretically flexible, as opposed to an a priori, category. In writing about racial dynamics there is a marked tendency to assume what most needs to be explained: what race *means* in a given sociohistorical context.

The Structural Approach. Beginning in the 1970s, and with greater frequency in later years, a "postrevisionist" or *structural* approach to race in Brazil began to emerge. This perspective saw race as a central feature of Brazilian society. "Structural" authors sharply refocused the problem of racial theory. They did not seek to explain how racism had survived in a supposed "racial democracy," nor how true integration might be achieved. Rather, they looked at the way the Brazilian social order had maintained racial inequalities without encountering significant opposition and conflict.

In a brief essay originally published in 1971, Anani Dzidzienyo combined a critique of racial inequality with a discussion of both the macro- and microlevel cultural dynamics of race in Brazil. He challenged the "bias which has been a hallmark of the much-vaunted Brazilian 'racial democracy' — the bias that white is best and black is worst and therefore the nearer one is to white, the better." Further, he noted that "The hold which this view has on Brazilian society is all-pervasive and embraces a whole range of stereotypes, role-playing, job opportunities, life-styles, and, what is even more important, it serves as the cornerstone of the closely-observed "etiquette" of race relations in Brazil" (Dzidzienyo, 1971, 5).

Here, in embryo, was a far more comprehensive critique of Brazilian racial dynamics. Dzidzienyo argued that racial inequalities were both structural and linked to a hegemonic racial ideology. This "official Brazilian ideology achieves *without tension* the same results as do overtly racist societies" (Dzidzienyo, 1971, 14; emphasis in the original). Structural inequality and the system of racial meanings were articulated in a single racial order; each served to support the other.

Carrying on this approach in a more recent contribution of great importance, Carlos Hasenbalg developed a new synthesis of race and class, building on, but also departing from, the work of Fernandes (Hasenbalg, 1979; see also van den Berghe, 1967). In Hasenbalg's view, post-*abolição* racial dynamics have been steadily transformed as Brazilian capitalism has evolved; thus, far from being outmoded, racial inequality remains necessary and functional for Brazilian capitalism. The essential problem, then, is not to account for the persistence of racism, but rather to explain the absence of serious racial opposition, what Hasenbalg calls "the smooth maintenance of racial inequalities."

Both Dzidzienyo and Hasenbalg recognize that in the Brazilian system *racial hegemony* created an essential link between the cultural and sociopolitical logics of race. Neither the powerful ideological complex of "whitening" and "racial democracy" nor the brutal structural inequalities between black and white would have been sustainable on its own. In this sense, these writers adopted early versions of a racial-formation perspective.

Important problems, however, remain unresolved by the structural theories, for they still bear some of the marks of class reductionism. To be sure, these analyses grant Brazilian racial dynamics a significant degree of autonomy. But in the structural approach the ability of elites "smoothly" to manage racial inequalities is still based on their historical manipulation of class conflict. In Hasenbalg's view, this manipulation took on its characteristic form when the elites decided to encourage massive European immigration, thus displacing black labor after *abolição* (Hasenbalg, 1979, 223-60). Plentiful supplies of white labor prevented the emergence of a racially split labor market, such as developed in the United States, and effectively defused racial antagonisms. In this way, the Brazilian racial pattern was consolidated in the ideal of "whitening," and later in the ideology of "racial democracy." Thus the system of racial categorization, as well as the ideological and political dynamics of race in general, were *consequences* of capitalist development in the post-*abolição* years.

This account does not take into account the fact that racial ideology was entirely present at the supposed foundations of Brazilian capitalist development. Indeed, it was in part because of their fear of blacks that the Brazilian elite turned to European immigration in the first place (Skidmore, 1974, 130-31, 136-44). Thus, Hasenbalg's argument would operate equally well in reverse: the course of development followed by Brazilian capitalism was shaped in significant measure by preexisting racial patterns. However significant the absence of a split labor market was to the development of Brazilian racial dynamics, it was clearly not determining; at most it was one factor among others. Indeed, a reasonable argument could be made that the political authoritarianism — the *coronelismo* (rule of a "big boss," usually in the countryside), paternalism, clientelism, and other factors that characterized elite-mass relationships in the first republic and beyond — was a carryover from slavery into the post-*abolição* framework in which capitalist development began in earnest. Thus, not only the framework of Brazilian class relations, but also, in large measure, the traditional political structure, have their origins in racial dynamics.

Racial Formation: Comparative Perspectives

Race is simultaneously an obvious and obscure phenomenon. In the United States, for example, everyone "knows" what race is, while at the same time it is difficult to specify how many racial groups there are, the salient characteristics of each group, and the terminology with which these groups should be described. In Brazil, of course, race is an even more flexible category. The implications of this insight remain unresolved, despite significant debate. Does this imply, as Harris thought, that race becomes a relatively insignificant variable in comparison to class in determining one's "life-chances"? This would suggest a pure class reductionism. Does the Brazilian pattern imply that the supposedly defunct racial ideology of "whitening" remains in force? This would suggest not only a permanent depoliticization of race, but a ferocious racial hegemony such as that charged by Abdias do Nascimento (1968, 1978). Or does the Brazilian pattern imply that racial meanings and constructs might indeed be open to rearticulation? Could the traditional clientelism and populist authoritarianism that up to now has characterized Brazilian racial politics (and politics in general) be ruptured, such that a black movement would become a more viable political alternative than before? Nothing in either the revisionist or the structuralist literature enables us to answer these questions.

Racial-formation theory seems particularly well suited to deal with the complexities of Brazilian racial dynamics. Developed as a response to reductionist approaches, this perspective understands race as a phenomenon whose meaning is contested throughout social life. Race is seen as a constituent of the individual psyche and of relationships among individuals; it is also an irreducible component of collective identities and social structures. The processes by which racial meanings are decided, and racial identities assigned, are inherently discursive. As with any discursive process, more than one interpretation, more than one meaning, can exist at any given time. The political character of racial formation stems from this: elites, popular movements, state agencies, religions, and intellectuals of all types interpret and reinterpret the meaning of race constantly.

The articulation and rearticulation of racial meanings is thus a multidimensional process, in which competing "projects" intersect and clash. These projects are often explicitly, but always at least implicitly, political. "Subjective" phenomena — racial identities, popular culture, "common sense" — and social structural phenomena, such as political movements and parties, state institutions and policies, market processes, and so on, are all grist for the mill, all active components of racial formation. Wherever racial categories become salient markers of individual and collective identity, race emerges as a key axis of contestation and accommodation (Omi and Winant, 1986).

Comparing racial-formation processes in Brazil and the United States provides new insights about both countries. At first the two societies present themselves as a set of opposites, and indeed many analysts have suggested as much. The following antinomies are often proposed: in the United States, racial identity is rigidly assigned and racial significance is overtly recognized; in Brazil, identity is flexible and racial meanings are hidden. In the United States, the state and political processes are directly implicated in racial dynamics; in Brazil, the state and politics are, at most, indirectly racial. Yet, on closer examination, a more complex pattern emerges, in which the political dimension of race plays a central role.

Racial Identity. Many writers have discussed the differences between racial identity in the United States and Brazil, proposing such concepts as "hypo-descent" to account for the rigidity of color lines in the United States (Harris, 1964, 56), and "hypergamy" (Bastide, 1965, 26) to account for the flexibility of racial identity in Brazil. At the time of the UNESCO studies the United States appeared far less racially tolerant than Brazil, the restrictions of racial identity far more pronounced. Today, after three decades of movement activity, the reverse is probably true. Racial identity has been politicized to an unprecedented extent in the United States, with enormous cultural and indeed personal consequences. In significant measure, the political terrain opened up by "new social movements" was first explored by the black movement, which brought a racial perspective to bear on problems of sex, science, the arts, "taste," and even the environment (not to mention traditionally political topics).

The Brazilian system was not challenged in this way, not only because the system of racial categorization withstood opposition better, but also because the military dictatorship was at pains to dampen all forms of social conflict. The result was that the process of *branqueamento* (the process of "whitening") continued without large-scale political or ideological opposition. Significantly, racial categories shifted nevertheless. As Pierre-Michel Fontaine has pointed out, "black" is becoming a more marginal racial identity: "[While] the definition of blackness is . . . historically receding to a narrower band at the darkest end of the spectrum, the definition of whiteness has been concurrently expanding to encompass darker shades of white at the other end" (Fontaine, 1979, 149). Thus in Brazil, too, racial identities change over historical time. If overt challenge to these identities was not possible because neither the system of racial hegemony nor the military dictatorship permitted it, these identities were still challenged by other more hidden means. Not merely contestation of the racial order but also its accommodation has consequences for racial identity.

Racial-formation processes also shape racial meaning or signification, not just identity. This has been true in both the United States and Brazil. In the United States, the racial implications of many social, political, or cultural issues are commonly recognized and debated (although not always openly — consider the question of racial "code words" and euphemisms like "law and order"; in Brazil the term *boa aparência* means "white"). Thus, racial signification is quite extensive, even if the racial dimensions of many issues are still not commonly recognized as such.[7]

In the postwar period, Brazilian racial identities and meanings have certainly been transformed more apolitically and slowly than in the United States. It should be recalled, however, that the United States, too, has experienced long periods during which the racial order seemed immune from change. Indeed, the period extending from the end of Reconstruction in 1877 to the advent of the modern civil rights struggle in the post-World War II years can be seen as one of only glacial change in the U.S. racial order.[8]

In the Brazilian case, even though the racial order possessed a formidable ability to thwart change, racial-signification processes have been transformed in recent years. Some quick examples must suffice here: as Fontaine suggests, "status whiteness" is less secure today than it was in the past (1979, 1981). A national political figure like Leonel Brizola finds it opportune to refer to his program as "socialismo moreno" (Dillon Soares and do Valle Silva, 1985).[9] The issue of Africa, not historical Africa or mythical Africa but contemporary Africa — for instance, support for the front-line states and opposition to Brazil's relationship with apartheid — is finding its way onto the agendas of Brazilian blacks, creating a racially based foreign-policy constituency whose interests obviously are not solely defined by African concerns.

The Racial State and Politics. In postcolonial Brazil there has never been an official, legally enforced distinction among the races, such as that of apartheid or Jim Crow (Nogueira, 1955). Rather, the opposite has occurred: both the state and popular wisdom have denied the legitimacy of color prejudice. Politically, this has had the effect of making racial inequality difficult to oppose, for two reasons. First, it has obscured the source of the problem. No Brazilian figure plays the role of a Bilbo or Eastland, no law or social policy institutionalizing racial inequality has existed since abolition in 1888, and no "separate but equal" principle was ever enunciated. Second, it has undermined the integrity of racial resistance. No official segregation meant no black church or black colleges, no segregated space to serve as a breeding ground of nationalism, of black consciousness, of counter-hegemonic racial discourse. Even the *terreiros* (places of worship, usually in a special room of a private house) of Candomblé and the Escolas de Samba have been integrated for decades, generating a "folklorization" of black culture that has had the same co-optative and debilitating effects as *branqueamento* in general (Borges Pereira, 1983, 1984). While these institutions do represent crucial black cultural resources, they are not generally perceived as political terrain.

In short, because Brazilian segregation was never absolute, its existence could always be denied; because it was never absolute, no absolutely black political terrain could ever be generated. Traditional political strategies — paternalism and clientelism — were always available when elites had to deal with potential black opposition.

These traditional political patterns, I suggest, cannot counteract racial opposition as effectively as before. They have, in fact, been significantly challenged in the last decade or so. Of course, this did not occur without the airing of familiar charges and ideological claims — black organizations were racist for bringing up the issue of race, prejudice was absent in Brazilian society, and so on — but these accusations clearly lack some of their past weight. Over the past decade, traditional racial patterns have been deeply, perhaps irrevocably, transformed. A politicization of race is beginning, a far-reaching chain of events that has the potential to reshape Brazilian politics. This process can best be understood in the terms of racial-formation theory.

Contemporary Brazilian Racial Formation

Some Key Trends in Brazilian Racial Formation Today. Still tentative and uncertain, contemporary Brazilian racial formation appears to consist of four interrelated elements, each essential for the others' existence. These may be characterized as follows:

A heritage of black opposition. Contemporary racial mobilization takes place in a historical context of opposition, rebellion, and egalitarian critique that spans the history of Brazil. There are significant precedents for almost every political current evident in the country today; the organizational efforts of the 1930s, expressed through the Frente Negra Brasileira, still constitute the highest level of black political struggle achieved thus far in Brazil.

Of the many black organizations that anticipated developments in the 1970s and 1980s, the Frente is surely the most important. Although it experienced a good deal of internal tension, the Frente mobilized large numbers of blacks, particularly in the São Paulo area, in the 1930s. It was suppressed by Vargas in 1937, after declaring itself a political party (Fernandes, 1978, 2: 7-115). The black community sustained a large number of organizations and publications throughout the first half of the twentieth century, and particularly in the period of the Frente. In such journals as *O Clarim da Alvorada* and *A Voz da Raça* the black movement debated issues of identity and politics in a quite modern fashion (Blair, 1965; Bastide, 1973, 129-156). Though imperfectly known and somewhat compromised by its linkages to traditional Brazilian political models, this heritage nevertheless remains crucial for the new movements. It was embodied by the participation of key "veterans" of the earlier movement currents in the founding of the most important contemporary racial-movement organizations, the Movimento Negro Unificado Contra Discriminação Racial (MNUCDR, later MNU).

Probably the most important single figure, whose activism in the black movement spans the decades from the Vargas period to the present, is Abdias do Nascimento. Nascimento was involved in the formation of the Comité Democrático Afro-Brasileiro in 1945; he was instrumental, along with Guerreiro Ramos and Edison Carneiro, in organizing the Congresso Brasileiro do Negro in 1950; he was the moving spirit behind the Teatro Experimental do Negro in the 1940s and 1950s, and he was a founder (apparently something of an *éminence grise*) of the MNU in 1978. As the originator of the philosophy of *Quilombismo*, Nascimento also possesses one of the few truly "nationalist" or "Afrocentric" voices in Brazil.

Rearticulation of racial themes. Rearticulation is the process of rupturing and reconstructing the prevailing *commonsense* logic of race. At its core, it involves challenging individual and group identities.

In order to transform an existing pattern of oppression, it is necessary to demystify that pattern, to demonstrate its vulnerability, its illogicality. But since common sense — for example, racial stereotyping — always has a certain logic, the elements of the old common sense have to be taken apart, disarticulated, deconstructed. These elements are in general not only political, but also familial, religious, linguistic; they are cultural norms and folkways; of necessity they are familiar things, taken for granted, part of everyday life. Everything from political style to style of dress, from child raising to language, from cooking to artistic form is fair game for racial rearticulation. These elements are reinterpreted, recombined, even reinvented in the rearticulation process, ultimately emerging as a new common sense.[10] Rearticulation is thus both a political and an intellectual project. It connects the world of ideas with that of the everyday. A deep interdependence links intellectuals (in the Gramscian sense of that term), social movements, and everyday life in the project of rearticulation: no movement is possible without the participation of intellectuals, but at the same time, there can be no political framework for rearticulation in the absence of a movement, indeed one that is deeply aware of the everyday life of its members.

Since the *abertura* began in 1974, nearly every component of Brazilian racial identity has been at least partially rearticulated, though, of course, traditional common sense retains a great deal of force as well. Much of the challenge has been intellectual; a review of the recent literature on race suggests that a very broad rethinking is under way. Among the main themes that have been reinterpreted in major studies over this period are the following: the legacy of slavery (Chiavenato, 1986); the meaning and extent of democracy for blacks (Valente, 1986); the nature of racial inequality and cultural difference (Moura, 1977, 1983; Sodré, 1983); the relationship between Brazilian blacks and blacks elsewhere in the world—notably in the United States and in Africa (Gonçalves, 1987; Dzidzienyo, 1985; Selcher, 1974); the psychological meaning of gradations in skin color (Souza, 1983); and the significance of such Afro-Brazilian religious and cultural traditions as Umbanda and Candomblé, samba and carnaval (Fry, 1982; dos Santos, 1977; Brown, 1986; Bastide, 1978; Brito, 1986; Araujo, 1983; Sebe, 1986).

Explicitly black political mobilization along two chief axes: cultural awareness and antidiscrimination. Beginning in the mid-1970s, there has been a proliferation of activities and organizations manifesting these tendencies. Of these, probably the most significant were the "black-soul" movement (da Silva, 1980; Fontaine, 1981, 153-56) and the Movimento Negro Unificado (MNU).[11]

Expansion of the political terrain. Finally, the process of *abertura* and the democratic transition provided a context for racial politics and made race a subject of political debate and maneuver.

Democratic opposition in general, traditionally compromised and co-opted by elite control, *coronelismo*, and corporatism, faced additional difficulties in the aftermath of 1964. The decades-long process of military rule rendered ineffective many of the traditional patterns of political conflict in Brazil; it eliminated others outright. Thus, the popular strata had to adopt new forms of struggle and contestation. Here, the new social movements—human rights groups, women's groups, residential associations, and very important in the Brazilian context, Christian base communities (CEBs)—became important political actors. The new social movements expanded the terrain of politics. They addressed issues that formerly had been seen as personal or private—that is, not as legitimate themes for collective action—as public, social, and legitimate areas for mobilization. Black-movement activity became possible as part of a larger effort to reconstruct civil society.

These four interrelated processes constitute the components of the contemporary Brazilian racial-formation process. I offer this model in a preliminary fashion, in order to further our understanding of what is still a limited and tentative challenge to Brazilian racial dynamics. To be sure, the transformation of racial identities and meanings, the creation of a new racial common sense, demands a fairly thoroughgoing confrontation with the hegemonic system, at least if we are to judge from the U.S. experience in the 1960s. Thus far Brazilian blacks have only begun to overturn the previous racial common sense, that of "whitening" and "racial democracy"; they have questioned the invisible and transitory position to which these racist ideologies had condemned them, but they have not yet been able to consolidate an alternative view, much less diffuse it among the black population that constitutes the majority of Brazil's citizenry.

Recent racial politics in Brazil can be illuminated by comparison to U.S. events in the postwar period. Racial dynamics serve, perhaps permanently, as the central indicator of democratic prospects in both the United States and Brazil.

Racial Formation and Democratic Transition

Beginning in the 1950s and more intensively in the 1960s, the black movement initiated a "great transformation"[12] of the U.S. political universe, creating new organizations, new collective identities, and new political norms; challenging past racial practices and stereotypes; and ushering in a wave of democratizing social reform. The black movement, then, brought about a significant "transition to democracy" in the United States.

Because it successfully presented its racial agenda in terms of established democratic ideals and aspirations, the black movement permitted the entry of millions of racial minority group members into the political process. These actors brought about reforms that exposed the limits of all previously existing political orientations — conservative, liberal, and radical. In their assault on the meaning of race and the contours of racial politics, minority movements transformedthe meaning and contours of U.S. politics itself. Indeed, they made identity, difference, the "personal," and language itself political issues in very new ways. For example, the idea that "the personal is political," though properly associated with the women's movement, has its origins in the black movement, as Carson shows in his history of the Student Nonviolent Coordinating Committee (SNCC) (Carson 1981).

In a word, the new movements "politicized the social." They changed the nature of politics; what had been understood in terms of conflict of interests (class conflict, interest-group conflict, elite competition) now also had to be understood in terms of conflict of *meanings*. Furthermore, the new movement mobilization was "contagious"; though catalyzed by the black movement, it soon spread to other racial minorities, women, peace, gay, and environmental activists, the disabled, and the aged. The black movement became the source of a new political logic in the United States.[13]

How may this "great transformation" of race in the United States be compared with the origins of a modern black movement in Brazil? Such a comparison is useful, I think, in two ways. First, it emphasizes the role of democratic transition in shaping racial issues; second, it demonstrates what I have called the "contagious" character of social-movement politics.

To speak of democratic transition in the contemporary United States may strike some as exaggerated. Yet with respect to racial minorities, and especially in the case of the modern civil rights movement, such a perspective is quite reasonable. Blacks in the South were disenfranchised; they were subject to official discrimination; they confronted terror, both state sponsored and "civilian," if they protested. Brazilian death squads and Klan night riders may not have followed identical protocols, but their commitment to torture and murder in defense of established inequalities may legitimately be compared. I am not seeking to make a global point here, but rather a limited one: the modern U.S. black movement arose in an undemocratic setting, and sought for its constituents the same basic rights of free expression, political representation, legal protection, and social justice to which Brazilians aspired under the military dictatorship.

To illustrate the utility of this comparison, consider the two parallel cases of the social movement upsurge in the United States and the Brazilian *abertura*. In the former case, the established political framework was stagnant, marked by the purging of the left by McCarthyism and the onset of the cold war, and the paralysis of the ruling bloc (the New Deal coalition and the Democratic party, Eisenhower notwithstanding). The inability of the Democrats to initiate reform was a result of southern legislative power, which was in turn based on black disenfranchisement. The emergence of the black movement involved a tactical alliance with the modernizing, liberal, northern wing of the Democratic party. Later, the black movement generated both radical-minority currents and the whole range of "new social movements" in the United States, thus leading to the resurgence of the first real political opposition since the repressive postwar consensus had been formed.

In Brazil similar processes seem to have occurred in reverse order: democratic transition had a catalytic effect on black political mobilization. This was true both because of the fragility of racial opposition and because of the historically limited character of Brazilian democracy itself. Military rule was faced with popular opposition and the partial stagnation of its political project by the middle 1970s. A reform-oriented faction attained power within the armed forces, which espoused the program of *abertura* (Stepan, 1988). As the reestablishment of civilian rule drew nearer, the first real political opposition emerged since the early 1960s, although the long-term future of democracy in Brazil remains in doubt.

The *abertura* meant that radical democratic themes — religious, feminist, localist, but chiefly "humanistic" — were encountered in new ways (or for the first time) as social movements appeared to articulate them. For many people, particularly those of humble origin whom the traditional political processes had always been able to ignore, the new social movements provided the first political experiences of their lives. For those of the middle classes — priests, journalists, lawyers, health workers, educators, and others who shared the democratic and egalitarian aspirations — the new social movements offered a political alternative to leftist and populist traditions that the military dictatorship had effectively stalemated (Scherer-Warren and Krischke, 1987; dos Santos, 1985, 47-48; Boschi, 1987; Schmink, 1981; Cardoso, 1983; Mainwaring, n.d.).

Brazilian blacks were intimately involved in these events. They were among the *favelados* (slum dwellers), the landless *boias frias* (impoverished, migratory agricultural workers), the metalworkers. Although by tradition they did not organize *qua* blacks, the interrogation of social and political reality and the quest for *citizenship* emphasized in many movement activities placed a new focus on racial themes.

Blacks took advantage of this *abertura* in many ways (Mitchell, 1985). Participating in the panoply of oppositional social movements that confronted the dictatorship, many blacks acquired fresh political skills and awareness. Among those mobilized were black activists in *favela* associations, in CEBs, and in rural struggles for land (especially in the Northeast); blacks who participated in strike activity (especially in the ABC region of São Paulo), and blacks involved in cultural activities and organizations;[14] black students (Turner, 1985), blacks concerned with issues of African liberation, black researchers and intellectuals involved in studying Afro-Brazilian history and culture, and black women involved in feminist activities.

This latter group merits a note of its own. As in the United States and many other countries, Brazilian black women play a crucial role in new social-movement activities (Carneiro and Santos, 1985). They have challenged both sexism in the black movement and racism in the women's movement. For millions of black women recent decades have seen precipitous declines in living standards. The military dictatorship's assault on democracy and the erosion of living standards inherent in the Brazilian "miracle" had particularly disastrous consequences for women, particularly for the millions of poor black women living in rural poverty and in the *favelas*. As a result, both social thought and social action took new turns. Researchers and activists linked to the black and feminist movements became interested in "subjugated knowledge" (Harding, 1986). They sought to reconceptualize the economic role of women in Brazilian society, developing in particular the concept of *chefia feminina* (economic management by women) among lower-class black families.[15] They also focused attention on the linkages between racial and gender-based inequalities.[16]

Of those "subjugated" by race, gender, and class, a few became "intellectuals" of movement groups such as *favelados* and *moradores* (neighborhood residents) associations. Other black women were

Ialorixas (roughly, priestesses) of candomblé (Rufino, 1987, 8). Others were involved in CEB activity, and still others were among the handful of black women in the universities.[17]

A host of projects and ideas has been generated by these women. Notably, they have called upon both the feminist and black movements to address not only the vast inequalities of race and gender in Brazil, but also the interaction of these inequalities in terms of identity and sexuality:

> All ideological constructions, European representations of romance, of passion, and of love always took the white woman as their muse. The black woman was never given the status of muse. . . . In relation to the black woman, what is the perspective we have on her? It is to view her as an erotic fruit, a thing to be plucked and eaten (Vanderlei José María, cited in Carneiro and Santos, 1985, 45).

In a tentative and preliminary way, then, Brazilian black women have begun to articulate an alternative view of themselves, based on their location at the intersection of racial, gender-based, and class "subjugation." This process, accompanied by significant levels of participation by women in the black movement, suggests in itself the magnitude of the conflict over racial meanings and identities in the Brazilian context.

Thus, as the *abertura* advanced and democratic opposition consolidated and expanded, blacks began to mobilize and organize as blacks. With the creation of the MNU in 1978 a level of racial politics was achieved that began to approach that of the Frente Negra Brasileira of the 1930s.[18] More recently, still other black organizations have come into being, notably the Grupo União e Consciência Negra, which claims organizations in fourteen Brazilian states, the Centro de Articulação de Populações Marginalizadas (CEAP), the Centro de Referência Negroméstica (CERNE), and the Instituto Palmares de Direitos Humanos (IPDH), and the magazine *Journal Da Maioria Falante*. These are the means by which blacks are participating in the struggle to create democracy and social justice in Brazil.

Although it is still too early to tell, ultimately even the meliorist term *racial democracy* may be rearticulated. What had once been a formula for denial may now become a search for identity and social justice. What had once obscured the meaning of race in Brazil may now be transformed into a more substantial challenge of racial identities and meanings.

Thus, the black movement has begun the laborious process of self-definition and political contestation over the last decade. Although it reveals many relative disadvantages when compared to its U.S. counterpart, the movement also exhibits many similarities. Notably, the range of ideological positions encountered compares readily to those in the United States. "Entrism" (the effort by marginalized groups to operate in the political mainstream), socialist positions, and "nationalist" currents are all clearly in evidence.[19] Strong debates and dissension characterized the development of the MNU, for example, as Abdias do Nascimento's effort to elaborate an "Afrocentric" ideology for the organization — *Quilombismo*[20] — was criticized by more radical democratic currents (González, 1985, 130). There have also been major debates about the role of feminism within the movement, and about the relationship of race, sex, and class in general.

As in the United States, there is the combined threat and opportunity of co-optation. State "absorption" of racial demands is taking place. Black oppositional activity has stimulated various government entities to establish mechanisms of liaison with the black community.[21] At the national level, there is now an Assessoria para Assuntos Afro-Brasileiros in the Ministry of Culture. Several state governments, particularly those of São Paulo and Rio de Janeiro, also have established agencies to foster cultural events and to investigate complaints of discrimination.

Alongside such "nationalist" currents as that of *Quilombismo*, "entrists" in the movement, both radical and reform oriented, have urged greater organized black participation in trade unions and political parties. Nascimento himself has been a PDT (Democratic Workers party) activist and served a term as a federal deputy from Rio, although he failed to win reelection. Many radical blacks have joined the PT (Workers party); within that organization they have created a Commissão de Negros that operates at both the national and regional levels. One of the few national black leaders, Benedita Souza da Silva, is a PT federal deputy, who often combines her antiracist activities with defense of women's rights (da Silva, 1986). There are also blacks in centrist and even rightist political parties. In general, however, even those blacks who are most committed to "entrism" continue to criticize the political and union entities as insufficiently committed to racial equality.

In Place of a Conclusion

The Brazilian black movement exists. This is a momentous achievement. To reach this point blacks had to overcome the entrenched racism and systematic self-deception that has historically characterized Brazilian society. Further, they had to insert themselves in a society-wide process of democratic opposition under quite precarious circumstances. The black movement in Brazil not only had to define itself in opposition to traditional ideologies and antidemocratic forces; it also had to situate itself in a democratic current whose other participants it could not entirely trust.

Today, nearly every Brazilian black will acknowledge the experience of racism (most whites continue to deny its existence). There are still, however, few black political organizations in the strict sense of the term. The MNU has not been able to sustain a national presence, though some of its local and regional entities continue to be active. Although there are many local groups of all sorts, Brazilian blacks still have relatively few organizational options. Activists tend to be intellectuals, based in universities, state agencies, or cultural entities. The vast majority of blacks — which is to say, the majority of Brazil — continues to encounter enormous difficulties simply in attempting to survive: unemployment, inadequate educational opportunities, nonexistent social services, police harassment, and of course the reality of an ever-worsening economic crisis whose main victims are at the bottom of the socioeconomic system. Nor can the left be excluded from the list of problems facing blacks; in many ways it continues to collude with racism by practicing a fierce class reductionism, by refusing to acknowledge the independent significance of race.

This situation is compatible with the limited character of redemocratization in Brazil. My model, you will recall, suggests that in Brazil the degree of racial mobilization reflects the degree of democracy available. Today, in the throes of a deep crisis that is every bit as much political as it is economic, the transition to democracy has clearly encountered major obstacles (O'Donnell, 1988). There is great uncertainty even about near-term events, such as the outcome of the draconian economic policies initiated by newly elected President Fernando Collor de Mello.

Nevertheless, "at the risk of seeming ridiculous," I should like to express my belief that there is no turning back now. "Whitening" and "racial democracy" (in the paternalistic sense of the term) are dead. The black movement, facing enormous difficulties, is alive, alert, questioning, debating, demonstrating. Racial formation is at work. The genie is out of the bottle. No racist elite will be able to contain it again.

NOTES

Research for this article was supported in part by a Fulbright grant. Thanks to Maria Brandão, Heloisa Buarque de Holanda, Michael Hanchard, Carlos Hasenbalg, Gay Seidman, Tom Skidmore, and George Yúdice.

1. The term *black* is used advisedly. As is well known, Brazilian racial terminology distinguishes in a variety of ways among those who in the U.S. context would be classified as "black." *Preto, crioulo, negro, mulato, pardo, moreno, branco da Bahia* are only a few of the terms used. These categories are also gendered, a fact that distinguishes them from English usage; for reasons of space I have given only masculine forms of the nouns here. Since what is at stake in this nomenclature is social meaning, use of any terminology necessarily involves a political dimension. On another point: in this essay I focus attention on racial problems involving blacks. This obviously does not exhaust the issue, since Brazil has substantial native (i.e., "Indian") and Japanese-Brazilian populations, as well as less significant numbers of Chinese, Arabs, etc.

2. Chapter III of the draft articles prepared by the Constituent Assembly's Commissão da Ordem Social proposed, among other items, criminal sanctions for racial discrimination and the incitement of racial hatred; it prescribed "compensatory measures" for "persons or groups who are victims of proven discrimination" and defined these measures as "giving preference to determined citizens or groups of citizens, in order to guarantee their equal participation in and access to the labor market, education, health, and other social rights." The draft constitution also required the Brazilian government to break diplomatic relations "with countries that adopt official policies of racial discrimination"; it granted Indians the right to their lands in perpetuity and nullified all actions of dispossession carried out against them; and it proposed to achieve strong programs of workers', women's, and even disabled persons' rights. Even though these measures are not included in the final document, their appearance in the draft indicates a significant politicization of racial issues (as well as other social movement demands—see below). The measures cited are taken from the full draft constitution published by *O Estado de São Paulo*, June 18, 1987, p. 23.

3. See, for example, Pierson (1967), Tannenbaum (1947), Freyre (1959). For reasons of space this essay focuses on contemporary issues of race. I do not consider the origins or history of racial dynamics or ideas in Brazil. For good sources on these topics, see Skidmore (1974), Viotti da Costa (1977, 1982, and 1985, esp. 234-46).

4. Thales de Azevedo, Roger Bastide, Florestan Fernandes, Marvin Harris, and Charles Wagley, among others, were associated with the UNESCO project. Wagley (1967) is a convenient collection of papers from the rural phase of this research. Bastide and Fernandes (1959) is the chief product of its urban phase. The importance of these

studies for Brazilian social science, and more indirectly for racial dynamics themselves, cannot be overestimated.

5. These arguments led Eugene Genovese to defend the admittedly conservative Gilberto Freyre (as well as Frank Tannenbaum and others) from the admittedly radical and "materialist" attack of Harris. Genovese (correctly in my view) perceived in Freyre a far more complex and "totalizing" view of the meaning of race in Brazil than he found in Harris (Genovese, 1971, 41-43).

6. Thus the impoverished Northeast — the traditional locus of Brazilian poverty and underdevelopment, and the focus of Harris and Azevedo's studies — is also disproportionately black, while the urbanized and industrialized Southeast is disproportionately white.

7. Monetary policy, say, or the current debates about the content of humanities curricula.

8. This is not to say that nothing happened; clearly, crucial events took place: the race riots in 1919 and during the war years, the Garvey movement and the Harlem Renaissance in the 1920s, and many other challenges to the racial order as well. That system, however, was not fundamentally assaulted, and did not crack open, until the postwar crisis initiated by the civil-rights movement.

9. Leonel Brizola, former governor of the state of Rio de Janeiro and leader of the left-populist PDT, was a leading candidate for the Brazilian presidency in 1989. As Dillon Soares and do Valle Silva point out, this slogan did not notably affect election results. My point here is that the mere use of racially oriented rhetoric is a significant development.

10. The fundamental categories here are derived from the work of Antonio Gramsci. Probably the most significant work to explore these processes, and the one which has most influenced my approach, is Laclau and Mouffe (1985); see also Portantiero (1982).

11. On the MNU, see González, 1985; Fontaine, 1981, 156-59; María Ercilia do Nascimento, 1989.

12. I use this phrase, with apologies to Karl Polanyi, to suggest the drama and significance of the political shift that the racial-movement upsurge represented in the postwar period.

13. It is important to note that this logic is not inherently democratizing, as neoconservatives and new rightists in the United States have demonstrated. "Reactionary" rearticulation has developed in the age of Reagan: the charge of "reverse discrimination" or the demand for "community control" of schools (used today to fight equal employment of school integration efforts) illustrate this possibility. See Omi and Winant (1986), 109-35; Omi and Winant (1987).

14. Such as the Palmares group, *terreiros* of candomblé, *afoxés*, and *blocos africanos*, etc. Cultural and religious groups are entirely central in black organizational efforts in Brazil, and in recent years have more frequently linked their traditional vocations with political themes. For example, *afoxés* are groups of religious orientation, based in Candomblé. They dance and sing in African languages, and participate in carnaval. Formerly outlawed, they were legalized in the late 1970s. In Salvador the *afoxés* have formed *blocos* that are not only active in carnaval, but also serve as "nationalist" organizations, performing educational tasks (racial *conscientização* — "consciousness-raising"), organizing favelados and *moradores* groups, etc.

15. An important consequence of this work is its challenge to the schizoid image of the black woman as either suffering mother "who pays with blood, sweat, and tears the

price for the disorganization of the black family," or turned-on sex object (Oliveira, Porcaro, and Araujo, 1987; see also Barroso, 1982; Oliveira, Porcaro, and Araujo Costa, 1981). Although this topic resembles the one debated in the United States during the 1960s and 1970s, too close a comparison would be misleading. The entire "welfare dependency" framework is irrelevant to Brazilian conditions, and there are other dissimilarities as well.

16. The MNU includes antisexist points in its statement of principles, for example (González, 1985).

17. For data on years of education by race, see IBGE (1980).

18. The foregoing discussion relies heavily on Joel Rufino dos Santos (1985), Mitchell (1985), and González (1985).

19. For U.S. references, see Omi and Winant (1983), 2:38-40.

20. See Nascimento (1985).

21. In the United States, black-movement successes were met with sophisticated state strategies that I have analyzed elsewhere in terms of "absorption" and "insulation" (Omi and Winant, 1986, 81). Predictably, in Brazil there are big debates about the extent of service, versus the degree of co-optation, offered by such organizations. The state tendency to establish a bureaucracy when confronted by opposition is very strong.

BIBLIOGRAPHY

Araujo, Ari, "O Samba e o Negro no Brasil," *Estudos Afro-Asiáticos* 8–9 (Rio de Janeiro: Conjunto Universitário Cândido Mendes, 1983).

Azevedo, Thales de, *Cultura e Situação Racial no Brasil* (Rio de Janeiro: Editora Civilização Brasileira, 1966).

Barroso, Carmen, ed., *Mulher, Sociedade, e Estado no Brasil* (São Paulo: Brasilense, 1982).

Bastide, Roger, "A Imprensa Negra do Estado de São Paulo," in Bastide, *Estudos Afro-Brasileiros* (São Paulo: Editora Perspectiva, 1973).

————, "The Development of Race Relations in Brazil," in Guy Hunter, ed., *Industrialization and Race Relations: A Symposium* (New York: Oxford University Press).

————, *The African Religions of Brazil: Toward a Sociology of the Interpenetration of Civilizations* (Baltimore: Johns Hopkins University Press, 1978).

Bastide, Roger, and Florestan Fernandes, *Brancos e Negros em São Paulo* (São Paulo: Companhia Editora Nacional, 1959).

Blair, Thomas, "Mouvements Afro-Brésiliens de Libération, de la Période Esclavigiste à nos Jours," *Presence Africaine* (1965).

Borges Pereira, João Baptista, "A Cultura Negra: Resistência de Cultura e Cultura de Resistência," *Dédalo* 23 (1984).

————, "A Folclorização da Cultura Negra no Brasil," in *Eurípides Simões de Paula: Livro In Memoriam* (São Paulo: n.p., 1983).

Boschi, Renato R., "Social Movements and the New Political Order in Brazil," in John Wirth et al., eds., *State and Stability in Brazil: Continuity and Change* (Boulder, Colo.: Westview Press, 1987).

Brito, Ieda Marques, *Samba na Cidade de São Paulo (1900-1930): Um Exercício de Resistência Cultural* (São Paulo: USP, Faculdade de Filosofia, Letras, e Ciências Humanas, 1986).

Brown, Diana, *Umbanda: Religion and Politics in Urban Brazil* (Ann Arbor: University of Michigan Research Press, 1986).

Cardoso, Ruth C. L., "Movimentos Sociais Urbanos: Balanço Crítico," in Sebastião Velazco e Cruz et al., *Sociedade e Politica no Brasil pos-64* (São Paulo: Brasilense, 1983).

Carneiro, Sueli, and Thereza Santos, *Mulher Negra* (São Paulo: Nobel/Conselho Estadual da Condição Feminina, 1985).

Carson, Clayborn, *In Struggle: SNCC and the Black Awakening of the 1960s* (Cambridge, Mass: Harvard University Press, 1981).

Chiavenato, Júlio J., *O Negro no Brasil: Da Senzala à Guerra do Paraguai*, 3d ed. (São Paulo: Brasilense, 1986).

Costa, Manoel Augusto, ed., *O Segundo Brasil: Perspectivas Socio-Demográficas* (Rio de Janeiro: Ebano, 1983).

da Silva, Benedita Souza, "A identidade da Mulher Negra—a Identidade da Mulher India," paper presented at the Conferencia Nacional Saúde e Direitos da Mulher, October 1986.

da Silva, Carlos Benedito Rodrigues, "Black Soul: Aglutinação Espontânea ou Identidade Etnica: Uma Contribuição ao Estudo das Manifestações Culturais no Meio Negro," paper presented at the Fourth Annual Meeting of the Associação Nacional de Posgraduação e Pesquisas em Ciências Sociais (ANPOCS), 1980.

Degler, Carl N., *Neither Black nor White: Slavery and Race Relations in Brazil and the United States* (New York: Macmillan, 1971).

Dillon Soares, Glaucio Ary, and Nelson do Valle Silva, "O Charme Discreto do Socialismo Moreno," *Dados*, vol. 28, no. 2, 1985.

dos Santos, Joel Rufino, *O Movimento Negro e a Crise Brasileira (São Paulo: FESP, 1985), mimeo.*

dos Santos, Juana Elbein, *Os Nago e a Morte—Pade, Asese, e o Culto Egun na Bahía* (Petrópolis: Vozes, 1977).

dos Santos, Theotônio, "Crisis y Movimientos Sociales en Brasil," in Fernando Calderón Gutiérrez, ed., *Los Movimientos Sociales ante la Crisis* (Buenos Aires: CLACSO/United Nations University, 1985).

Dzidzienyo, Anani, "The African Connection and the Afro-Brazilian Condition," in Pierre-Michel Fontaine, *Race, Class, and Power in Brazil* (Los Angeles: UCLA Afro-American Studies Center, 1985).

———, *The Position of Blacks in Brazilian Society* (London: Minority Rights Group, 1971).

Fernandes, Florestan, "The Weight of the Past," in J. H. Franklin, ed., *Color and Race* (Boston: Beacon Press, 1969).

———, *A Integração do Negro na Sociedade de Clases*, 2 vols., 3d ed. (São Paulo: Atica, 1978).

Fontaine, Pierre-Michel, "Models of Economic Development and Systems of Race Relations: Brazilian Development and the Afro-Brazilian Condition," paper presented at the meetings of the working group on "Temas e Problemas da População Negra no Brasil," Annual Meeting of the Associação Nacional de Pós-Graduação e Pesquisas em Ciências Sociais (ANPOCS), 1979 (mimeo).

———, "Transnational Relations and Racial Mobilization: Emerging Black Movements in Brazil," in John F. Stack, Jr., ed., *Ethnic Identities in a Transnational World* (Westport, Conn.: Greenwood Press, 1981).

Freyre, Gilberto, *New World in the Tropics: The Culture of Modern Brazil* (New York: Knopf, 1959).

Fry, Peter, *Para Inglés Ver* (São Paulo: Zahar, 1982).

Genovese, Eugene D., *In Red and Black: Marxian Explorations in Southern and Afro-American History* (New York: Pantheon, 1971).

Gonçalves, Williams da Silva, "Brasil, Atlântico Sul, e o Conflito da Africa Austral," *Estudos Afro-Asiáticos* 13 (Rio de Janeiro: Conjunto Universitário Cândido Mendes, 1987).

González, Lelia, "The Unified Black Movement: A New Stage in Black Political Mobilization," in Pierre-Michel Fontaine, ed., *Race, Class, and Power in Brazil* (Los Angeles: UCLA, Afro-American Studies Center, 1985).

Harding, Sandra, *The Science Question in Feminism* (Ithaca, N.Y.: Cornell University Press, 1986).

Harris, Marvin, *Patterns of Race in the Americas* (New York: Walker, 1964).

Hasenbalg, Carlos A., *Discriminação e Desigualdades Raciais no Brasil* (Rio de Janeiro: Graal, 1979).

————, *Raça e Desigualdedes Socioeconômicas no Brasil* (Rio de Janeiro: IUPERJ, 1983).

————, untitled presentation, *Estudos Afro-Asiáticos* 12 (Rio de Janeiro: Conjunto Universitário Cândido Mendes, August 1986).

IBGE (Brazilian Institute of Geography and Statistics), *Censo Demográfico* (Brasília, 1980).

Mainwaring, Scott, "Urban Popular Movements, Identity, and Democratization in Brazil" (n.d.), ms.

Mitchell, Michael, "Blacks and the *Abertura Democrática*," in Pierre-Michel Fontaine, *Race, Class, and Power in Brazil* (Los Angeles: UCLA Afro-American Studies Center, 1985).

Mouffe, Chantal, and Ernesto Laclau, *Hegemony and Socialist Strategy: Towards a Radical Democratic Politics* (London: Verso, 1985).

Moura, Clovis, *Brasil: As Raízes do Protesto Negro* (São Paulo: Global Editora, 1983).

————, *O Negro: De Bom Escravidão a Mau Cidadão?* (Rio de Janeiro: Conquista, 1977).

Nascimento, Abdias do, "*Quilombismo*: The African-Brazilian Road to Socialism," in Molefi Kete Asante and Kariamu Welsh Asante, eds., *African Culture: The Rhythms of Unity* (Westport, Conn.: Greenwood Press, 1985)

Nascimento, Abdias do, ed., *O Negro Revoltado* (Rio de Janeiro: Edicoes GRD, 1978).

————, *O Genocídio do Negro Brasileiro: Processo de Um Racismo Mascarado* (Rio de Janeiro: Paz e Terra, 1978).

Nascimento, Maria Ercília do, *A Estratégia da Desigualdade: O Movimento Negro dos Anos 70* (Master's dissertation, PUC-São Paulo, 1989).

Nogueira, Oracy, "Preconceito Racial de Marca e Preconceito Racial de Origem," paper presented in the "Symposium Etno-sociológico sobre comunidades humanas do Brasil," *Anáis do XXXI Congresso Internacional de Americanistas* (São Paulo, 1955).

O'Donnell, Guillermo, "Challenges to Democratization in Brazil," *World Policy Journal*, vol. 2 (Spring 1988).

Oliveira, Lúcia Elena Garcia, Rosa María Porcaro, and Tereza Cristina Nascimento Araujo, *O Lugar do Negro na Troca de Trabalho* (Rio de Janeiro, IBGE, 1985).

————, "Repensando o Lugar da Mulher Negra," *Estudos Afro-Asiáticos* 13 (Rio de Janeiro: Conjunto Universitário Cândido Mendes, March 1987).

Omi, Michael, and Howard Winant, "Race and the Right: The Politics of Reaction," in John Stanfield, ed., *Research in Social Policy*, vol. 1 (Westport, Conn.: JAI, 1987).

_____, "By the Rivers of Babylon: Race in the United States," Pt. 2, *Socialist Review* 72 (Nov.-Dec. 1983).

_____, *Racial Formation in the United States: From the 1960s to the 1980s* (New York: Routledge & Kegan Paul, 1986).

Pierson, Donald, *Negroes in Brazil: A Study of Race Contact in Bahia* (Carbondale: Southern Illinois University Press, 1967 [1942]).

Portantiero, Juan Carlos, *Los Usos de Gramsci*, 2d ed. (México, D.F.: Folios Ediciones, 1982).

Rufino, Alzira, "Mulher Negra: Uma Perspectiva Histórica," paper presented at the III Encontro de Poetas e Ficcionistas Negros Brasileiros, Rio de Janeiro (Santos: pamphlet, 1987).

Scherer-Warren, Ilse, and Paulo J. Krischke, *Uma Revolução no Cotidiano? Os Movimentos Sociais na América do Sul* (São Paulo: Brasiliense, 1986).

Schmink, Marianne, "Women in Brazilian Abertura Politics," in *Signs* 7 (Autumn 1981).

Sebe, José Carlos, *Carnaval, Carnavais* (São Paulo: Atica, 1986).

Selcher, Wayne A., *The Afro-Asian Dimension of Brazil's Foreign Policy, 1956-72* (Gainesville: University of Florida Press, 1974).

Silva, Nelson do Valle, "Cor e Processo de Realização Socioeconômica, *Dados*, vol. 24, no. 3 (1980).

Silva, Nelson do Valle, "Updating the Cost of Not Being White in Brazil," in Pierre-Michel Fontaine, ed., *Race, Class, and Power in Brazil* (Los Angeles: UCLA Afro-American Studies Center, 1985).

Skidmore, Thomas E., *Black into White: Race and Nationality in Brazilian Thought* (New York: Oxford, 1974).

Sodré, Muniz, *A Verdade Seduzida* (Rio de Janeiro: Francisco Alves, 1983).

Souza, Amaury de, "Raça e Política no Brasil Urbano," in *Revista Administração de Empresas*, vol. 2, no. 4 (1970).

Souza, Neuza Santos, *Tornar-se Negro* (Rio de Janeiro: Graal, 1983).

Stepan, Alfred, *Rethinking Military Politics: Brazil and the Southern Cone* (Princeton, N.J.: Princeton University Press, 1988).

Tannenbaum, Frank, *Slave and Citizen: The Negro in the Americas* (New York: Vintage, 1946).

Turner, J. Michael, "Brown into Black: Changing Racial Attitudes of Afro-Brazilian University Students," in Pierre-Michel Fontaine, ed., *Race, Class, and Power in Brazil* (Los Angeles: UCLA Afro-American Studies Center, 1985).

Valente, Ana Lúcia E. F., *Política e Relações Raciais: Os Negros e as Eleições Paulistas de 1982* (São Paulo: USP, Faculdade de Filosofia, Letras, e Ciências Humanas, 1986).

van den Berghe, Pierre, *Race and Racism: A Comparative Perspective* (New York: Wiley, 1967).

Viotti da Costa, Emília, *Da Monarquia à República: Momentos Decisivos* (São Paulo: Grijalbo, 1977).

Viotti da Costa, Emília, *Da Senzala à Colonia*, 2d ed. (São Paulo: Diffusão Européia, 1982).

Viotti da Costa, Emília, *The Brazilian Empire: Myths and Histories* (Chicago: University of Chicago Press, 1985).

Wagley, Charles, ed., *Race and Class in Rural Brazil* (New York: Columbia University Press, 1972).

Theater after the Revolution: Refiguring the Political in Cuba and Nicaragua
Randy Martin

In the center of Havana is the Plaza of the Revolution. At one end, steps rise to a towering monument and review stand where Fidel Castro has delivered some of his most important speeches. Facing the concrete spire across the plaza is a wall-sized portrait of Che Guevara affixed to offices of the Revolutionary Armed Forces (FAR). At the other two sides of the square stand the National Library and the National Theater. Icons of politics and culture frame this largest of public gathering places. Millions gathered here to cheer Castro's denunciation of those who fled from Mariel. Hundreds of thousands danced to the combined force of the town's two most popular bands, Los Van Van and La Orquesta Revé, in a tribute to Che's sixtieth birthday. These are the spectacles with which the revolution is likely to be identified, events that graft political and cultural centrality onto this physical center. Yet most days the plaza is empty. Crossing the plaza midday is more likely to make one dizzy with sun than with revolutionary fervor. But if one keeps going, across a field of weeds in the direction of a row of apartment towers, just a block from the cemetery and the neighborhood that borders it, La Timba, there stands a place of more modest spectacles, a church converted by a group of young actors into a theater where daily rehearsals are in process.

In many respects, this group, Teatro Buendía, enjoys the privileges of being in Cuba's cultural center. The actors are graduates of the highly selective Instituto Superior del Arte (ISA), which assures them work in their chosen profession. Until recently, graduates of the ISA dispersed and did an initial two-year civil service with established theater groups throughout the country. Buendía's actors, on the other hand, have been able to remain together as a cohort in Havana, forming a theater aimed self-consciously at the representation of youth. Their acting technique, repertory, and theater space are directed toward a public — those who grew up in the three decades after Batista's ouster — whose voice has yet to be heard from in shaping the direction that Cuba will take. The theater is a gathering place, a public sphere of a different sort than the plaza. It presents an enactment of possibilities for a group that historically has been marginal.

Theater's capacity for articulating historically marginal voices is apparent in the postrevolutionary context of Nicaragua as well as Cuba. As in Cuba, margin and center are articulated only in relation to one another, producing an emergent theatrical form based in the Nicaraguan countryside but aimed at figuring national development. Figuration is a complex process. It serves both as a representation of an existing situation and an effort to calculate what could be. In this sense, theater becomes a form of historical reckoning. Its dramatic conflicts play to its historical protagonists, for theater is occasioned only by gathering a public. In the effort to create and make viable this alternative public sphere, theater as an institution signifies the dynamic of margin and center that it seeks to articulate in performance. It becomes, therefore, a privileged domain in which to figure the trajectories of development that revolutions present. The tensions, antinomies, and interpenetrations of margin and center stand not only for cultural differences within and between Cuba and Nicaragua, but figure as well in the contours of state and society. Specifically, the degree to which state power is centralized impacts upon cultural production in a way that displays its present moment and its prospects for development.

Whatever the particular significance of theater turns out to be in Cuba and in Nicaragua during its decade of Sandinista rule, its study from the perspective indicated here raises some intriguing questions about the future of socialism. Is it conceivable that a struggle between margin and center, articulated through the specificities of each country's political economy, replaces the struggle of classes? In Nicaragua's mixed economy of the 1980s, this question was, at the very least, premature, and its relevance to the strategy of the socialist forces after the election of 1990 will have to be ascertained. In Cuba the concrete political expressions of the margins have yet to make themselves fully apparent. This makes theater all the more valuable for posing the questions, for in its history the struggle over the direction of socialist development may more readily be etched. With this project in mind, I will return then to Teatro Buendía and place it in an historical context, then repeat the exercise for its theatrical counterpart in Nicaragua.

Shifting Voices in Havana

Buendía, whose name is taken from the family in the Gabriel García Márquez novel *One Hundred Years of Solitude*, was formed in 1985 as an outgrowth of acting students' work with their teacher Flora Lauten. Lauten, herself an accomplished actress and playwright, continues to direct the group. The freshly converted church that houses their theater is white on the outside and black on the inside, with tall shutters to let in light and a high-domed ceiling. Beneath the church-theater are a rehearsal hall and dressing rooms. The actors themselves converted the theater over the course of many months, a building activity echoed in the program of voluntary labor to construct much-needed housing, the microbrigades. The area in which the theater is located is dotted with clusters of these housing projects, some rising over twenty stories. As a new area of development in a city with tremendous pressures for increased housing, the new neighborhoods contain residences without much else. Young people can go over the hill into Havana's bristling strip, La Rampa in the Vedado section, but there is little for them in the neighborhood. Buendía intends to address this need.[1] They have developed a piece, actually a reworking of a 1954 play by Rolando Ferrer, *Lila, la mariposa* (Lila, the butterfly), that speaks directly to the problems of youth in Havana.[2]

Clearly, a single theater cannot transform a marginal demand into a central one. The themes that *Lila, la mariposa* addresses, however, figure the present political and cultural marginality of youth in a way that may betoken certain future movements. The play is a sort of Cuban *Streetcar Named Desire* with Lila the fallen woman who is the owner of a sewing shop. The play as scripted opens with Lila already mad and unable to tend to the store. She progressively succumbs to the disquietude in her life until she commits suicide at the end of the second act, and is mourned by the community in a funeral procession during the third act.

Flora Lauten has wholly restructured the play, adding text, deleting the third act, and placing its contents at the beginning of both Acts 1 and 2. *Lila* opens with the pronouncements of a chorus, now three women who work as seamstresses in a shop run by Lila's sister. Initially, these three announce Lila's death before she is carried onstage by her mourners. In the original, these three were Yoruba goddesses (an adaptation of Afro-Cuban idioms not uncommon in Cuban theater) who comment upon the action from upstage. For Buendía's production, they have been brought downstage as the worldly employees who banter and interact with the audience, at times teasing the public and at other times soliciting their input. They both parody the action and instigate problems within the play—as the influx of what lies beyond the text.

Lila's tragedy, her loss of agency, has brought her to fetishize the radio. Upstage, Lila is alone with her radio, while downstage the three seamstresses enact current radio jingles and fragments of radio plays familiar to the audience. Lila at first listens to the seamstresses' radio programs, then mimics them, then dialogues with them. The suggestion of suicide comes from the radio. In one of the fragments from a radio drama, one of the seamstresses is singing and another responds, "If I hear that song again I'm going to kill myself. It's so awful." Lila begins to mimic this line as well. Reproduction becomes consciousness. The symbolic of mass communication shifts to the psyche. The live action of Lila and her family continues to be interrupted, first by the radio, then by her own dreams, which together freeze into a single narrative of melodrama.

With each intervention by the radio, Lila is more and more transformed into the romantic victim, the femme fatale, lost in a 1950s misogyny. Lila's own dreams also deal with a substitution of herself as child for the place of her children who are just coming to the age of sexuality. Her niece Adelfa and her son Marino pursue each other. Adelfa is at the center of many boys' attention. Lila (mis)places herself as Adelfa and swoons into her son's arms when he enters the sewing shop where he lives and Lila dreams.

Lila, like Blanche Dubois, has her gentleman caller, an author whose best days are also past. His book, written twenty-five years ago, is still precious to Lila. In a dream, he comes into the shop to romance Lila, and her ecstatic memory passes into the confusion of the present. All of these dreams have been inserted into the script by director Flora Lauten. Lila is a woman who cannot be left alone, whose submission to the suggestion of the media, of the broadcast, is so total as to become her society. Yet this is a society of consumption, of the spectacle, so Lila, too, will be consumed by it. In a second dream sequence, it is Marino, her son, who enters just as she is about to kill herself (or at least she announces this—we already know the outcome of her threats at the beginning of the play).

Her death is a premise, and the play seeks its causes in a retrospective and speculative fashion. The scissors, the instrument of death, are hidden in the audience by one of the three seamstresses. This makes the public complicit in both killing and protecting Lila, as the audience is wedged between the knowledge of her death and her need for help. Once the scissors are found and Lila's second death is certain, the audience is made to decide where to cut.

The melodrama of the first act yields to the cabaret in the second. The live band that accompanies the play shifts from lilting strains of flute and guitar to saxophone and drums in a dirty blues. The three seamstresses, like the rest of the cast, have now donned nightclub garb and sing their lines to the audience through a microphone. The mourners, inspired by a dazzling solo from Lila, dance around the three.

Marino's chase of Adelfa is repeated, but this time Adelfa is called home by Lila before the two fulfill their attraction. In this second act, Marino becomes the protagonist, the responsible voice demanding to know his own identity. At first, he is doubled in a female Marino who penetrates the many-surfaced cabaret with a return to the depths of the Romantic mode. The two sing sweetly and earnestly of the place of love. This doubling of Marino soon multiplies into the entire cast—who all become Marinos—but only after Marino has demanded from the audience: "Who am I?" "Am I alone?" The cabaret continues carelessly through all of this until Marino stops the action and declares, "No one has answered my question." Now the entire cast becomes Marino. They move to the audience and ask the myriad questions from a teenager's daily life: "Why should I stay at home?" "What must I do to become a man?" "Why do I need to work?" "Why don't I like the sea as much as I used to?"

The demand for identity becomes a shared responsibility of the audience. The transposition of the inner circle of the family (the up-stage action where the family activities had been confined) into caba-ret (which occupies the entire theater) changes what had been an insulation from conflict into a terrain of contention. By the end of the production (and presumably after the theater turns into a café) this terrain will be bequeathed to the audience. The mingling of modes from the first and second acts embraces the public by confusing the kitsch outside the family with the caring inside, thereby creating a public sphere composed of both. Hence there is the possibility, the hope, that Marino will not repeat his mother's fate of isolation and solitary reception. In this sense, the cabaret is attacked by the more romantic structures that offer the possibility of directing serious in-quiries when it would seem that no single utterance mattered. This turn from the humor of the cabaret to the high seriousness of youthful existential dilemmas perhaps serves to invest the marginality that youth experiences with a critical tension necessary for reflection with-out abandoning either voice.

The church-theater that is Buendía's home itself is intended to open a space for such dialogue. The spatial problem of an inside and out-side to the family, which Buendía's Lila so thoroughly divides and then compromises, is expressed concretely in the surrounding environs that house some of Havana's newest housing projects. The demands for space, fueled by population growth of 50 percent in the thirty years since the revolution, have contributed to a high number of mar-riages and divorces among young people as marriage becomes the only legitimate way of procuring "a room of one's own." Unlike the Soviet Union, where there appears to be a countercultural movement that might include a drift away from the historically defined family unit, the Cuban scene seems to avoid both of these rifts. The ongoing relation to the family becomes essential.

The revival and reorganization of this prerevolutionary play into two acts presents a view of an earlier time ridden with decay and foreign influence to a young audience unfamiliar with the play and distant from its historical context. Lila's passivity in the face of the media invasion figures as a kind of neocolonial portrayal. The diffi-culty of responding to the voice of authority is questioned directly in the second act. The "mass" cultural element is replaced by Cuban popular forms. While Cuban television, introduced in 1950, did produce distinctive forms like the telenovela, the juxtaposition of mass and popular idioms in the two acts poses the problem of participation in cultural production. The amateur arts, carnaval, and public dances generate greater attendance than the highly popular cinema. The generational shift in protagonist, which occurs in the second act, suggests a movement away from dependency as a narrative of Cuba's recent cultural history.

Lila reflects on imitative prerevolutionary culture as well as the Cuban present. The play speaks in two voices. One, a romantic, heroic voice that finds Marino moving from his mother's desire to a fully protagonistic role, fits nicely with the existing rhetorical form of that supreme Cuban revolutionary, Fidel Castro. This romantic voice is attacked by a second, a cabaret voice, which displaces the high seriousness of heroic politics for a more permeable and dialogic form. This is the other dilemma of youth posed for the Cuban situation. The singularity of the heroic voice poses the problem of how new voicings can be heard in political discussion. Scarcities of space, experiences of marginality may demand expression in rhetorical forms that distinguish themselves from those associated with the revolution's official voice. The heroic voice that has served as an instrumentality of the revolution may no longer be practiced so universally. In short, the play announces the decline of a rhetoric of instrumentality within the state and the possibility of a greater and more critical instrumentality for the cultural sphere.

The Past and Future of Cuban Theater

Teatro Buendía figures a break from certain rhetorical forms that pervade the Cuban present, as well as certain tendencies within the history of Cuban theater. From the earliest evidence of theater, the imprints of colonialism, and as such of the political economy as a whole, have made their mark on the trajectory of cultural development. While in Nicaragua colonialism depended on an indigenous work force and a domestication of its culture (traces of pre-Columbian cultural forms survive to the present day in *El güegüence*, a drama that pits local wit against colonial administration), the complete decimation of the domestic population of Cuba led Spain to import labor. Little is known, for example, about the *areíto* other than that it was a form of dance-theater found on the island by Spaniards in the six-teenth century.[3] Since the early part of the nineteenth century, how-ever, theater has been a prominent feature of the Cuban cultural scene. While the theater buildings tended to be modeled after Euro-pean opera houses,[4] theatrical forms, such as the Teatro Bufo, mixed parodies of western operas and dramas, and dialects of slaves and immigrants, with comedic forms based on caricatures of Afro-Cuban culture.[5] The Bufos were identified by the Spanish as separatist, and they came to fulfill this prophecy. During one performance at the Villanueva theater in January 1869, the popular singer Jacinto Valdés cheered the *independista* hero Carlos Manuel de Céspedes. The next day the police descended on the theater. By the 1940s, aspirations for self-determination had a working-class expression, and Paco Alfonso was making what has since been referred to as a pamphleteerial thea-ter aligned with the Cuban Communist party.[6]

It was not until the 1950s that a theater group emerged that was devoted to what Cuban critics have called a "scientific" approach that systematized each stage of the production process, from training of actors to directing to script analysis to mounting the play. The prob-lem of a self-conscious technique for the theater had a parallel in the need to perfect the tactics of several failed attempts at revolution (Cas-tro's attack on the Moncada barracks in 1954 and the near-disastrous landing from the yacht *Granma* that returned him to Cuba from exile in Mexico). Yet this move toward a perfectible technique could also be seen as a response to the rather thin political theater of Alfonso, on the one hand, and the laissez-faire technique of the apolitical drama of the small subscription theaters in Havana called *salons*.[7]

Theater paralleled the development of the revolution, but the two did not cross paths. Theater, incarcerated by its insularity and attachment to a particular class, focused its critique, as did its coun-terpart in the West, on the estrangement of that class from the promise of a capitalist society. As there was no explicit function for theater in the attack on the state, an assault on the inability of past Cuban theater to establish its aesthetic credibility, to be taken as other than mere entertainment or simple message, gave an oppositional character to the emerging theater within a domain of high culture. As theater in the 1950s was not a popular form and depended upon an urban elite audience, it could develop in its productions a critique of that audience's class ambiguity in relation to larger political choices. The theater of Miller and Williams takes on special significance in this context, and it is no wonder that these two can be called the most significant figures in Cuban theater at the time of the revolution.[8]

The company Teatro Estudio embodied this strain of realist theater most strongly and came to influence much of the theater for the next thirty years. Vicente Revuelta, a founding director, had a hand in training many of the actors now working professionally, and the majority of professional companies are led by those who at one time worked at Teatro Estudio. Postrevolutionary cultural policy only intensified this centralization, which privileged that one particular group. In his now famous speech "Words to Intellectuals," delivered in 1961, Castro addressed himself to the question of those uncommitted to the revolutionary process and those whose artistic formalisms made the political nature of their art difficult to discern. Castro asked, "What kind of support do our intellectuals deserve?" and responded, "Within the revolution, everything, against it, nothing."[9]

Although no artistic form was officially endorsed by the state, the climate was such that certain artists had difficulty in showing their work, or they left Cuba. In theater, another of the founding members of Teatro Estudio, Roberto Blanco, left during this period. He returned in the 1970s and now mounts the most expensive and formalist productions, and is one of the directors most appreciated by the critical establishment. The tightening during the 1960s centralized both criticism and innovation within Teatro Estudio. One (1966) play, *La noche de los asesinos* (The night of the assassins), by José Triana, used realist allegory (a son turning against his father) to display artistic disaffection.[10]

While Stanislavskian acting technique remains the basis of training for Cuban actors, it is not the only dramatic influence. Revuelta had traveled to Germany to study Brechtian acting in the 1960s and brought back the prompt book for *Mother Courage* (mounted in 1962). He also invited Eugenio Barba, Jerzy Grotowski, and a host of European experimentalists. Hence, Cuban theater does not reflect a singular influence so much as a hegemonic one. The same could be said for the development of a national drama. Spain, the Soviet Union, and Latin America are now the main foreign influences. Still, the proportion of Cuban writers being staged exceeded 70 percent by the 1970s after being well below 10 percent during the 1950s.[11]

The influence of Teatro Estudio on acting technique was institutionalized in 1976 after the just-founded Ministry of Culture, headed by Armando Hart, formed the university-level Instituto Superior del Arte. Revuelta, his sister Raquel, Blanco, Berta Martínez, and other Teatro Estudio alumni became the principal theater instructors in the ISA.

More broadly, the formation of the Ministry of Culture made possible the professionalization of the arts, although on terms different from those in the West. Playwrights, for example, earn over one thousand dollars for every script written as guaranteed by the ministry. Actors, however, have a tougher time. In place of a market that would assure unemployment among actors, the Cuban solution has been to plan the numbers of actors needed given the spots available. The admission to the ISA is quite rigorous, demanding both academic and artistic talents. Years of the curriculum are devoted to philosophy and history. In the past years the numbers of students in the theater class have run as follows: 1977, sixteen; 1978, twenty-nine; 1981, eighteen; 1982, eleven; 1983, fourteen.[12] In 1986, of sixty-four students continuing in the scenic arts (including all technical aspects such as lighting and design), two were graduating.[13] Other material aspects of Cuban culture have expanded since the introduction of the ministry as well. For example, the number of art galleries has expanded from 44 in 1981 to 138 in 1985, and bookstores have multiplied from 266 to 316 in the same period, with the number of books published annually from 1967 to 1985 tripling from 500 to 1539. So, too, has attendance at cultural functions and installations tripled between 1967 and 1985, from 75,237,000 to 228,870,000. This meant that in 1985, on the average, Cubans went to some aficionado event (popular community-based amateur productions) ten times; 16 and 35 mm cinema four times each, respectively; musical functions twice; public libraries once; while one in five persons attended professional theater. Expanded attendance and increased functions are directly subsidized by the Ministry of Culture. While many events are free, even the most expensive seats at the ballet cost under three dollars. The cultural budget also burgeoned from 63.3 million pesos in 1981 to 102.9 million pesos in 1985 (in 1990 1 peso = $1.25).[14] Increased funding for culture must be seen in the context of an expanding productive base in which the Global Social Product (material production minus services like tourism) increased from 14,063.4 million pesos in 1975 to

26,904.1 million pesos in 1985 and a per capita shift in income from 1,512 to 2,664 pesos in the same period.[15] The increase in production and consumption is carried by the continued industrialization of the work force, which rose from 49 percent to 55 percent during this time.

While theater is on surer material footing than it has ever been and audiences are at record levels, there has been of late some skepticism expressed about the aesthetic development of theater. Vicente Revuelta asserted recently that with few exceptions, theater in Cuba was anarchic and without purpose. He indicated that theater would have to be revitalized outside of Havana.[16] Revuelta's is not the only critical response, nor is this the first time an attempt has been made to depart from the centralizing allure of Havana. The formation of Teatro Escambray in 1968 and the growth and decline of the Teatro Nuevo movement it inspired in the mountainous region around Santa Clara were also efforts at decentralization.[17] Albio Paz, one of the founders of Escambray, has had a commitment to developing theater outside of Havana since his work with provincial theater brigades in 1963, and he now directs the Teatro Mirón in the port city of Matanzas. His theater has maintained a commitment to popular performance through annual tours of factories and towns in the region and in the use of theatrical elements from carnaval, circus, and folklore in collective creations such as *Con el gato de chincilla o la locura a caballo* (1987), *Fragata* (1989), and *El circo de los pasos* (1990). On the eastern side of the island, the Cabildo Teatral Santiago, under the general direction of Ramiro Herrero, has concentrated Afro-Cuban sources from various regions, along with Christian iconography and national historic figures, in their work for the past twenty years in what came to be known as *teatro de relaciones* (for example, *De cómo Santiago Apóstol puso los pies en la tierra* [How the Apostle Santiago put his feet on the ground] [1970], and *Baroko* [1990]). The Cabildo deploys anthropological and sociological techniques to gather theatrical materials.

Currently, there appears to be a different kind of development within the Havana theater scene, one that might indicate a certain type of movement away from the centralization that has characterized the first thirty years of postrevolutionary Cuban theater. The timing of this initiative is interesting to note. Its main impetus would seem to be from young actors, writers, and directors who, for the most part, were born after 1959. The impetus from within the ISA gave rise to Teatro Buendía. Other groups are following, some composed of actors and directors without professional training. Notable among these is Victor Varela's Teatro Obstáculo (Obstacle Theater), which, before receiving any state support, mounted a piece, *La cuarta pared* (The fourth wall), in Varela's living room. They performed dozens of times there for audiences of eight before being invited to do a run in the National Theater, after which they returned to their household performances.[18] New dance groups have been formed, some by young choreographers who left established companies, like the National Ballet of Cuba, as in the case of Caridad Martínez, Rosario Suárez, and Mirta García, who started the Ballet Teatro de la Habana in 1988. Marianela Boán, formerly with Cuba's national modern dance company, has also started her own group, Danza Abierta. Some young visual artists have been extremely active in providing a critical lexicon for popular culture and politics that they have at times taken to the streets, as a performance art they call *acción plástica*.

These projects would have been unimaginably difficult even in the mid-1980s. All materials for the theater, spaces for performance, and money for expenses and salaries come from the Ministry of Culture through special businesses that supply materials to the existing professional groups. In 1989, the ministry was reorganized and initiated a program in which projects can be proposed by a director or group and funded individually. The administrative center for theater has been moved into a building of its own and given greater budgetary autonomy. This newly created entity, the National Council of Scenographic Arts of the Ministry of Culture, is both a functioning bureaucracy charged with the administration of a budget and the planning of cultural output, now in response to proposals submitted by directors for projects, and is itself a source of livelihood for scores of intellectuals. The council is headed by Raquel Revuelta, artistic director of Teatro Estudio, and a range of established and emerging critics, playwrights, and directors. This situation makes possible both the assimilation of these critical energies and a power base for the younger intellectuals within the broader contours of policy development.[19]

The Cuban cultural policy now emerging represents a departure from the conventional mechanisms of both markets and centralized planning for the production and dissemination of artistic work. This decentralization does not eliminate planning altogether, but rather shifts the emphasis from building theatrical institutions to making available the resources for theater. The community can take initiatives without appeals to state control or a profit motive to determine whether those initiatives were worthwhile. In the first year of the new system, over seventy requests were made in the city of Havana alone, roughly half from new directors. More than half of the requests were funded and over a dozen constituted new groups. While Buendía antedates these changes by several years, it is not responsible for them. Rather, the shifting of margin and center, to which the new policies are sensitive, are figured in Buendía's work as well as that of other companies. The interaction of theater and its institutionalization recorded here is an instance of the movement of social processes in postrevolutionary Cuba. While the specific content of margin and center is not the same in all revolutionary contexts, some similar dynamics will be observable in the case of certain Nicaraguan theater groups.

Decentering Theater of Nicaragua

The material presented here on Nicaraguan theater was gathered before the Sandinistas' electoral defeat in 1990. It stands both as a measure of the critical cultural impulse that developed during the Sandinistas' rule and, more broadly, as a suggestive version of socialist possibility. Although this account is situated within the ten years of Sandinista governance, the theoretical questions it makes available may be relevant beyond the Nicaraguan context.

The debate in Nicaragua during the 1980s over the degree of centralized authority concentrated in the national state apparatus was tempered both by the war and by Nicaraguan history. The Sandinistas made a major policy shift in 1983, when the war was building up steam.[20] There was a recognition that a guerrilla war in the mountains could not be fought from distant headquarters in Managua. This had been key to the Sandinistas' own victory and it was this experience that they drew upon to shift their own strategy. As a consequence, military command was regionalized. The decentering did not stop there, however. Economically, the Nicaraguan economy is quite diversified with some regions specializing in cattle, others cotton, and still others coffee. This, too, lent itself to planning at the provincial and municipal levels. The new constitution established a greater measure of autonomy for municipal elections and facilitated the election of opposition candidates or coalitions in villages and towns across the country. The reasons for this sensitivity to diversity, mapped in geographical terms, do not lie simply in a pressure to pluralize. Managua, the current capital of Nicaragua, was itself established to placate a century-long feud between two warring urban centers, León and Granada. The need to balance regional differences, with or without the hegemony of capital, has evidently been, therefore, a deep condition for national unity and one for which the Sandinistas had fought. For this reason, one can suspect that the move toward decentralization undertaken in these war years may have a lasting impact, albeit one with an uncertain political tendency as attested by the marches led by conservative mayors against the Chamorro government early in 1991.[21]

This impact was felt not only in the realm of the political economy, but could be observed in the domain of culture as well. Indeed, while the economy and polity were most directly constrained by war, cultural expressions flourished in many different directions, including the proliferation of scores of theater groups in neighborhoods, workplaces, and mass organizations. The Ministry of Culture in Nicaragua was established soon after the revolution. Initially, it too had assumed a policy of centralization. Projects in the provinces were to be reviewed, assessed, and funded directly from the ministry in Managua. Budget cuts soon made this type of financial support implausible, and the ministry shifted from its role as a funding producer to become an encouraging promoter of cultural events in the countryside. Responsibility for support of cultural workers shifted to their union, the Asociación Sandinista de Trabajadores Culturales (ASTC), and full-time salaries were paid between 1986 and 1988. By February 1988 fiscal constraints contributed to the dismantling of the Ministry of Culture itself and its reorganization as a department within the Ministry of Education. Subsequent cuts led to the formation of the Institute of Culture, an entity formally independent of the government and hence able to receive foreign assistance directly, a format retained by the Chamorro government. Available support remained quite limited and was concentrated on a few groups in the capital. These reorganizations left groups outside Managua all the more reliant on regional, or their own, resources (tours abroad or agricultural commodities) for survival. By the end of the decade only one provincial theater group was still working.

The feasibility of this decentralization was not simply economic. It also had to do with the historic regional cultural diversity of Nicaragua and Somoza's disinterest in developing a singular national culture. Rather, imported culture was showcased in the National Theater (inaugurated December 6, 1969), while Somoza occupied himself with his family's baseball team, the Five Stars (named after the general).[22]

Unlike Cuba, Spanish colonialism in Nicaragua proceeded through a subjugation and enlistment of the local population into large-scale agricultural production. As the indigenous population was itself culturally diverse and the presence of colonialism uneven (the Spaniards left the Atlantic Coast to the British and Americans, whose colonial strategies featured administration over assimilation), each area of Nicaragua developed its own peculiar forms of cultural expression. This is still the case. The region of Masaya is renowned for its Marimba music, while the Segovias feature an almost flamenco-sounding guitar music. Bluefields has a maypole (palo de mayo) dance derived from those of the English court. The influence of German migration to the coffee-growing region of Matagalpa is evident in the polkas that can be found there. Each town has its annual festivals to celebrate the fruits of its harvest as well as church processionals and theater pieces that mix Catholicism with elements from indigenous pre-Columbian forms. One such popular mobilization is El Tope, when residents of Diriamba, Jinotepe, and San Marcos take statues of their respective patron saints from the church altars and carry them along the highways, in a procession of music, dance, and fireworks, to "meet" in the small church in Dolores.

All of this cultural activity made the countryside a rather rich cultural field that, unlike Managua, has retained a greater degree of local control over semiotic production by transmitting cultural contact into popular performance. Utilizing these cultural pathways and proclivities for assembly, a single theater company could reach tens of thousands, giving it a proportional equivalence to mass media in a country of three million inhabitants. Radio had been common in the rural areas, but not television, and cinema is limited to trips into town. The capital is awash in contemporary cosmopolitan culture, and the grounds for transmitting these forms into the historic forms of

Nicaraguan experience is less apparent there. Sandinista cultural policy facilitated a wide variety of films, music, and television programming. The film industry was only being established, and television production was limited apart from the news and coverage of civic events. The dissemination of North American cultural products, especially, was amply in evidence during Sandinista rule in the more than twenty movie theaters in Managua; in the fifteen state-run and fifteen to twenty-five private radio stations throughout the country,[23] many of which play North American top-forty tunes for break-dancing youth on dirt plazas; and on the two television stations that circulated old American westerns, which had been dubbed in Spanish in Mexico. After the Sandinistas' electoral defeat in 1990, one channel was taken up by Univision, the Spanish-language station based in the United States, and the other station programmed several news and public-affairs slots and increased the fare of telenovelas; a third station run by the Sandinistas is scheduled to begin broadcasting in April 1991. *Barricada*, the FSLN's official paper, and *Nuevo Diario*, one sympathetic to the Frente, continue to publish, along with *La Prensa*, whose masthead no longer includes President Chamorro's name.

Yet precisely the problem of how to respond to this fluid and disembodied cultural presence shaped the work of at least one Managuan theater group during the 1980s. It served as a mediation of these imported forms, providing a parody that generates certain critical tools for its public. This group, Grupo de Teatro Experimental Miguel de Cervantes, performed in cinemas and high schools and brings references to western pop music, break-dancing, and cinema directly to its performances.[24]

A quite different theatrical expression emerged in the countryside. Two groups combined theatrical and agricultural production on collective farms. The more established of the two, Nixtayolero, was formed by Alan Bolt, who, during the 1970s, was a national cadre in the guerrilla movement of the FSLN, and had organized agitational theater in the cities. In 1979 and 1980 he worked directly for the Ministry of Culture and ran its theater school in Managua. This first of several incarnations of the school (in 1989 it moved to the National Theater and began a four-year program with assistance from Sweden) soon collapsed for a variety of reasons. Unlike Cuba, there were no professional groups for the graduates to join. Their energies were diverted to television and radio, or in other directions outside Nicaragua. The small salon theaters that existed in Managua before the revolution could provide neither the infrastructure nor political sympathy for the cultural impulses that followed it. Nor were the theatrical expressions that emerged with the revolution oriented toward the extant dramatic literature by Nicaraguan authors, much of which had gone unperformed. A theater festival for national authors was one of the first projects planned by the new administration of the Institute of Culture, headed by Gladys Ramírez de Espinosa, who had acted with the Teatro Experimental de Managua since the 1950s. While there has never been a national theater company in the formal or official sense in Nicaragua, the Comedia Nacional has been perhaps the only consistent theatrical presence since its founding in 1965 by Socorro Bonilla Castellón, but it has not had the kind of central impact on subsequent formations that Cuba's Teatro Estudio enjoyed over the same period, despite its use of the Teatro Nacional Rubén Darío for rehearsals since the 1970s. With the exception of the few years of Sandinista subsidy, Nicaraguan actors have had to find means of subsistence apart from the theater, and in Managua this tended to detract from the time they could spend in the theater.

During the 1980s, the theater group Nixtayolero was distinct from its urban counterparts because it occupied an actual site of economic and cultural production. Since 1990 many in the group had to move off the farm for economic reasons, although the economic and cultural projects continued. From the group's small farm, or *finca*, in the coffee-growing region of Matagalpa province, thirteen people of largely peasant origin and from many of the country's seven departments came together under Bolt's direction. Each person was in charge of a certain agricultural project designed both to make the cooperative self-sufficient economically and to provide new agricultural techniques and products to *campesinos* in the area, who, after five hundred years of colonial presence, have had their diet reduced to a single variety of rice and beans. The regional diversity of the actors provided the group with the range of forms of music, dance, and theater to be found throughout the countryside. Intertwined together, these marginal forms appropriately constitute a more representative national culture than one constructed from the center, and they attest to the cultural strength of the margins and the political power of the regions.

The second of these two "community theater movement" groups that was able to continue working until 1988, Teyocoyani, made a piece in 1985 that displayed the dynamics of these relations quite forcefully. It was a collectively produced work, *Juan y su mundo* (Juan and his world), which, like Buendía's *Lila, la mariposa*, contained two acts that divide the work into a pre- and postrevolutionary saga. Before the piece begins, folk songs of the León region mix with the national songs of the revolution. This music continues as narrative when two of the musicians climb atop a bamboo platform upstage and continue to sing, and (like the seamstresses of "Lila") announce the action, comment upon it, and listen to and judge what transpires in a testimonial dialogue with the players and public.

The first act of *Juan y su mundo* played so much like a kind of fairy tale of the revolution as to provide a parodic backdrop for the more confounding second act. "Juan," as introduced before the play by the actor who portrayed him, is the archetypal *campesino*, costumed in black and white indicating that he contains the capacity for both good and evil. Without land or means to support his family, Juan in these "twilight times" is readily enticed to do the devil's work. He becomes the interlocutor of coercion, beating his fellow *campesinos* into submission and forcing his wife to provide the devil's brigade with sexual favors. The devil is not Juan's only exteriority. An angel intervenes and challenges Juan's conduct and the devil's privilege. The two forces do battle, and with the predictive force of hindsight, the white-clothed angel prevails. Juan has been saved for the second act.

Juan did not himself make the revolution. Yet, because it is made in his name, he is able to reap its fruits. When the action resumes, Juan, along with the *campesinos* he had formerly betrayed, is offered a cooperative by the angel, now an agent of the government. The cooperative is composed of all of the dreams the *campesinos* can name, and the angelic agent crafts them out of thin air. When the angel departs, the dreams revert to their prior gaseous state and the cooperative is simply a plot of land upon which to materialize them. The first harvest is successful, but a tractor will be needed to assure continued productivity. Juan is sent into the city to secure a loan.

The bus depots of Managua are located in three large markets. When people get off the buses, they are immediately confronted with this economic nexus of country and city. Juan's arrival here presents all of the corruptions of the market in a mixed economy. Government inspectors come to buy under the table what they have just surveilled on top. Juan makes it past the market to arrive at the bank where an immense bureaucratic machinery and an empty hall provide no access. From a corner, an official beckons and Juan is relieved of the deed to the cooperative that he would have used to secure a loan. Returning with a useless bank note, he reaches the cooperative and finds his *compañeros* sleeping. He regards them for a moment, reaches into a basket, and steals off with the cooperative's remaining funds. On his way out he is stopped by the angel from the first act, who demands that he reflect on what he is doing. The devil then heralds him, only to be ignored. Juan walks offstage and the bards join the cast in song. The decision is left with the audience in a third act improvised as discussion with the actors.

This piece was viewed, in a sense, out of its context. Typically, these performances occurred before the people characterized in the play. In the countryside or on the war front, *Juan y su mundo* evoked the very distance and marginality that are so central to the future of Nicaragua. This particular performance was presented before an audience at the Autonomous National University of Nicaragua (UNAN) in León. In this very auditorium important meetings of student supporters of the Sandinista Front took place and earlier works of political theater were performed. This particular crowd of urban intellectuals persistently questioned the ambiguity of the play and its ending during the "third act" intended for their input. They suggested that the play did not provide strong enough guidance to its *campesino* public and was not clear enough as to the sources of shortages and scarcity that Juan's cooperative encountered. What this UNAN audience recapitulated in the third act was the very tension between center and margin that the play offered as its predicament. The intellectuals responded, however, as an already marginalized voice demanding a return to the center, to their properly directive role.

That the play would seem to "work" on both sides of the divide that it inscribes only underscores the inseparably relational aspect of the center-margin problematic in Nicaragua. Juan's departure is as much a problem for the *campesinos* he leaves as for the intellectual's city that he may be heading for. Juan, as character and social actor, anticipated the economic dilemma of those unable to maintain independent plots in the countryside and migrate to a city that can scarcely provide for them (Managua's population had tripled during the war).

Juan also articulated the political quandary of how to grant increased autonomy to the regions without their leaving the revolution. Finally, the play's blending of regional idioms indicated the cultural conundrum of rural roots as national culture compressed into the currency of mass media that can no longer be exchanged in the countryside (regional folk musics are the source of a burgeoning recording industry in Nicaragua whose products remain in the city, as reproductions are scarcely consumed in the countryside). At the same time, *Juan y su mundo* was a rather modest instance of a public sphere with certain functions that parallel the state, yet are formally outside it. Here, social problems were articulated and rehearsed in performance.

Decentered Development?

What all of these tensions declare is the pervasiveness of the margin-center problem in the overall development of these two countries. The theater figures not only the particular aspects of these problems but the foregrounding of the problem per se. It would be difficult to imagine a piece of theater as generally distressing as "Juan y su mundo," being produced in a war-torn Nicaragua without the possibilities of a decentering road of development as a distinct prospect. It was friendly to a revolutionary process with diverse trajectories. Indeed, upon my return to Nicaragua early in 1991, this type of critical articulation in the theater was strikingly absent, both with respect to established groups and, from all accounts, at the grass-roots level. The 1980s saw theatrical productions that were critical of the government from the left and the right. In the new conjuncture, the possible and appropriate forms of participation had to be adumbrated without an appeal to artistic purpose that extended beyond the aesthetic dimension, and the theater was thrown back upon its immediate conditions of production.

The Cuban case presents a different play of margin and center. Marino is quintessentially an urban youth whose push and pull from the local center of the family hurl him into an uncertain future. The romantic closure of words to be obediently followed on the radio is permeated with the raucous and unbounded cabaret. Marino turns to romance while being seduced by cabaret. In this process his singular voice is fragmented and multiplied into many. While there is little reason to doubt that Havana will remain the party's center and Cuba's core, *Lila, la mariposa* may very well be figuring a meiosis, a growing smaller that results in a greater multiplicity. It raises the question of a postrevolutionary era without the singular romantic voice to give guidance and certainty, and at the same time, it depicts a demand for an embrace of uncertainty.

Revolutions are never simple processes, but there are times within the fevered struggle for power that forms of communication must of necessity be quite direct. While even the briefest scrawls of graffiti should be understood as signs that condense multiple meanings and references into a single image, their communicative function, despite their formal complexity, could be characterized as an instrumental one in relation to politics. Here, communication is quite clearly a means to an end. Its presence affirms a certain transgression that simultaneously gives evidence to and supports those engaged in a "frontal assault" on the state. The message of oppositional possibility is borne both by the contents of the sign and by its very existence. In this sense, a symbolic war may continue in places where a contest of bodies may be too dangerous. This revolutionary sign is always, at the very least, a placeholder for armed conflict and, at most, an extension of battles that make the presence of an underground movement felt at all times.

Theater played precisely this type of role in the Nicaraguan revolution. The mere act of assembling people to witness the representation of rebellion was a transgression of the state's control over the public sphere. Theater groups composed of students would perform in the urban barrios of León or Managua, sometimes completing their sketch before being chased by the National Guard. Masked fighters of the Sandinista Front would perform in the mountains while one of their rank stood guard. That these were the conditions that generated a new impulse in Nicaraguan theater would be full of significance for the forms of theater that followed the Sandinistas' accession to power.

In Nicaragua the traces of that revolutionary process remained highly visible. The faded slogans against Somoza resided under fresher red and black slashes of paint that carried forth the Sandinista Front. These competed with markings from the Nicaraguan presidential campaigns promoting the Independent Liberal or Conservative parties (1984), the UNO coalition (1989-90) that brought Violeta Chamorro to power and invections against the mothers of *yanquis*.

Due to persistent international conditions of the 1980s, the revolutionary character of Nicaraguan culture dried much more slowly than the painted messages on these plaster walls. Yet the straightforward instrumentality of revolutionary culture to the movement it supported changed dramatically in the decade since 1979, both from an organizational and an aesthetic point of view. In both instances, theater shifted from a handmaiden of revolution to a much more critical force with an organizational identity of its own. The boundaries of this autonomy and the aims of this critique must be understood within the historical process that made them possible and as a measure of the political culture in a postrevolutionary context. Since the role of culture after a revolution must respond to the conditions that generated that revolution as much as the direction of development that post-revolutionary processes take, cultural forms can nowhere be identical. It is conceivable, however, that certain problems faced by countries experiencing socialist development overlap, that the history of socialism is itself a resource for emerging social formations, and that theater with a revolutionary heritage unburdened by the demand to prove its solvency on the market may take on certain common characteristics.

To these ends, a comparison is in order. It turns out that the particular circumstances for theatrical development in Cuba are distinct yet subject to some of the same constraints as those in Nicaragua's socialist-led decade. Theater at the time of the Cuban revolution had none of the political instrumentality of the Nicaraguan case. Not that theater makers were inactive in the movement against Batista, but Cuban theater already had a more continuous history and an established audience. This was particularly true in Havana, where plays predominantly from the Western canon were performed in small halls frequented by professionals and the petite bourgeoisie. While this type of theater existed in Managua, it lacked these revolutionary sympathies and was overshadowed by an explosion of popular theater in the early years of the revolution.[25] Even a decade after the Sandinista revolution much of the urban theater depended on non-Nicaraguan directors (from Mexico, Colombia, El Salvador, Argentina, and Spain), although the ASTC concentrated more effort on supporting these theaters.

If the great burst of Nicaraguan postrevolutionary theatrical activity began in the countryside, it took some time to get there after the

Fidelista victory in 1959. The closest thing to a situation of political instrumentality for the Cuban theater emerged ten years after the revolution, when a group of actors from the most established theater in Havana took to the hills of Escambray in an ideological assault on the counterrevolutionary Jehovah's Witnesses. Before and after that period, theater seemed to have a more even development than many of the other artistic media in Cuba. An organizational centrality was established early on, and a continuity of aesthetic form marked the movement from a pre- to a postrevolutionary context.

In Cuba, as in Nicaragua, the process of making political culture has been far from simple. What is intriguing is that a cultural sector with a measure of organizational autonomy (aesthetic independence had existed from the beginning) from the state organ, the Ministry of Culture, is only now developing, thirty years after the revolutionary break. Unlike popular Western presentations of Soviet *glasnost*, in which an opening emerges somewhat metaphysically from an ontological closure in culture and the economy, the emergence of a semiautonomous cultural sector must be viewed within its own distinctive history. Just as the immediate position of theater within the Nicaraguan revolution can be seen as shaping its position after the revolutionaries come to power, so is the course of Cuban theater a consequence of its historical trajectory that presented professionalization as its first priority. In both of these cases, there are certain paradoxes and turns that may appear counterintuitive: How does Nicaraguan theater change so rapidly from a relation of such profound instrumentality to the revolution to play then a function of providing criticism within it? Similarly, why does Cuban theater, which is not formally incorporated into the frontal assault of the revolutionary process, remain so thoroughly integrated with the state for as long as it does? These questions have been far from resolved here, but the capacity to pose them seems in itself a justifiable gain to the appreciation of political culture in Nicaragua and Cuba. Particularly in Nicaragua, the critical liveliness of theater is complicated by its placement within a broader critical field that both enabled and challenged Sandinista governance.

Theater is certainly not unique as a domain of cultural expression that embodies the constraints of an entire social order. What might be suggested as the privileged position of theater is its ability to enact the dynamics of this contradictory process before a public. In the course of this enactment one sees with certainty the myriad constraints: the location of the theater, the cost of admission, the demographics of the audience, the limits of training, the relation between dramatic litera- ture and national dramaturgy, and so on. More important, perhaps, for an understanding of the promise of a future that revolutions claim, is the theater's presentation of utopian possibilities onstage. In this, the utopian vision must be located within the cultural history that gives rise to the theater itself. The presentation of lived possibilities onstage is woven out of existing currents. Hence, while theater may not be able to predict the future any better than econometrics, it may con- dense certain possibilities latent in current circumstances and pre- sent them concisely and coherently.

Cultural policy under socialism is also a manifestation of state plan- ning. Cuba and Nicaragua developed relatively centralized and decen- tralized socialist states. This essay has attempted to assess the signifi- cance of this difference on cultural production and, in turn, use the figurational possibility of theater to identify potential developments in the state and society. The strategy here was to move from a reading of a particular production that links that history to the anticipation of its future to the broader affinities of culture and politics that present the problem of the relation between organizational and aesthetic form. It is hoped that this movement reveals the complexity of the center-margin problematic as an index of the historical dynamics of socialism. Center and margin are not positions but exist only in rela- tions that are multiply determined. Managua's cultural peripherality, in relation to both multinational culture and national cultural produc- tion, presents it as a weak center that decenters the prospects of devel- opment to the countryside. Culture and politics crystallized in Havana after the revolution (as before), but its apparent centrality is deceptive if seen as monolithic or solid. Processes of decentering are visible there as well and figured prominently in the theater. The utility of the margin-center metaphor resides above all in the analytic fluidity it per- mits. As socialist development erodes class-based ownership of social wealth, its history continues along lines that permit new distributions of power. Socialist impulses emerge under many conditions that are fluid and by no means assured. Yet the persistent appearance of such impulses suggests that the historical movement they propose cannot be easily extinguished. The search for evidence of this movement leads toward less-familiar constructs of the representation of politics.

NOTES

1. Cuban sociologist Ester Suárez has explained the resurgence of theater in the last several years as the result primarily of young people's interest in the theater. This generation brought up on television has spent enough time inside the house in front of the box (interview with Ester Suárez, July 22, 1987). A number of young playwrights have been able to get produced on the basis of this demand, notably Yulky Cary (*La rampa arriba, la rampa abajo*), Abilio Estévez (*La dolorosa historia del amor secreto de José Jacinto Milanes*), Alberto Pedro (*Fermán como Verónica, Weekend en Bahía*); some of these have been published in the theater journal *Tablas*.

2. Rolando Ferrer, *Teatro* (Havana: Editorial Letras Cubanas, 1983).

3. Edwin T. Tolon and Jorge A. González assert that there is no indigenous influence in Cuban theater today. For their account of early theater, see *Historia del teatro en la Habana* (Havana: Universidad Central de Las Villas, 1961), 9. See also Rine Leal, *La selva oscura*, vol. 1 (Havana: Editorial Arte y Literatura, 1975), for a history of theater in Cuba from colonial contact to the mid-nineteenth century.

4. See, for example, Hernando Serbelló, Pilar Ferreiro, and Carlos Venegas, *El teatro la caridad* (Havana: Editora Política, 1983).

5. For a history of this period, see Rine Leal, *La selva oscura: De los bufos a la neocolonia*, vol. 2 (Havana: Editorial Arte y Literatura, 1982).

6. Paco Alfonso, *Teatro* (Havana: Editorial Letras Cubanas, 1981).

7. This analysis of recent Cuban theater history is dependent on interviews and research conducted in July 1987 and in June 1988, 1989, and 1990 (tapes in possession of author), including interviews with a number of critics and directors, among them, Armando Correa, Rine Leal, Ignacio Gutiérrez, Vicente Revuelta, Gilda Hernández, Laura Fernández, Roberto Blanco, and Vivian Tabares.

8. For an account of theater at the time of the revolution, see Rine Leal, *En primera persona* (Havana: Instituto del Libro, 1967).

9. I am indebted to George Yúdice for this insight. Castro's speech is published in *Revolución, letras, arte* (Havana: Editorial Letras Cubanas, 1980).

10. As an indication of support for a group deemed "within the revolution," the play was awarded a prize by the official community of critics and in 1986 was judged as the second most significant Cuban production by a similar assemblage — after *Fuenteovejuna*, also directed by Vicente Revuelta for Teatro Estudio (see Haydée Sala Santos and Miguel Sánchez León, "Una encuesta sociológica: Las diez mejores puestas en escena," *Tablas* (Jan. 1986), 62-70). Blanco, Revuelta, and Berta Martínez, listed in the same *Tablas* poll of critics as the top three Cuban directors (with more than half of the vote split between them in a field of twenty-seven directors), together formed Teatro Estudio, and the latter two are still associated with it.

11. Magaly Muguercia, "Informe no confidencial," *Tablas* (Feb. 1986), 8.

12. Información Estadística Seleccionada Informe, Sobre el Trabajo del Ministerio de Cultura (1985).

13. Ministerio de Cultura, Plan Anual de Superación (1986).

14. Informe Sobre el Trabajo del Ministerio de Cultura (1985).

15. Anuario Estadístico de Cuba (1985).

16. Interview with Vicente Revuelta (July 27, 1987); tape in possession of author.

17. The first important break came in 1968 with the formation of the Teatro Escambray by Sergio Corrieri and a group of actors from Teatro Estudio. By 1971 the group had a base in the mountains of Escambray and was making work (notably *La*

vitrina, directed by Elio Martín) through a social investigation of small farmers being wooed by the antirevolutionary Jehovah's Witnesses in what came to be known as the "lucha contra bandidos" (struggle against bandits). In the wake of Escambray's success, the Ministry of Culture funded a series of similar projects that in the late 1970s came to be known as the Teatro Nuevo movement. These groups were also based in the Escambray region and used similar investigatory procedures. The groups that followed Teatro Escambray, however, never broke their dependence on Havana either financially or aesthetically. Actors tended to maintain homes in Havana, and the groups lacked an impetus from below that would sustain them (interview with Elio Martín, July 30, 1987). By 1980 the Teatro Nuevo movement was already on the wane, and today the Teatro Escambray is the only group that remains. See also Roberto Orihuela, ed., *Lucha contra bandidos* (Havana: Editorial Letras Cubanas, 1983).

18. For a fuller discussion of Varela's work and recent cultural currents in Cuba, see Randy Martin, "Cuban Theater after Rectification," *Drama Review* 125 (Spring, 1990).

19. Some discussion of these emerging policies can be found in "Proyecto: Sistema de organización y funcionamiento de las Artes Escénicas," unpublished ms. (Cuban Ministry of Culture, Dec. 25, 1987), and "Proyecto para el perfeccionamiento organizativo de las Artes Escénicas" (Cuban Ministry of Culture, Mar. 1989).

20. For a discussion of various aspects of early Sandinista policy, see Thomas Walker, ed., *Nicaragua: The First Five Years* (Praeger, 1985).

21. A compact history of these interventions can be found in Karl Bermann, *Under the Big Stick: Nicaragua and the United States since 1848* (Boston: South End Press, 1986).

22. Interview with Pepe Prego, secretary of the theatrical section of the Association of Sandinista Cultural Workers, July 1986. Other materials are drawn from fieldwork done in Nicaragua during the summers of 1985 and 1986 and in January of 1989 and 1991.

23. Armand Mattelart, *Communicating in Popular Nicaragua* (New York: International General, 1986), 9.

24. For a fuller discussion of theater and popular culture in Nicaragua, see Randy Martin, "Nicaragua: State and Theater without Walls," *Social Text* 18 (Winter 1987), and "Country and City in Nicaraguan Theater," *Drama Review* 116 (Winter 1987), 58-76. In 1990, this group was reconstituted by the same director, Néstor Méndez, as Tohil.

25. The scholarly and critical apparatus for documenting and evaluating theater is not as elaborate in Nicaragua as it is in Cuba. Jorge Eduardo Arellano has compiled material that illustrates theatrical activity since colonial contact, in *Boletín Nicaragüense de Bibliografía y Documentación* (Aug. 1988-Jan. 1989), 58-59. An overview of Nicaraguan theater can also be found in Franz Galich, "Teatro Nicaraguense," forthcoming in *Revista Iberoamericana* published by the University of Pittsburgh.

Bad Poetry, Worse Society

Iumna M. Simon and Vinícius Dantas

Translated and abridged by Holly Staver

Poesia Jovem (1982), an anthology of 1970s poetry, represents a new direction in poetry made by and designed for an adolescent audience.[1] It was aimed at a youth culture identified with the playful and uncommitted registering of everyday experience. Analogous to rock music that is no longer nonconformist and rebellious, it is part of a movement called "marginal poetry," which broke with contemporary literary values, particularly with the formal and existential restraint of the avant-garde.[2] By the end of the 1970s marginal poetry had given rise to a number of derivative movements. And it clearly had been domesticated to a considerable extent (despite or because of its marginality). It broadly responded to young consumers who thus acquired a poetry to fit the standards of the culture industry.[3]

Young Brazilian poets were lured to this trend that dispensed with literary tradition and formal craft. Literary scholarship is rare even among Brazilian elites, so this devaluation of literary tradition found fertile ground in a culture characterized by a low level of education and a taste for mass media. Whatever countercultural and antiliterary value was expressed by marginal poetry in its earliest stages, it soon disappeared. By the mid-1980s, in fact, its poetic production had become as homogenized and standardized as consumer commodities, and obviously without the infrastructure required by the consumer industry. This poetry conveys the life-style, behavior and affectivity of a new sensibility at a moment when it can no longer be expressed as subjective experience. Given the impossibility of individual style, poetry has to be grounded in the anonymity of collective experience.[4]

To reduce the characteristics of the new Brazilian poetry, as some critics do, to cultural imitation or external influence is not particularly helpful. In fact, the development of the movement after the political "opening" of 1978 can be monitored in the gravitation of earlier "marginal" poets toward pop music. Their work thus gained a circulation and popularity that few poets of the past had known.[5] This poetry also uses clichés and gestures of irreverence and nonconformity, while refusing to assume obscurantism in a society living under the crushing burden of conservatism and authoritarianism. Here it is useful to recall the dynamics of democratization, the rapid failure of the campaign for the direct election of the president of the republic, and the transitional phase of a civilian government chosen by an electoral college.

Limited to a small number of cultural elites in contact with developed capitalist societies, marginal poetry nevertheless has an unsuspected potential for mass consumption; after 1978 it became amenable to dissemination in magazines, recordings, radio, and television.[6] Whatever attitude we take toward it, this poetry is an increasingly important aspect and the inevitable index of literary sensibility for any evaluation of cultural change. On the other hand, it is not an isolated phenomenon in Brazil. Consider, for example, the situation of the poetry produced over the last few decades. The most important avant-garde movement of the 1950s, concrete poetry, and the leftist nationalist poetry movement of the 1960s obstinately fought for a poetics of direct communication with the public. Some argued that poetry ought to reach the distracted urban dweller, others that poetry should awaken the alienated consciousness of the exploited worker. However, the readership of these earlier movements did not exceed five hundred readers, the majority of whom were middle-class intellectuals. Those poets were misunderstood, persecuted, boycotted, and went through hell. But what about now?

"Without a utopian perspective, the avant-garde loses its significance," theorist and poet Haroldo de Campos declared in 1984, without really going into the historical or cultural consequences of this crisis.[7] Only then did he finally acknowledge that, having lost its relevance, the avant-garde is no longer worth emulating. The space of the avant-garde had disappeared, and any avant-garde intervention is no longer motivated by a spirit of criticism. Nor does it meet with the resistance of a hostile public. Long-term projects that involve opposition to the status quo belong to the past, and there are no visible signs of their slogans and tactics. The foregoing epitaph of the avant-garde, pronounced by one of its foremost theoreticians and practitioners, was late in coming. After all, during the 1960s critics had already noticed the loss of radicalism and negativity among the utopian avant-garde. Other, more skeptical thinkers even suspected that Brazilian avant-garde movements were no more than opportunistic reflections of the so-called historical avant-gardes of the 1910s and 1920s.[8]

Nevertheless, Haroldo de Campos's declaration touches on a vital point: the absence of any vestige of hope for a transformative project or practice, the hope that had powered avant-garde initiatives and provided them with a totalizing goal. At the present time, the future holds no promise and the very idea of utopia has been lost. Yet for de Campos, poetry continues to be a worthy, valid experience, an experience of "the concretion of signs," that can still defy despair and permit an ultimate norm of action. For a poet like Haroldo de Campos — rooted in the "classical" conception of modernity, which warrants him the comprehension of poetic language as an autonomous structure — what now takes on value as a positive ideal is the creative present (its "nowness"), through which the poet maintains a dialogue with words and signs. Hence his addendum: "This poetry of presentness, as I see it, should not, however, undertake a poetics of abdication, should not serve as an alibi for eclecticism and facility." With the waning of the influence of the avant-garde, it is necessary to preserve poetry as a positive value, a linguistic ideal opposed to pastiche and redundancy. In de Campos's diagnosis of contemporary despair, it becomes apparent that he has been forced to rethink his premises in the face of present adversities, salvaging a critical element and maintaining a cautious attitude toward contemporary sensibility. Can the objective of not debasing poetry be enough? To what extent is poetry in itself a transhistorical value unaffected by the impoverishment of postmodern sensibility? Is the convention the poet chooses the result of historical and cultural conditions to which she or he reacts by questioning them, or does it correspond to the ideals of modernity with which the poet is charged and obliged, at all costs, to comply? These questions are irrelevant to a generation of poets who take little interest in modernity as such, are not particularly given to reflection, and for whom the postutopian is an empirical, though not necessarily unpleasant, experience. This sensibility goes back to 1968 — Tropicalismo, the best films of Júlio Bressane, Rogério Sganzerla, and Glauber Rocha, which responded in part to the military dictatorship, the turbulent climate of armed struggle, and the crisis in political representation.

Gradually this disenchantment lost its links to politics and repression, revealing a similarity to the complex effects of advanced consumer society. Neither the oppositional movements nor those that produced radical and avant-garde art escaped this co-optation. The failure of projects for change, the feeling of impotence and cynicism, and the lack of options, at first attributed to political factors, magically became the everyday experience of postmodernity in Brazil.

The increasing importance of relations with international capital made the country ever more vulnerable and, at the same time, accentuated the flow between center and periphery, which, in turn, deeply affected the economic and cultural spheres. With the failure of 1960s ideologies, it was easier to see the paradoxical mixture of wealth and misery, although there has not been enough critical reflection on the impact of all this on aesthetics. The ideologies of nationalism and developmentalism, which had acted, until then, as reference points for Brazilian artists, became irrelevant given the unequal and reckless modernization of the country — whose social and political cost was most severe among the working classes — and the exclusion of the majority of the population from consumption. This state of affairs directly affected cultural production. Modernization had become intrusive and violent, comfortably coexisting with the perpetuation of social backwardness and vast poverty that a modern consumer society now reproduced. Such contradictions affected Brazilian artists who, although closer than ever to international artistic tendencies, were also caught within a backwardness that excluded them from, and was inappropriate to, the hegemony of the modern. The best songs of Caetano Veloso evoke this predicament with ironic sweetness and bold melancholy.

The Tropicalista generation lived the transition from populist democracy to military authoritarianism in perplexity and despair. In contrast, the generation that started writing at the beginning of the 1970s, already familiar with political exhaustion and the immobilization of transformative projects, witnessed without hope or illusion the effects of accelerated modernization. It was the media that reorganized cultural and artistic debates. An increasingly well-organized culture industry laid down rigid rules for participation in the market. The entire first crop of marginal poetry (through approximately 1979) staked out an independent alternative space for production and consumption that opposed commercial publishing channels and emphasized an artisanal mode of production, distribution, and reception. The traditional conditions under which poetry had been produced in Brazil (frequently self- or group-financed) suddenly took on a new meaning. The prevailing interpretation of this poetry reads an ambiguous political message into its individualist, artisanal mode of production and into the fact that it was a project undertaken by youth.[9] Was this "political response" a matter of poetic content and form, did it envisage a new social experience, could it be translated into other sociocultural relations and values, and did the artisanal mode of production work against political intentions? The very figure of the marginal poet came to be identified with the street vendor, selling in bars, along movie and theater lines, promoting shows, recitals, happenings, and even demonstrations in order to market the poetic product and open new channels of distribution.

But it is necessary to keep in mind that this marginal experience was meaningful only during the years of political repression and censorship, when artistic production was excluded from public space. This historical contingency was an important factor. Existential practices and behavior imbued the poetry of the younger generation, conferring a symbolic value that surpassed its poetic content. When there were signs of a political "opening" toward the end of the 1970s, all of this production was accepted, published, and promoted without any difficulty by the large publishing houses. This official endorsement of marginal poetry paradoxically brought to an end the theoretical debates over publishing, sales, and distribution alternatives. Since the question of poetic value had always taken second place to reception (for example, the seduction of the reader mattered more than poetic content), the movement was left empty handed when the artisanal mode of production no longer had any value. The program of the marginal poets was limited to two points: the denunciation of the authoritarianism of the avant-garde and the intellectualist tradition associated with João Cabral de Melo Neto, and the call for a "strategic retreat" to the Modernista poetry of the 1920s.[10] Even the term *program* has to be understood loosely, since in fact this was formulated by the literary critics who surrounded the first marginal groups, theorized for them, and sought to define clearly their literary politics.[11]

Succumbing to market and publishing industry forces, what remained of this poetry was its *poetic form*, which can perhaps give us objective criteria for evaluating its contents and understanding the consequences of its devaluation of the literary. What one critic of contemporary Brazilian literature identified as a "strong desire for re-subjectivization"[12] provoked by the rediscovery of intimate experience would not appear to compensate for the loss and intentional rejection of the "objective lyric" from João Cabral to Concrete Poetry. The writing of marginal poets undeniably attests to re-subjectivization, but also to the fact that subjective experience is no longer what it always was. It is now inscribed in a sociohistoric situation in which subjectivity, the problem of identity, is rather a symptom of anonymity, isolation, atomization, and the loss of the referent. Re-subjectivization makes the poetic subject coincide with the empirical subject; literary representation becomes relative because it is less distanced from reality. There is still a process of elaboration, involuntary or otherwise, since representation involves a *formal* rearrangement of its elements. The confessional and biographical register, the irreverent monitoring of everyday life, and the raw recording of feeling, sensation, and the random are poetic solutions that, in the end, impose an *informal and antiliterary kind of stylization*. The recurring characteristics are easily recognizable: colloquialism, unpretentious subject matter, a conversational relationship with the reader, humor, extravagant metaphors rendered in everyday language, simplicity of syntax and vocabulary—all techniques that may include simultaneity, collage, ellipse, and brevity.

A preference for graphic effects, word games, and puns marks the influence of the earlier avant-garde. Now the literal and the informal predominate: the raw material of verse is given in a prosaic tone, half mélange and half pastiche, whimsically put together out of a spectrum of old Modernista diction that lapses into the rhetorical, polemical, surrealist, and pseudophilosophical. The objective is to accommodate all the disruptive strategies of modern poetic language into an easy, flowing sensibility and to naturalize the poetic perception of the poem by means of everyday speech. Those effects of irony and parody, so common in Modernista poetry, that the ironic colloquial tradition derived from changes in register—moving from an elevated erudite pitch to everyday speech—are here indistinguishable and homogeneous. The result is transparent and truncated figuration, chaotic and simple, in keeping with nonselective, direct, and immediate perception.

A Brief Anthology of Marginal Poetry

I'm more given to mischief than responsibility
fonder of music than brawling
more disposed to vice than virtue
pedestrian yes sir
a corporate annual report
peering through dark city clouds

—Charles

I'll trade a wad of poetry for an ugly groupy's love
I'm a romantic cubalibre dancing to the moon

—Charles

I'll make you a trade right now if you're game
an epic poem in ten cantos
for a lullaby
the whole work week
for a moment of carousing
what I no longer am
for what I never was
my careless ashes
for your heavy diamonds

—Eudoro Augusto

I cut my dentist's appointment
cut college
cut some other things
and came to see you
it was an irresponsible change in the weather

—Ronaldo Santos

first thing in the morning I wrote some shitty poems
one wasn't too bad
pissed off I tore up the shitty ones
son of a bitch it's fucking stifling hot
reread the better one
felt satisfied
the record scratched on
lunch was getting cold
didn't shower
you know I get up late
called but only the circuits answered
got on my jeans
any bus
any destiny
any business
there's no theater of life

— Guilherme Mandaro

Rotgut

as if it weren't enough
falsies
sour wine
modess rubbing my wet thighs
as if it weren't enough
the boredom piling up
plucking and quartering chickens
aborting
offspring of hangovers
but the nights with you
— they're useless and innumerable too.

— Leila Miccolis

Vida Bandida [Bandit life]*

Kicked the motherfucker while he was down
betrayed my best friend

---

*This poem resembles a hit record by Brazil's most renowned rock group, Lobão.

chains brass knuckles and switchblade
the paper was full of praise
blood and beatings late at night
you've got to live the bandit's life
ain't no use trying to play it safe
the heat's coming down on you and life is tough
but one shot won't bring you down
running with teary eyes
is not for everyone
but smiles come easy
when the cash flows freely
you should've seen the chick's eyes
as she climbed the hill
it's all fun and games up there
they haven't yet invented money
I can't take
                              — Bernardo Vilhena

no, my heart isn't bigger than the red light district
it's much smaller

it won't hold all the whores & pederasts
all the crazy punks & beggars
all the filthy & suicidal killers

my heart is too small
for my own evil ways
                              — Adauto de Souza Santos

Visitors

la chair est triste my ass
the pale-faces were never moved
by the gut rhythm of the congas
the driving pleasure of maracas
they've never been to Madurreira
nor fell on their faces in the gutter
for the love of a crazy dark-skinned girl
                              — Eudoro Augusto

Devaluation of the literary was a means to give evidence to the subject's vitality and to the register of experience that, according to "marginal" credo, had been banished from Brazilian poetry since the poetic and intellectual meditations of João Cabral. Of course, this argument turns things around, as if poetic technique were not the translation of experience into formal problems and poetry's formalized contents were not learned in the world. It also encouraged a return to pure lyricism, which was intended to restore neoromantic expressiveness by using a transparent, informal, and quasi-spontaneous language in contrast to poetic technique. In other words, subjectivity was to displace cold technical experimentation and restore living experience to poetry. Marginal poetry could thus bear witness to its time; it could become the form of individualization that, at the very least, might express the conflicts experienced by the younger generation in its urge to transgress, to revolt against family, education, or class. Even if these experiences were very mundane and their literary expression awkward, the fact that they were documented was of general significance in itself. What is both surprising and disappointing about marginal poetry, however, is the fact that although it attempted to adopt a testimonial and confessional mode, stylization was superimposed on immediate experience. Experience became stylized transcription.

The poetic solutions to the figuration of ambivalent feelings—of chaos and passion, pleasure and horror, seduction and solitude, affinity and animosity, personal vitality and general anonymity—are conveyed primarily by means of the devaluation of the literary: emotional experience has no qualities as such, nor can style and literariness dignify it. The devaluation of the literary becomes a proxy for the expression of individual subjectivity. The reader who sits down to leaf at random through many pages of this poetry, sampling poets and poems of various tendencies and groups, from different centers of production, will recognize something vague and generic, without uniqueness, a kind of poetic figuration of an objective historical phenomenon, stylized in a noncommital and futile manner: there is a certain hedonistic pleasure in playing with the devaluation of sensibility itself.

In short, a collective sensibility—with standardized sentiments, emotions, sensations, and reactions—here expresses itself without denouncing the presence of a personal voice behind the multifaceted mask. The confusion and mixture of dictions, the routinization of disruptive operations, and the naturalization and resulting banalization of the power of suggestion of the poetic image add up to a devaluation of style. Although related to different social conditions of production, an analogous phenomenon was recently described provocatively by Fredric Jameson who, writing from a sociohistorical point of view, described pastiche as one of the symptoms of the transition from "classical" modernity to postmodernity:

> The great modernisms were . . . predicated on the invention of a personal, private style, as unmistakable as your fingerprint, as incomparable as your own body. But this means that the modernist aesthetic is in some way organically linked to the conception of a unique self and private identity, a unique personality and individuality, which can be expected to generate its own unique vision of the world and to forge its own unique, unmistakable style.[13]

According to Jameson, pastiche is "blank parody" (that is, it lacks the critical and satirical motivations of parody) or "neutral practice," given the impossibility of individual styles in an era in which the subject, as personal identity, no longer exists. In other words, the epoch of classical bourgeois individualism has come to an end.

More than one spokesperson of marginal poetry (when it still had "style" and was limited to the groups that founded it) remarked on this collective tendency toward anonymity that, in turn, came to imply undifferentiated values and criteria, and complete banalization. In 1975 Antônio Carlos de Brito wrote:

> A good deal of marginal work suffers from this devaluation of artistic form and technique, and ends up repeating itself in a general, undifferentiated way that makes it hard to tell one author from another, one poem from another, one vision from another. Everything starts to look like everything else.[14]

In the same year, Heloísa Buarque de Hollanda officially anthologized the movement with this reservation:

> The apparent facility of writing poetry today may lead to serious mistakes. A significant amount of so-called marginal work is already watered down and trendy. Thus, the serious problematization of the everyday and the mixing of styles lose their power as transformative and formalized elements, becoming *mere subjective registers* without any greater symbolic and, therefore, poetic value.[15]

To the contrary, we argue that the new poetry is not subjective enough and its literary devaluation fails to achieve its intentions. Those poets who privileged the personal and the autobiographical as the most genuine way of expressing events, including political ones, should be excepted from this statement. Francisco Alvim and Roberto Schwarz practiced a sort of unemphatic and quite ironic chronicle of the infamies of political repression, exile, bureaucratic life, and the family. In fact, both of these established writers identify themselves with the movement for strategic reasons. In the poems of Francisco Alvim, the subjective autobiographical notation of events acquires a pathetic force of revelation that extravasates the poetic economy. This unmistakable poetic voice, although sometimes degenerating into the *poema piada* (joke poem) and coded self-revelation, confirms the fact that subjective register and personal style cannot be disassociated.

We arrive, therefore, at a paradox: what is taken to be the re-subjectivization of poetry is, at bottom, no more than the general state of contemporary sensibility. And after all, if literary creation presupposes universality, why should the general expression of a sensibility limit poetic quality? Doesn't the collective and anonymous subject of this work offer the theoretical advantages we might correctly require from poetry? Literary history offers interesting examples in this respect. Second-rate literature, we know, expresses the most characteristic features of sensibility in the styles, mannerisms, fashions, and tastes of the times. Occasionally, these general characteristics not only predominate but are also cultivated as conventions (for example, the baroque and arcadian). Historical avant-gardes adopted a strategy: rampant individual styles were replaced by the exploration and affirmation of a form that, once dominant, would become the new convention. João Cabral confronted in 1945 this challenge of how to create personal works from existing ones (the great works of Modernismo) when these possessed such singular features that they inhibited the expression of equally singular personal qualities in the young poets of the Generation of '45. He accepted this challenge as a positive one:

> Work whose extension is determined by its historical position may very well lead to the creation of a general Brazilian expression constituted not by the coexistence of a small number of distinctive and dissonant voices, but rather by a broader, more general voice, capable of integrating all the dissonances into one chorus.[16]

If the crisis of modernity can be interpreted as a crisis of individual style, it is also true that some poets have chosen a collective and general style in order to affirm themselves individually. This is how the Concrete Poetry project envisioned its goal, both objectively and programmatically. Marginal poetry, however, works in the opposite way: there is neither a common linguistic project to carry out, nor any utopia programmed as a goal. A multitude of experiments with many disparate and divergent characteristics come to express a general feature of contemporary sensibility, which is rendered by an informal and antiliterary stylization. The devaluation of the poetic thus comes to coincide with the content of the sensibility in question.

The *Jornal Dobrábil* of Glauco Mattoso, one of the most fascinating poetic texts of this period, deserves mention here in passing. It takes advantage of this very state of nullification of the subject and stylistic undifferentiation to articulate a perverse strategy. The author uses the newspaper format as a device to establish an anonymous identity. Everything acquires the status of a humorous but degraded poetic text, and poetry is equivalent to excrement. A pastiche of all available discourses, styles, mannerisms, proverbs, and quotations, sometimes altered by parody and nearly always scatologically and pornographically perverted by the contexts in which they are used, creates a kind of subjective elephantiasis that is both unexpected and obsessive in its gratuitous and limitless machinations. The self-conscious antiliterary anonymity is converted into a vertiginous effect. The poem offers an aberrant and menacing image of how the sensibility we have described can be carried to the extreme of depersonalization.[17]

In sum, these desacralized poems offer a chaotic and banal picture of everyday life that reflects the total desacralization of an equally chaotic and absurd world. Given this no-holds-barred sensibility, it is difficult to detect whether the poems are any less banal than the reality that inspired them. The fact that it is stylized invalidates the hypothesis that attributes the antiliterary to the lack of culture among our new literary elite, to mass education, and to the loss of a historical referent in the absence of critical thought (although it may be connected to many of these factors). Some marginal poets cultivate high literary values and scholarship, like Geraldo Carneiro, Afonso Henriques Neto, and Eudoro Augusto, but the artistic results of their trend are less interesting than trivial devaluation of the literary.

Devaluation is not simply risky; it amounts to a threat, as the poem tends to accommodate aberrant aspects of reality, naturalizing and playfully accepting the techniques of modern poetry—shock, estrangement, and discontinuity. The banality of reality coincides with the banality of poetic technique, although this is not only confronted in a natural and straightforward way, but is also comfortably enjoyed.

Anomie attracts and eventually invades this poetry, whose very language dispenses with poetic technique as a way of validating and reflecting on experience. Thus the poet expresses affirmatively the collective basis of his or her feeling, rather than denouncing and exposing what he or she has personally suffered and how his or her sensibility has been touched. Thus, poetic revelation, however whimsical and strange, however natural, cannot be critical, much less unsettling.[18] One of the more intellectual poets of this movement wrote doubtfully of the risks of the antiliterary in a proverbial but poetically elusive quatrain:

> In the violence
> that language imitates
> isn't there something of violence
> strictly speaking?[19]

Compared to North American confessional poetry (at its height in the 1960s) by authors like Sylvia Plath, Anne Sexton, and Frank O'Hara,[20] Brazilian marginal poets seem to have witnessed the effects of modernization without those inner wrenchings or upheavals in the personal and social universe that are inevitably experienced in the everyday life of advanced consumer societies. They write, then, of the devaluation of sensibility from the stable perspective of a middle-class dining room. Anonymity, fear, anguish, despair, homogenization are neither wrenching nor threatening experiences. In this poetry the social ground seems firm even while everything around it, including this ground itself, undergoes modernization. On one hand, there is degradation and violence. Yet, surprisingly, there is also considerable pleasure, something light, ingenuous, a compulsive brightness. True, ways of writing of these and other unsettling experiences vary considerably according to the subject, the intention, and the inflection. There are many cases where references to details of everyday life—minor pleasures, love affairs, flirtations, walking around, holidays, eating out, a night on the town, parties—are always forgettable because instantly replaceable. All this appears to be based on comfortable predictability and tedium; but there is always an opportunity to have fun. Chacal writes in his famous "Fast and Low":

> there's going to be a party
> where I'm going to dance
> 'til my shoe begs to stop
> that's where I'll stop, take off my shoes
> and dance the rest of my life.[21]

Even in the poetry of Ana Cristina César, conflicts and divisions, the ambiguities of multiple small events with their seductions, anxieties, and desires, are graced by syntactical flirtation. A chic affectation conceals the brink of a great ruin behind elisions, silences, and style, always concluding with an elegant image. These unsettling feelings appear in one line or another, in some authors more than in others, and often focalized against the background of explicit references to violence, the city, the lives of ordinary people, the police, and so on. Thus the poet's sensibility itself is compared to the marginal, the outlaw, the poor person degraded by poverty ("the poet in delirium / is the punk of the race," proclaims the most rabid outsider of the marginal poets). This common analogy is also a stereotype of the drug experience. In "gang" perception, threats of police repression, physical destruction, and despair resemble the problems and situations of the most wretched. This "populist sensibility" includes smatterings of effusive and ardent sentimentalist and nationalist clichés. This sensibility is less a matter of political appropriation than an idealization of social reality, expressed by devaluation of the poet and poetry. Concrete social experience is emptied into the brand name of marginality. The postures of the poet become equivalent to those of the poor: ignorance becomes the equivalent of anti-intellectualism; to be déclassé, the equivalent of petit bourgeois transgression, having no prospects, the synonym of rejecting progress. The stylized devaluation of the literary thus imposes a class perspective, which is then projected in the guise of a social condition. Images of urban chaos, poverty, and perdition give rise to genuine sentiments, whose doubt and uncertainty are questionable because they are not based on the social experience of devaluation itself, and thus take undeniable pleasure in privilege.

The hermetic, tight linguistic weave of modern poetry gives way to a pragmatic literal language that has no mystery or nuance. Polysemy, opacity, and the questioning of expression only appear in the form of the humorous poem, gloss or parody. In order to forge an immediate and spontaneous bond with life, this bold antiliterary attitude takes a pragmatic approach to communication. Poetic language is rendered facile so that it may be easily consumed. Its simple and transparent everyday revelations promote a complicity based on personal affinity in order to attract the reader: "not the pretty little poem / but its way of being read by you," according to a marginal quasi-manifesto. This poetry "descends from the tower of literary prestige and appears in a performance that, by restoring the connection between poetry and life, reestablishes the nexus between poetry and public."[22] Evidently, the problem does not reside in the flow of poetic communication, but rather in the implications of the devaluation through which the attempt is made to seal the communicative pact. Transparent, simple, and literal, yet chaotic, fragmentary, and dispersed, the poem is reduced to a sensitizing experience, a therapy that occurs outside of the verbal medium. Yet poetic form does not dissolve because it is stylized. In our view, this stylized solution simulates literary devaluation and denies poetry the capacity to bear witness and reveal its social and historical implications.

This is a problematic solution because the poem promises a personal and affective relationship that its subjective and stylistic anonymity make it impossible to fulfill. This is also an apologetic solution because the experience of devaluing the literary is an option of the privileged. Not only is it a class pleasure, something that limits its critical scope, but it is also a hedonistic version of the discrimination inherent in Brazilian modernization. The uneven development of this process, which intensified during the 1970s under the authoritarian regime, is the sociohistorical precondition for this poetry. However, the contradictions and the violence of modernization are not revealed in the poems; they capture only the symptoms, the ambivalent feelings and sensations mentioned earlier. It is the very ideology of modernization and its most obvious expression, class privilege, that is reproduced. This poetry does not value itself as a formal experience that transcends the general features of this sociohistorical context. The coexistence of devalued poetic form, the poverty of subjective register, and the celebration of modernity say a lot about the position of people who lived the experience of literary devaluation while accepting the benefits of "progress" and consumption. Pleasure, satisfaction, and cheerfulness thrive on a generalized devaluation. The pleasure principle of poetry yields to the everyday reality principle, and banalization is its most literal and comfortable illustration.

Nevertheless, the new idea of poetry configured in this situation is one of the most remarkable accomplishments of Brazilian poetry. Thanks to the nature of its stylization, it takes the ideals of the culture industry to their limits and promotes a pragmatic, communicative reconciliation between poetry and the public. The historical irony is that this was a project of the 1950s. Concrete Poetry conceived of the "poem-product, the useful object," according to the almost mythical principles of constructivism. As we have seen, this led to a farcical repetition of earlier debates and utopias. Now, however, this farce is leading us back to reality, cutting us off from the "perceptible universe of forms" of that happy idealism. Unlike Concrete Poetry and the poetic avant-garde in general, which envisioned a transformative utopia guiding its strategies and pointing toward a future global revolution in which poetry would be privileged, contemporary Brazilian poetry is bounded by the banality of the everyday, the disagreeable horizon of the present. This has a catastrophic effect on poetic language, which is reduced to a kind of routinized vernacular, incapable of opening up to the multiplicity of life experiences and languages. Nevertheless, this contemporary sensibility has the virtue that it neither inspires idealizations nor promises what it cannot deliver: to change the world through poetic form.

NOTES

This essay was originally published in *Novos Estudos CEBRAP*, 12 (June 1985), 48-61. The poems included here were translated by Elizabeth Marchant and Holly Staver.

1. Heloísa Buarque de Hollanda and Carlos Alberto Pereira, eds., *Poesia Jovem. Anos 70* (São Paulo: Abril Educação, 1982).

2. For a minimal bibliography on this work, see H. B. Hollanda, *26 Poetas Hoje* (Rio de Janeiro: Editora Labor do Brasil, 1976), and *Impressões de Viagem* (São Paulo: Brasiliense, 1980); C. A. Pereira, *Retrato de Epoca* (Rio de Janeiro: Editora Funarte, 1981); A. C. Brito, "Tudo da minha terra: Bate-papo sobre poesia marginal," in *Almanaque*, no. 6 (São Paulo: Brasiliense, 1978), 38-48. Though not extensive, this small bibliography, in addition to the articles mentioned above, includes some items of interest.

3. This proliferation, not yet sufficiently analyzed, is best documented in the already mentioned anthology *Poesia Jovem* and in *O que é a Poesia Marginal?*, an instructive little book by Glauco Mattoso (São Paulo: Brasiliense, 1981). In the latter, an overview of the history of recent work, the author demonstrates the inadequacy of definitions and the extraordinary reach of the phenomenon that went beyond the con-

trol of the groups in Rio de Janeiro that initiated the movement.

4. We base this diagnosis upon Fredric Jameson's suggestive reflections on the cultural symptoms of postmodernity in the late capitalist context of "postindustrial society," whose application to the Brazilian case entails obvious risks. See, especially, Jameson's "Postmodernism and Consumer Society," in H. Foster, ed., *The Anti-Aesthetic. Essays on Postmodern Culture* (Port Townsend, Wash.: Bay Press, 1983), 111-25.

5. It should suffice to mention that in 1940 one of Brazil's major poets had to pay the cost of publishing an edition of his poems out of his own pocket so that he might have a volume of poetry in circulation after being accepted into the Brazilian Academy of Letters. At that time Manuel Bandeira, fifty years old, was recognized as one of the most important modernist poets. See M. Bandeira, *Itinerário de Pasargada*, 3d ed. (Rio de Janeiro: Editora do Autor, 1966), 119.

6. Today, Brazil possesses impressive machinery for the production of best-sellers. Only a little while ago, editions reached two thousand copies at the most and never sold out. Now they are multiplying. The publishing market modernized as well, and despite the persistence of deficiencies in distribution, it now functions in conjunction with other media. It is not unusual for a successful work to be turned into a TV series, a film, play, or the subject of journalism, etc.

7. See Haroldo de Campos's long reflection, "Poesia e Modernidade," published in two parts: "Da morte da arte à constelação" (*Folhetim*, no. 403, Oct. 7, 1984), and "O poema pós-utópico" (*Folhetim*, no. 404, Oct. 14, 1984). An itinerary of the several phases of Concrete Poetry, up to the crisis in the avant-garde, is described in our introduction to the volume *Poesia Concreta* (São Paulo: Abril Educação, 1981).

8. These positions, with varying shades of meaning, are adopted in more than one text by a number of critics, some well known, including: Octavio Paz (*Children of the Mire*), Hans Magnus Enzensberger (*The Aporias of the Avant-Garde*), Michael Hamburger (*The Truth of Poetry*), Daniel Bell (*The Cultural Contradictions of Capitalism*), and T. W. Adorno (*Esses Anos Vinte*). It should be noted that in Brazil *Modernismo* (1920s and 1930s) corresponds to the "historical" avant-gardes and that the Concrete Poetry movement of the 1950s and subsequent movements are called *Vanguarda* or avant-garde. (Eds.)

9. H. B. Hollanda and A. C. Brito, "Nosso verso de pé quebrado," in *Argumento*, 1, 3 (Rio de Janeiro: Paz e Terra, Jan. 1974), 81.

10. H. B. Hollanda, *26 Poetas Hoje*, 8. The proposal to recuperate 1922 Modernismo's "most valuable contribution," that is, "the poetic incorporation of the colloquial as an innovative element, and a break with high academic discourse" (ibid., 8-9), which had served until then as a characteristic quality of marginal poetry's "reconquest," is, in itself, meaningless. Colloquialism was undeniably an innovation of the Modernista movement, subsequently incorporated into modern Brazilian literature, with varying means of adaptation and combination with erudite literary language. Even the "classicizing" tendencies, typical of the poetry of the Generation of '45, or the post-Modernista diction of Carlos Drummon de Andrade, which finds its equivalent in almost all the traveling companions of Modernismo, from Mário de Andrade to Cassiano Ricardo, are stripped of pedantic syntax and vocabulary. This elevated, rather solemn pitch did not hinder the linguistic opening up to all available verbal registers. In addition, the linguistic reform of Modernismo systematized scientific prose and facilitated the incorporation of speech into dramatic dialogue in Brazilian theater and cinema since the 1940s. We should not forget that since 1972, with the commemoration of the fiftieth anniver-

sary of the Semana de Arte Moderna by the Medici government, the elements of innovation and rupture have finally found their consecrated resting place in the official pantheon.

11. This precarious anti-vanguardist and retro-modernist theoretical program was, in fact, entirely drawn from positions earlier argued by José Guilherme Merquior, in a 1968 essay, "Capinam e a nova lírica," included in *A Astúcia de Mimese* (Rio de Janeiro: José Olympio Ed./Conselho Estadual de Cultura de São Paulo, 1972), especially 179-87. Meanwhile, everything that converged to weigh in favor of a curiously and explicitly conservative defense of the reflexive, classicizing diction of the "philosophical lyric" (interpreted as the pinnacle of post-modernista evolution, but at the same time as an obstacle to the new poetry) was also used to celebrate spontaneity, intuition, and an informal lack of commitment.

12. José G. Merquior, "Comportamento da Musa: A Poesia desde 22," in *O Elixir do Apocalipse* (Rio de Janeiro: Nova Fronteira, 1983), 68.

13. Jameson, "Postmodernism and Consumer Society," 114.

14. Brito "Tudo da minha terra," 43.

15. Hollanda, *26 Poetas Hoje*, 10; emphasis added. In *Impressões de Viagem*, Hollanda reconsiders that critical reservation, positing marginal poetry's spontaneity and lack of artifice as the refusal of poetic language that makes possible the experience of banal daily reality as art—a conformist acceptance of everyday experience that, in our opinion, falls into an aestheticization of the banal.

16. João Cabral de Melo Neto, "A Geração de 45—III". *Diário Carioca* (Dec. 1, 1952).

17. Glauco Mattoso synthesizes his poetics as follows: "I start on the assumption that I am a plagiarist; I don't respect anyone's intellectual property. That is my point of departure. As a plagiarist, I mix my things up with other people's. It doesn't matter if the idea is mine or somebody else's. I put my name under things that aren't mine and I put other people's names on things that are mine. So, taking off from there, I began to publish a small newspaper. When I mentioned crosswords and puzzles, I was speaking of diversions, pastimes. That's how I approach poetry: a way of passing the time and keeping busy." Interview in *Rebate de Pares*, "Remate de Males," collection 2 (Campinas: IEL/FUNCAMP, 1981), 1.

18. The fundamentally vitalistic tendency of the new poetry—from which it seems even utopian elements are absent—privileges the transcription of "immediate life," as if it were enormous poetic *graffiti*. Its apparently simple, good-humored, and "uncommitted" language is not as critical as it might seem at first sight." H. B. Hollanda, "A Poesia Vai a Luta," *Alguma Poesia*, no. 2 (April 1979), 59.

19. A. C. Brito, "As aparências enganam," *Grupo Escolar* (Rio de Janeiro: Coleção Frenesi, 1974).

20. A good survey of the new tendencies in North American poetry may be found in the *Harvard Guide to Contemporary American Writing*, ed. Daniel Hoffman (Cambridge, Mass.: Harvard University Press, 1979), especially in the final chapters.

21. Chacal, *Drops de Abril* (São Paulo: Brasiliense, 1983), 11. An ambiguity should be noted in the double meaning of "dançar," which means the actual execution of the dance, and also (in slang) the degradation of one who takes pleasure in "screwing up." (trans.)

22. H. B. Hollanda, *26 Poetas Hoje*, 8.

Cultural Redemocratization: Argentina, 1978-89
Kathleen Newman

The Argentine daily newspaper *Clarín* regularly features on its back page the comic strips of the best graphic artists and political humorists of the nation: among others, Fontanarrosa, Tabaré, Crist, and Caloi. On August 8, 1989, Caloi's strip "Diógenes y el linyera," which chronicles the misadventures of a philosophically inclined dog and his down-and-out human companion, ran the following conversation between the two:

EL LINYERA: Hyperinflation has got to affect humor. There are many reasons to raise the price of jokes. The raw material is imported, because humor has left the country. The producers of our humor have increased the ridiculous, the absurd, the grotesque, and paradox. And if that weren't enough, with everything going up, consumption is going down.

DIÓGENES: How horrible! In the end, laughter will be a thing of the rich . . .

Not surprising sentiments given the problems facing Argentines that month. Just a month earlier, in July 1989, Peronist candidate Carlos Menem had assumed the presidency from outgoing Radical party leader Raúl Alfonsín. It was the first democratic transition of political power in decades, but, in response to the severe social and governmental crises of midwinter, including food riots in several cities, it occurred six months earlier than scheduled. In August, inflation was to come down by approximately three-fourths, from nearly 200 percent a month before, but daily life was fraught with problems: continuing increases in basic transportation fares and gasoline; bills such as gas, electricity, and water so high that one alone among them might consume a monthly paycheck; rotating blackouts because the power plants were in disrepair from the period of the last dictatorship

(1976-83); monetary shortages; disrepair of streets and parks; even shortages of cigarettes. In Buenos Aires, a city known for its fast pace, there were long lines of taxis parked curbside because few could afford the cost of the ride. In all, there was a sense of a nation at a halt. Caught between an external debt (tied to the political mysteries of the world debt crisis) and an incalcitrant military demanding pardons for those involved in the dirty war, that is, in the disappearances and torture of Argentine citizens that characterized the first years of the dictatorship, the new government would need to deal with an impoverished middle class and with the poor and working poor, who were facing ever more brutal conditions of existence. At the same time, on any weekend the outward appearances of disposable income among the upper classes were visible in Patio Bullrich: the packed, gleaming, new, and elegant shopping mall of Barrio Norte, a glass and marble redesign of the Bullrich family's stockyards. Perhaps that is why Diógenes, during August, was of the opinion that Argentina needed a "Robin Jajahud" — whose last name is the sound of laughter — to steal jokes from the rich and give them to the poor.

The return to civilian rule in 1984 was to have initiated a period of political redemocratization. The euphoria of the return to democracy, chronicled in film as the dancing political demonstrations in the background of Fernando Solanas's *Sur* (1987), gave way to recurrent political-economic crises of the mid-1980s to which Alfonsín's Radical party, again caught between the debt and the military, could offer no adequate response. The too white-collar image of the Radicals contributed to the return to worker-based Peronism, but it was a Peronism now ranging between the more center-left positions of Cafiero; the governor of the province of Buenos Aires, who lost to Menem in the primaries; to the more conservative positions of Menem, who, if his economic policies and his eventual pardon of military convicted for crimes in the dirty war can serve as evidence, seems to have made a pact with the right. This pardon, the word for which in Spanish is *indulto*, was misunderstood by the comic strip character Clemente as *insulto*.

The pages that follow present a brief and necessarily schematic account of the role of cultural production in process of redemocratization, a process that began before the return to civilian rule in 1984 and, given that by late 1989 "humor [had] left the country," can be considered to have ended with the decade. It is an account of the ways in which humor magazines, comic strips, novels, and films are a record of resistance during dictatorship, a domain of competing interpretation of the dirty war and of democracy during the euphoric days of the return to civilian rule, and, in these latter years of the transition from *radicalismo* to renewed but sharply conflictive *peronismo*, an arena of public debate severely reduced in scope and in vigor of critique by economic crisis. The ephemeral record of counterhegemonic cultural practices—art in the service of seemingly national or collective sentiments of hope, despair, humor, and disillusion as to the nation-state's future—registers four distinct periods since the military coup of 1976: (1) until 1980, a grim sense that the dictatorship was unending; (2) in 1981, the year of the *apertura* (opening, or decrease in the overt military presence in daily life), in 1982, the year of the Malvinas-Falklands War, and through the elections of 1983, a sense always of impending change; (3) from 1984 to 1987, an energetic confrontation with the State terror of the recent past and the possibilities of a democratic future; (4) from 1987 to 1990, very little sense of a potential solution to the nation's problems given its place in the ongoing process of global capitalist restructuring. Finally, these pages seek to review how it came to be that one of the last Argentine films to be released in 1989—there were no releases of new films after August for that year because it was recognized that there was no possibility of a film earning even enough to cover the cost of its production—was *Cipayos*, a slick, vapid dance film made for export, in which the "youth of Argentina" dance tango in the streets to save Argentina not merely from foreign occupation but from the alleged failures of the left, of the generation of their parents: all in all, a rightist interpretation of the nation's political future.

"Bodas de Humo": 1978

To return to the importance of graphic arts in interpreting the politics of culture in Argentina; in June 1978 a monthly satirical magazine *Hum(R) Registrado* (Registered Humor) published its first issue. The name is condensed on the cover logo, the final *r* appearing inside letter *0* (imitating the trademark symbol). The magazine would become bimonthly, and the name would later be further shortened to *Hum(R)*. A number of its editors and graphic artists had worked previously on other important humor magazines (a well-established genre in twentieth-century Argentina), and the work of some collaborators, such as Fontanarrosa, Quino, Tabaré, or Viuti (mentioned previously), appeared regularly in national newspapers. Though the magazine self-consciously promoted itself as a Marx brothers' editorial madhouse, the director Andrés Cascioli and editor-in-chief Tomás Sanz undertook the very serious work of pushing the limits of what was considered possible to even say, let alone lampoon, during the years of the dictatorship. On the magazine's fifth anniversary in May 1983 (no. 105), advertised on the cover as "EL 'PROCESO HUM(R)' CUMPLE 5 AÑOS," the regular editorial column began:

> After five years of priesthood, we are celebrating a journalist wedding anniversary of some kind. And we don't know what name to give you. We could call it the "Sad Anniversary" because in spite being satisfied with our work, the situation of the country depresses us. Perhaps we may have reached the "Steel Anniversary" for having had such patience, disposition and morality to overcome crises, discouragements and pressures of all sorts. Or are they the "Anniversary of Smoke" [Bodas de Humo], volatile and ephemeral as are all human endeavors, even those which seem to us worthwhile and lasting? (21)

The pressures were economic and political (in the latter case, phone calls and threats of the seizure of issues)[1] but the Anniversary of Smoke, as contradictory as it may seem, did not disappear. Rather, it entered into the ephemeral record of acts of resistance.

Hum(R) had two kinds of existence during the dictatorship, and both were crucial to the creation of an oppositional culture. *Hum(R)* was a satirical magazine to be read and a cover to be seen every two weeks. Cascioli himself always created the covers of *Hum(R)*, and he favored covers that stop passersby in their tracks in front of the thousand and one street-corner kiosks that sell mass magazines and newspapers (and a good number of small presses as well). These covers are colorful, exaggerated, and at times grotesque caricatures of famous singers, soccer players, movie stars, international political figures, and as the dictatorship wore on, infamous generals and admirals. The entry on Cascioli in the catalog for the 1981 graphic arts exhibition "Muestra de Humor" (Teatro San Martín) begins:

> Every two weeks, the covers that Andrés Cascioli draws for his magazine "Hum(R)" inundate the kiosks and hang in front of the

people's noses. And the public recognizes them: a monumental and changing Moira Casán [an incomparable burlesque artist], the green and solemn face of Palito [a singer], the alarmed or diabolic official or person in government . . . The caricatures of Cascioli are the graphic identity of his magazine, the face to the street, the reflection of his intention and his expressive intensity.

Cascioli's grotesques—huge noses, ears, distended bodies—run from the silly and sexist to the intensely political. In the latter category are his reworkings of the faces of the military in deep but muddy greens, browns, and yellows. One of the covers that stopped people in the streets in 1981—in a month in which there were a number of *rumores de golpe* flying about (rumors of an internal power struggle between the various branches of the junta or, as likely, the egos of the upper-echelon commanders)—depicted a certain general as a bad boy looking for trouble, a bully in short pants with his military uniform ripped and his face and hands covered with scrapes and cuts. It seemed at the time a measure of the disintegration of military power that their infighting could be so directly represented, but in truth, what was surprising *then* was just a preview of what was to come. By 1983, successive junta members had been, among other things, a chorus line under a crucified Lady Liberty (no. 105) and ghoulish white faces under "the tip of the iceberg" (no. 108) of war crimes. Videla and Hardinguey showed up as a Laurel and Hardy ("Stan Videl y Oliver Hardyndeguy"), court summons in hand, about to be crushed by a falling statue of blind justice (no. 109). The recombinant power of the Cascioli grotesques were foretold even in the first cover in 1978. In the days of the World Championship Soccer matches in Buenos Aires, he combined the long-haired soccer team director Menotti with the big-eared Minister of Economy Martínez de Hoz to produce a Menotti de Hoz, who announces, echoing the government's economic policy, "El Mundial se hace cueste lo cueste" (The Championships will take place no matter what the cost). In the context of the Mundial, which was promoted with patriotic fervor and during which progovernment stickers were distributed showing a heart in the national colors of white and celestial blue containing the words "los argentinos somos derechos y humanos" (We Argentines are upright and humane—a play on *derechos humanos*, human rights), this first cover was clearly "anti-patriotic."

The measure of what was permissible in 1979, when fear was still great, can be found in the kinds of death jokes that appeared in the first issues of *Hum(R)*. For example, in the second issue, January 1979, there is a drawing by Añil of a hangman sitting under his noose reading a paper. A sign tacked up on the side of his gallows reads, "open all day." In the third issue, there is a Fontanarrosa drawing of two men standing next to a bullet-ridden cadaver. One says: "Don't call the coroner. Call the dentist. It's a case of lead poisoning." These jokes are in no way overtly political, but they would be read as being encoded political protest. The first would have been taken to be referring to the death squads and the second to the official duplicity regarding political murder. These kinds of death jokes occur frequently throughout the years of the dictatorship. The strangest inversion of this standard of double reading, however, can be found in one of the issues published during the last year of the dictatorship. A color toy advertisement for a suspense game called "Terror en la noche" shows a haunted house. The caption below it reads, "when terror is a game." How did the Toytrade company expect this advertisement to be read? But then, in 1981, after years in which a green Ford Falcon was the preferred car of the paramilitary in their "operations," how did the Ford Motor Company executives expect a billboard along the lines of "Ford Falcon, An Argentine Classic" to be interpreted? The Toytrade "Terror" faces a full-page comic strip about a fat military man who keeps reminding people talking about elections that they have short memories concerning what happened during the dictatorship. In the strip, when the election arrives the fat general is shown heading off for Hawaii (not so far from the truth, as General Suárez Mason was found in hiding in California), announcing he's glad people have short memories. If, perchance, the Toytrade or Ford executives did have short memories, the cartoonists of *Hum(R)* felt the responsibility to remind them. Indeed, Ford Falcon jokes achieved terrible perfection under civilian government. In a December 1986 issue (no. 188), when the military was supposedly in a period of self-criticism, there is a cartoon playing on the word *auto*, which can mean either "self" or "car":

> Three "veterans" of the dirty war, two wearing regular and combat uniforms and one wearing the overcoat and dark glasses of a security-forces thug, are speaking together.
> "Look, for kidnapping there isn't anything as good as the Falcon."

"But what are you saying? It uses a lot of gas . . ."
"Besides the trunk is very small. It can't compare with the F-100."
Two passing civilians observe:
"It seems that self-criticism [*la autocrítica*] has begun."

The fifth issue of *Hum(R)*, October 1978, combines a parody of King Kong movies (it is possible the U.S. remake might have been showing in Buenos Aires at the time) with soccer mania: buy King Kong for the Boca team! This combination sustains a long soccer article at the beginning of the issue, but at the back is found the "Balada de King Kong" by a certain Jeremías Sanyú. In sixteen of the eighteen shots or boxes, King Kong is talking aloud about his life; a "crazy" soliloquy about, for example, how Patricia Derian (U.S. Assistant Secretary of State for Human Rights under the Carter administration) was tearing out her hair because he'd been invited to Argentina, and how much fun it would have been to have done "Candid Camera" here in Argentina—he could have gone to the government and said he was a delegation from Carter. In this sixteenth box, Kong is revealed to be standing on top of the Obelisk (a national monument at the center of two main streets, 9 de Julio and Corrientes). When King Kong commits suicide by jumping off the monument, the adults in a passing car assume it is one of artist Minujin's latest, but a child who exclaims, "Look, a *gorila* fell from the obelisk!" is told "Quiet kid . . . *gorilas* don't exist." *Gorila* is the slang term for military right-wingers or fascists. It is significant that in October 1978, *Hum(R)* could critique *gorilas*—and the people who didn't believe *gorilas* were running Argentina—in print. Along the side there is a correction notation: "Fe de erratas: el cuadro no fue autocensurado" (Printer's error: the strip was not self-censored). A few months later, in 1979, the year in which the Inter-American Commission on Human Rights visited Argentina, the tenth issue of *Hum(R)* contains a cartoon by Limura showing a radio announcer reading over the mike: "And now in our program of current politics, "The Hour of Truth," a news flash for our vast audience . . . It's 7:30 P.M. in the whole country!" The reading public, at least, had means by which to measure seeming political "truths."

By the elections of 1983, *Hum(R)* was replete with overtly political humor. In fact, since the year of the *apertura* and the disaster of the Malvinas the military has been excoriated on the covers and in the pages of *Hum(R)*. The September 1983 issue (no. 112) shows two security agents, guns drawn, hauling off Lady Liberty as a guard explains to a coronel that nothing is happening, "a small problem with the transfer order . . . to civilian government." *Transfer* was a slang word for taking a disappeared person from a torture or detention center to be killed. The cover of this issue, a parody of a Mel Brooks movie poster, shows "The Crazy History of the *Proceso*, Part VII," which starts with Videla and Viola as primitive man (*gorilas*) and ends with the institutional breakdown of the military. Were that not enough, in its film column the issue goes beyond the normal mention of how many minutes of a film were cut by the government censors.[2] The U.S. film *Missing* is described in detail because even though it wasn't allowed to be shown in Argentina, "sooner or later it will show up on our screens." The title of the article is "¿Qué pasa con *Desaparecido* (the disappeared)?"

From 1978 onward the pages of *Hum(R)* are the evidence of the existence of at least two nations within the same national territory. In their declared war against "subversives," the military did not merely deepen a civil war; they redefined citizenship. In this redefinition they excluded most of the national populace, some of whom they physically eradicated, the rest of whom became citizens of an occupied territory.[3] Thus, the laughter of *Hum(R)* is not a carnivalesque laughter, the kind of laughter that exists in a nation-state, that is, an inversion of social norms, the king ritually brought low. The laughter of *Hum(R)* is camouflage for a war of knowledge and of wits between two nations that coexisted in the same space. In the first aspect, knowledge, it is the dissemination by allusion and inference of information that could not otherwise be communicated in the mass media. It affirmed as public knowledge that which was said privately at home. In the second aspect, by time and again outwitting censorship through humor, the magazine became the bimonthly definition of the enemy as *brutos*, those who could only possibly rule by force. It is not that people took *Hum(R)* to be a subversive magazine, even though there was a definite politics to its editorial policies. It is that humor could be nothing less than oppositional. This is the one fact the editors of *Hum(R)* took seriously.

Representing Terror: 1981

Graphic art was not the only medium that became a cultural front line: literature, music, film, and all the arts that potentially reached a mass public had the same double life and double public as *Hum(R)*. Here, I am not using the war vocabulary merely as a metaphor. Survival in the first years for people who had been politically active — professionals, students, labor organizers, and others — did require the kind of strategies employed by, and the learned habits of, organized resistance fighters in occupied territories. These exigencies created for a broad sector of the populace the sense of a double life that was sustained by a collective knowledge circulating through anecdotes. There were anecdotes concerning how people escaped when the security forces came for them or about the problem of remembering telephone numbers after discarding one's address book so as not to implicate friends if one were taken. Resistance to State terror had an anecdotal repertoire:

> I turned this corner and had to jump aside because one of the green Ford Falcons was off the street and speeding along the sidewalk . . .

> I know others did destroy or hide books, but I decided not to because if they come to your house they've already got you on a list . . .

> the last time I ran into him was on Corrientes and we only talked for a few minutes. He was disappeared that afternoon . . .

> when the bus rammed the taxi in front of us, we forced the back door open, were out and lost in the downtown crowds before the police would have checked the witnesses' identity cards.

Novels and films were interpreted against such anecdotes, and the least political comment in works of art and/or entertainment was raised to the status of a political referent.

Two examples of this constant double interpretation in the year of the *apertura* were the award-winning novel that opened the year, Ricardo Piglia's *Respiración artificial*, and the award-winning film that closed the year, *Tiempo de revancha*, directed by Adolfo Aristarain.[4] In both cases, the promotion of the work contributed to its interpretation. The first Pomaire edition of *Respiración artificial* showed Buenos Aires apartment buildings against a red sky on the front cover and, on the back, against the same sky the words: "Tiempos sombríos en que los hombres parecen necesitar un aire artificial para poder sobrevivir" (Dark times in which men seem to need bottled oxygen to survive), thus suggesting an artificially sustained society in bloody times. In the case of *Tiempo de revancha*, the poster, which reproduced a shot not used in the film, bore the interpretative line: "Un hombre honesto hoy, algo muy peligroso" (An honest man today, something very dangerous). The shot is of the lead actor, Federico Luppi (an actor associated with such political films as *La Patagonia rebelde*), about to throw a bundle of dynamite, above a title that means not only *Time of Revenge* but of individual retaliation, a second chance to turn a defeat into a victory and to overcome, through gained knowledge, a hated enemy. *Una revancha* is the opportunity to vindicate oneself. It is the personal correction of an injustice. Both the novel and the film were a kind of artistic *revancha*, and at the time, in both cases, people wondered how Piglia and Aristarain managed to get away with it, how the censors did not catch the overt politics of the two works.

In Piglia's case, it is assumed that the novel was so highly encoded — so literary — that it required a skilled reader to move through the shifting narrative voices, the thrice-over embedded conversations, the complicated temporal relations, and the literary and philosophical allusions to reach the political material of the plot. This novel treats the disappearance of political activists and describes paramilitary violence and torture. The torture is narrated in a letter to a government official by a crazy woman who asks to be named an Official Singer. What she would sing or confess ("singing" is slang for confessing under torture) is having witnessed torture:

> At first I could only see the dead man. He was lying on a metal bed, covered with newspapers. There are others here, at the end of the hall, floor of tamped down earth. I close my eyes so as not to see the harm they have done him. (99)

It is also a novel that meditates on history, discusses at length the ideas of "a philosopher who spent years working in the reading room of the British Museum" (240), and contemplates the responsibilities of contemporary writers. Thus the year of the *apertura* began with a novel that publicly bore witness to the disappearances and torture, and which, like *Hum(R)*, commented under the noses of the military on the nature of cultural resistance.

In the case of *Tiempo de revancha*, the politics of the film were communicated by analogy and allegory. The plot concerns Pedro Bengoa, a demolition expert and one-time union leader, who procures false identity papers in order to be able to obtain work in the quarries of an international corporation. An honest man, he is driven by the company's disregard for workers' safety to participate in an extortion plot in which he will pretend to be speechless after an accident caused by a blast. What begins as an action to make the company pay becomes a chance to bring to light the dangerous working conditions at a court trial for disability compensation, and so Bengoa must maintain his feigned loss of speech under the surveillance of men who consider themselves above the law and who will use violence if they consider it necessary. Though the film is structured as a thriller, the corporation quickly comes to stand for the government. Its thugs, like government thugs, desire to silence and exploit the workers. Near the end of the film, in a scene where Bengoa is running through an impoverished, deserted section of the city to escape from corporation pursuers, a blue Ford Falcon with four thugs inside pulls alongside him — exactly as the green Ford Falcons were known to do — and the body of a worker who testified on his behalf is thrown from the car. The image was shocking not so much for its inherent violence, but for the fact that it directly represented State violence. The final shots move the analogy into allegory: Bengoa, in front of the mirror in his father's proletarian flat, looking himself in the face and knowing he cannot survive any other way, slowly and deliberately takes a razor and cuts out his tongue. In this last moment, Bengoa becomes the Argentine people. His is a calculated silence. The power to deny speech is wrested from the oppressor. It was a film that made explicit the function of calculated silence in a climate of fear.

To have read Piglia's novel or seen Aristarain's film in 1981 was to be able to take heart that writers, filmmakers, and other cultural workers were regaining for all of nonmilitary Argentina the right for citizens to exist in their own territory. With the return to civilian government, mass political mobilization, the end of censorship, and the re-creation of a public life, it might have seemed that the times of silence were over. The military could be publicly denounced, even if, in the end, only the military leadership has been brought to trial and sentenced for the torture and murder. It is unique in the region's history that a civilian government should even be able to bring to trial the previous dictators. On the other hand, it was still necessary to read the military's public messages and rumored private statements for their double meanings, their threats of coups, their intentions. Moreover, when the knowledge of what took place during the dirty war became *officially* public, the military was still interventionist. Photojournalism and television could show images of the dead and present the testimony of the survivors or their relatives. The accounts could be recorded and made public, as in the government commission report on the disappearances *Nunca más*. Yet, given the continuing dual nature of the Argentine State, how could the grieving ever come to an end?

In August 1984, eight months into civilian government, a small event took place that is indicative of the situation at the time: the Librería Clásica y Moderna held a roundtable discussion in celebration of the reissue of a book that had been banned during the dictatorship, Rodolfo Walsh's *Operación masacre*. This account of the police murders of a group of citizens during the Valle uprising in the mid-1950s has come over time to be considered one of Latin America's most important documentary novels. Piglia spoke at the event, which was attended by David Viñas, a major political novelist who finally had been able to return from exile. The fates of these three men during the dictatorship perhaps summarize the possibilities for cultural workers under the dictatorship: death, cultural resistance inside the nation, cultural resistance outside the nation. In spite of the fact that there could be no end to a national grief, there was the sense that these months were, in terms of cultural production, the closure of one period and the commencement of another. National culture was to be recuperated and revitalized, and Argentina was again to be part of a perceived internationalist (though Eurocentric) global culture. At this juncture, a new twist or doubling of the threads took place: Argentina became, after the fact, a transnational referent for terror at the very same time as its new democratic cultural institutions and practices were being shaped. Condemnation and renovation were not necessarily complementary practices; indeed, during the first three years of *alfonsinismo*, cultural production followed two tendencies: one, assessing the past, in particular the recent past; another, speculating on the present and the near future.

Past Terror, Future Politics: 1984 to 1987

The seven years of dictatorship heightened the populace's awareness of national boundaries and societal divisions, in particular the division between those who stayed and those who left. The two cultures of exile, internal and external, produced a geography that consisted of Buenos Aires and scattered places of exile at the far ends of the earth. Everyday life was either repression continuously experienced or a homeland forced into memory. Yet, for people who were outside the country during these years, both exiles and non-Argentines, there was difficulty imagining everyday life in Argentina after 1976 and what form resistance to the dictators took. Though Argentina was a place of terror in the years of the dirty war,[5] and the murder and torture committed by the military against Argentine citizens made grief a commonplace of national daily life, Argentina under dictatorship was at the same time a place where — as shown above — sectors of the populace, including the intelligentsia, did resist the military. Yet it was not uncommon in the mid-1980s to encounter the perspective, expressed by historian Eduardo Crawley in 1984, that "the great mass of the population preferred not to know — the facts were too hard to bear."[6] In fact, the "great mass" was divided in extremely complex ways. Argentine cultural production in the years of the dirty war was a record of *many* kinds of resistance. Yet the idea, expressed by Crawley, that the national populace was complicitous with the military in the dirty war had in the mid-1980s a certain currency both inside and outside Argentina. That is, a complexly divided collectivity was treated as a unified whole: Argentines as citizens were held *alone* responsible for something they *alone* could not have stopped. For example, the most widely known film to deal with the aftermath of the dirty war is Luis Puenzo's *La historia oficial*, which won the Oscar for best foreign film in 1986. *La historia oficial*, which for the first time brought to the notice of a good many U.S. citizens what had happened in Argentina, was not at all an accurate portrayal of State terror. Film historian Tim Barnard writes:

> *La historia oficial*, though thoroughly revisionist in its depiction of
> bourgeois anguish under the junta, has been praised for its ostensibly
> correct political line and the emotional power of its drama. . . .
> *La historia oficial* spearheaded, by virtue of its bland international
> style and thematic attention to the Argentine middle class, the
> Argentine film industry's reorientation towards the national middle
> class and the European and U.S. markets.[7]

It was a film that assumed the necessity of the expiation of guilt by the middle class and blamed the Argentine people *more* than the

Argentine military. Yet, if we remember that the film was made before the trials of the generals and the new limits of denunciation were not yet set, the film's indirect or tentative political analysis can be better understood. The film examined the assignment of responsibility for the criminal acts of dirty war, but it combined an anxiety about the indeterminacy of the nation's political future with an anxiety about the indeterminant status of Argentina the nation vis-à-vis other nations.

Political scientists Guillermo O'Donnell and Philippe C. Schmitter, who have worked extensively on the nature of the State during the dirty war and during the process of democratization, have written in *Transitions from Authoritarian Rule*:

> One major source of indeterminacy in the length and outcome of the transition lies in the fact that those factors which were necessary and sufficient for provoking the collapse or self-transformation of an authoritarian regime may be neither necessary or sufficient to insure the instauration of another regime — least of all, a political democracy.[8]

Part of Argentina's indeterminacy was that it was no longer, if it ever had been, an impermeable nation — a nation unto itself. The dirty war divided the nation's populace into two national peoples coexisting in the same territory. Nicos Poulantzas's observations in the 1970s on the attempted homogenization of national space under "States of exception," that is, the expulsion of declared subversive elements,[9] can be seen in the light of the Argentine experience of State terror to describe a process by which the "deterritorialization" of a national populace is not corrected or "reterritorialized" with the return to civilian rule. Thus, the analysis of State terror as a post-Holocaust question of how to recount horror was also a problem of the permeable and shifting definitions of what is "national" and what is "international." This can be briefly illustrated by two works first published outside of Argentina.

Exilio, a book published by Editorial Legas in Buenos Aires in 1984, explicitly invited the comparison of the experience of two well-known Argentines, poet Juan Gelman and writer Osvaldo Bayer, who had lived in exile in Italy and Germany, respectively. An essay by Bayer included in the volume had stirred controversy in Germany, when those who had commissioned the book initially refused to publish it. In the context of Argentina in the first year of civilian government, Bayer's words had a different impact:

Upon landing at Frankfurt I couldn't help but think of the anti-Nazi immigrants to Buenos Aires back in '36 or '37. I remember their pale faces, their European clothing, their watery eyes as they conversed in low voices in a table at "La Cosechera" in the Belgrano district, over coffee and an endless game of chess. Their faces . . . suddenly illuminated by a lightning flash as if someone had let slip the confidence: "Hitler will fall this spring, time to pack our suitcases."

That image seen with childish eyes has come full turn, and I, son of a land that had received them, now found myself in exile in the land that had exiled them. A savage, sarcastic, ironic go-round . . . always repeated. Perhaps a German boy was watching me when, in the "Ruhrblick" pub in Essen, I explained to Osvaldo Soriano that before Christmas the Videla dictatorship would break into pieces and it was time to prepare our bags. (45-46)

In considering how much the disappearances and the Holocaust have in common, Bayer was remarking a pattern in which the shifting of segments (in particular, the intelligentsia) of various national populaces from nation to nation in the latter part of this century was deeply connected with the world-economic determinants of genocide. It is also a reminder that the fates of Argentines and the fate of Argentina have *never* been a national question alone.

A nonfictional example of the representation of Argentine repression is John Simpson and Jana Bennett's *The Disappeared: Voices from a Secret War*, published in London in 1985. Though in many ways an excellent documentation of the dirty war and everyday life thereafter, the authors did not document acts of cultural resistance as clearly. For example, writing of Teatro Abierto, a cycle of short plays by twenty-one authors (among others, Bortnik, Cossa, Dragún, Gambaro, Gorotiza, O'Donnell, Somigiliana) performed in 1981, they state:

> The last time Carlos Gorotiza saw a play of his being performed on the Argentine stage was in October 1981. It was about the life of a group of exiles, and it was put on by a new group, the Teatro Abierto, at the Picadero theatre in Buenos Aires. One night, the theatre was badly burned by a group of arsonists, and it remained closed after that, its gates chained, its façade attacked by vandals, with warnings spray-painted on its walls advising people to keep away. The theatre group managed to keep working, but it was plain the military found it easier to do their work by intimidation rather than by the uses of decrees and formal orders. (223)

Simpson and Bennett were justifiably employing the Teatro Abierto arson incident as an example of cultural repression, but the description is misleading. The theater group did more than "manage to keep working." When Teatro Abierto moved to the Teatro Tabaris downtown, it was known in Buenos Aires that this was an act of resistance and that it was possible that there might be some further attack on the theater group or individuals (though, because it was late in 1981, it was less likely than it had been several years earlier that anyone would "be disappeared"). The theatergoing public also consciously chose to ignore the threat. People went to see the plays anyway, sometimes just to support an actor or author they knew to be blacklisted or under pressure. Teatro Abierto published the collection of plays, including an epilogue about the burning of the Teatro Picadero, calling for its reconstruction and announcing that they would ask *the State* for funds. Teatro Abierto, in keeping with its name, "opened" cultural space and reclaimed, for that moment and that time, personal and cultural sovereignty. In this passage, Simpson and Bennett momentarily fell prey to a too-exteriorized vision of national culture. Thus they did not sustain an analysis of the simultaneously national and international nexus of discourses in which resistance took place.

The question of responsibility for the dirty war raised during the first years of redemocratization was accompanied necessarily by the question of how to portray torture explicitly while avoiding sensationalism. The official documentation of torture in the Southern Cone region produced stark accounts of torture techniques. For example, part of the testimony of Teresa Celia Meschiati (Legajo 4279) in *Nunca más*[10] reads:

> They took me immediately upon arrival at "La Perla" to the torture room or the "intensive therapy" room. They undressed me and tied my feet and hands with rope to the bars of a bed that was suspended in the air. They put a wire on my right foot. The torture was applied gradually, using two electric prods that each had a different voltage: one was 125 volts, producing involuntary muscle movements and pain in my whole body as it was applied to my face, eyes, mouth, arms, vagina, and anus. The other, called "the daisy," at 220 volts left me with deep wounds I still have; it produced a violent contraction — as if all my limbs were being torn off at once — especially in the kidneys, legs, groin, and sides of the torso. (43)

Like the various Amnesty International reports,[11] *Nunca más* and *Brazil: Nunca Mais* make an effort to present the facts in a language as free as possible from drama. Accuracy and detail were needed for the legal condemnation of the torturers and the medical description of the results of torture. Others, then, took this language and used it for dramatic ends. Omar Rivabella, an Argentine newspaperman living in New York, published in 1986, in both the United States and in Great Britain, a novel about torture entitled *Requiem for a Woman's Soul*.[12] Its plot concerns a priest's attempt to piece together the story of a woman from scraps of paper smuggled out of a torture center. In the narration of the torture, the author appropriates a woman's voice but then reenacts in his writing a masculinized brutality:

> They took off my clothes and bound me to the bed but didn't remove the hood. I heard them drag in another body and place it on the bed next to mine. I could hear the other person gasping. The torturers started working me over. First they applied the *picana* from head to toe. Then they raped and sodomized me with something blunt and hard, and finally they beat me until I lost consciousness. (1987, 105-6)

Though the scene does not immediately appear to be different from the documentation in *Nunca más*, it is exploitative in that, after having created a female character who has endured countless acts of brutality, the author objectifies her as an object of torture. Note the differences between Meschiati's summary of her own torture, as starkly narrated as it is, and the invention of a woman's voice in which a torture scene is *repeated*.[13] At various points in this novel, the author positions the reader to *observe* the torture.

Women's writing on torture is notably different. Alicia Partnoy's autobiographical *The Little School: Tales of Disappearance and Survival in Argentina*,[14] written in exile, concentrates on the details of everyday existence that got her through her experience of torture. Her narration also chooses a simplicity of tone, but she does not reenact the sacrifice of the humanity of individuals. When, for example, she narrates the birth of a prisoner's child — a requisite in Rivabella's comprehensive presentation of torture — she does not tell of it as one terrible fact among many terrible facts, but rather gives that detail interpretative power:

> A new cry makes its way through the shadows fighting above the trailer. Graciela has just given birth. A prisoner child has been born.

> While the killer's hands welcome him into the world, the shadow of
> life leaves the scene, half a winner, half a loser: on her shoulders she
> wears a poncho of injustice. Who knows how many children are born
> everyday at the Little School? (121)

The principal way in which Partnoy's writing contrasts with male
writers on the question of torture is that she, perhaps like most
women, does not figure the Nation as Woman. The symbolism of nation and gender has a complex history, particularly with respect to the
formation of the European nation-state. In the case of Argentina, the
most well-known figuration of woman as nation involves writer
Rodolfo Walsh's daughter. After the suicide death of his daughter, a
Peronist *guerrillera*, Walsh wrote a letter recounting her final moments.[15] The house in which she was staying with other combatants
was surrounded early in the morning by the police, and a shoot-out
ensued. A policeman at the scene told how the firing ceased when she
and a companion stood on a parapet and said they would not allow
themselves to be taken alive. She was wearing a white nightgown;
Walsh commented specifically that "she wore one of those absurd
long nightgowns that were too big for her." María Victoria Walsh died
as the figure of Lady Liberty on the barricades,[16] and Walsh's account
of her death is cited time and again in writings on Argentina (my own
included) as emblematic of the dirty war. When Osvaldo Bayer writes
of María Victoria Walsh, citing again the description of the nightgown,
in a eulogy (reprinted in *Exilio*) to a German woman, Elisabeth Käse-
mann, who was disappeared in Argentina, he concludes:

> María Victoria with her absurd white nightgown that is covered
> with red. Elisabeth,
> a traveler in a distant country, her bags packed with utopias.
> Our women.
> Do not leave the last word to the executioners or the military. (123)

The destruction of "our women" here is the destruction of the nation-
state. As moving as Bayer's tribute is, it reveals a tendency to conflate
the State and the gender system and to assume the denial by a military
of the rights of citizenship to its own national populace to be analogous to the violation and eradication of a woman's body.

Film also contributed to this conflation of the State and the gender
system. In the first four years of civilian rule, there were 168 Argentine
feature films released, according to records of the Instituto Nacional

de Cinematografía.[17] In terms of entertainment, the films ranged from adaptation of Argentine novels such as Roberto Arlt's *El juguete rabioso* or Jorge Asis's *Flores robadas en los jardines de Quilmes* to Porcel and Olmedo "picaresque" comedies and sexploitation films about women behind bars, on motorcycles or in showers. The some twenty films that dealt with the dirty war can be divided into two groups: those that directly narrated terror and torture, and those which through allegory examined the nature of State terror. The film *Malayunta* (1986), directed by José Santiso, is an example of the latter:

> *Malayunta*: "A sculptor rents out a room in his apartment to a conservative middle-aged couple. Their differing values and habits lead to increasingly violent confrontations. It is both a comedy of manners and a horror film. And it is not always easy to tell which you are watching, in this devastating portrayal of how the conservative values of lower middle class Argentines contributed to the atrocities of the dirty war."[18]

In *Malayunta*, which is based on a play by Jacobo Langsner, the conservative couple (played by Federico Luppi and Bárbara Mujica) take over the sculptor's apartment, hold him prisoner, binding him with barbed wire until he "behaves decently." When the sculptor (played by Miguel Angel Solá) does not capitulate, the couple "disappear" him, butchering him with a large kitchen knife. The film, though released under civilian rule, exposes the silences of the period of dictatorship; in this, it is quite distinct from another of the allegorical films, *La película de rey* (1985), directed by Carlos Sorín. In *Malayunta*, the conservative couple stand directly for the rightist security forces that carried out the dirty war. In *La película de rey*, a tale of a film director obsessed with finishing a film about a crazy foreigner proclaiming himself king in Patagonia in the nineteenth century, no one character or set of characters stands for the Argentine military or oligarchy; rather, it is the land itself — its death-filled, hallucinatory landscapes shown in the final scenes to be ultimately controlled by the military — that is permeated with oppression. *La película de rey*, much like the internationally better-known *Hombre mirando al sudeste* (1985), directed by Eliseo Subiela, does not attribute the dirty war to the actions of a specific social sector or group, but rather to a generalizable human cruelty.

La noche de los lápices (1986), by Héctor Olivera, typifies the second category of films about the dirty war in which torture is shown on screen:

> *La noche de los lápices*: "The newest film by Argentina's most popular film director (*Rebellion in Patagonia, Funny Dirty Little War*), who has always created a blend of polished entertainment and topical social comment. Based on a true incident, a group of high school students demonstrate in favor of receiving bus passes to get to and from school. Branded as subversives, all but one disappear under the terror of the military junta. This film, based on the account of the only survivor of the group, Pablo Díaz, is causing a sensation in Argentina, where it has just been released, at a time when several military officials are standing trial for the incident depicted."[19]

In this film, the depiction of torture "causes a sensation" but it does not produce an understanding of the experience of torture or of its causes. *La noche de los lápices* can be read against the dark comedy *No habrá más penas ni olvido* (1985). Based on the homonym novel by Osvaldo Soriano, it includes scenes of the left peronist leader of a small town being beaten to death and therefore demands that the viewer directly confront physical brutality. It can also be read against the historical film *Asesinato en el Senado de la nación* (1984), directed by Juan José Jusid, which includes scenes of the use of electric shock torture in 1935. *La noche de los lápices*, however, showed on screen an aspect of the dirty war that had no other direct visual representation: the daily lives of the disappeared before their extermination. The scenes of the blindfolded teenagers speaking to each other from their separate cells, of their activities apart from torture and sexual abuse, made the interim between disappearance and death "appear." For this alone, the film stands as one of the most important cultural assessments of the dirty war. But the film also foregrounded, in the final scenes, the emotions of the young man who was released and his girlfriend, who had been a leader among the young activists and who was not released. Her image, the image of the woman defiled and exhausted, is the unfortunate synthesis of all that the nation lost. The realist representation becomes a problematically gendered allegory. It is the gendering of allegory that characterizes the final film of the period of redemocratization, a film which, while it is not the last in date of release, closes the period in terms of possibilities of representation of the dirty war: Fernando Solanas's *Sur*.

Proyecto Sur: "1987 y después"

Like his previous *Tangos: El exilio de Gardel*, and very much unlike
the revolutionary film for which he and Octavio Getino had been best
known, *La hora de los hornos* (1966-68), Solanas used the Argentine
tango tradition to express in dance, with lyrics as counterpart to and
commentary on scenes, the emotions of those whose lives were irrevocably changed by the dictatorship. The promotional material for
the film presents the director's affirmation that the film is "una historia de amor," concluding:

> *Sur* speaks to us about finding each other again and about friendship.
> It is the triumph of life over death, love over resentment, liberty over
> oppression, desire over fear.

> I also want to say that *Sur* is an homage to all those who, like my
> character the stutterer, knew to say no. They were the ones who
> maintained their dignity. They said no to injustice, oppression, the
> surrender of the country.

> Dear friends, here is *Sur*. It was made with all my heart and it now
> belongs to you.

The professed friendship and collective affection of this film is exactly
its political strength and its analytical weakness. The exquisite compo-
sition of the shots — patterns of reflections of faces in windows and
mirrors and framing of characters in doorways and corridors — serves
to enhance the love story between a political prisoner, Floreal, released unexpectedly from jail, and his wife, Rosi, from whom he is
estranged because of her extramarital affair during his years of im-
prisonment. The images are meant to capture moments of the past
and reorder them, to change the memories of State terror into more
bearable, formulaic stories of strength in the face of adversity. Set on
the empty night streets of a southern neighborhood of Buenos Aires,
Sur narrates the allegorical journey home of Floreal, in the company
of El Muerto (Death), the joyous specter of a friend murdered by the
paramilitary during the dirty war. During the journey, Floreal encoun-
ters, in wafts of luminous blue fog, the ghosts of his mentors, heroic
old men who organized and led the battle for social justice in the
unions and in the military in the 1930s. The viewer, particularly the
politically committed viewer addressed by Solanas as one who had

the "dignity to say no," is given the opportunity to rejoice in a long heritage of struggle.

Yet as positive as it may be for a national culture in the midst of redemocratization to honor those who struggled in the recent and distant past, problems of political analysis arise because *Sur* conflates the political passions of the characters with their individual romantic relations and sexuality. The character of Emilio, flawlessly played by Ulises Dumont, epitomizes the honorable, selfless *militante*. In one of the funniest scenes in the film, in which the military authorities categorize the library of Argentine political culture, via sonorous refrains of "subversivo" or "pornográfico" on the soundtrack, Emilio has the privilege of explaining to the keepers of order that if they cannot understand "Proyecto Sur" it is because they belong to the North: they are agents of imperialism. In another striking moment, in which the paramilitary break into Emilio's home and engage in a shoot-out in the darkened hallway, the viewer is invited to interpret the death of Emilio and his wife as a dignified culmination of years of political militancy. Knowing the moment of death has come, Emilio's wife chooses to die behind the improvised barricade with him: she brings two glasses of wine for a last toast, he brings a handgun. When they are slaughtered the viewer does not see their bodies, but, rather, their pet parrot flying up from behind the barricade, cursing the intruders. The triumph of "desire over fear" is, here, one of hindsight: it is not a greater celebration of life to romanticize the death of comrades. It is a falsification of history to retroactively proclaim dignity for the fallen or for the survivors: in a dirty war, dignity is not even a category and survival is not a matter of *voluntad*.

Likewise, the drama of Floreal and Rosi's extramarital liaisons and their return to one another is to be glossed as an evaluation of the left's behavior under dictatorship or in exile. When Rosi states she loves both Floreal and her lover Roberto, a French emigré to Argentina who was Floreal's coworker and friend but stays to await the return of Floreal, she is opting for Argentina over France, for loyalties both to homeland and to those with whom ties were formed under the dictatorship or in exile. The filmmaker's anxieties about his return to his homeland are projected onto the female character: this is apparent in the shot of the couple's reunion in which the viewer sees, from Floreal's point of view, Rosi's face encompassed by his own reflection in the glass pane of a window. Rosi's character had double duty: she bears the anxieties and divided loyalties of the person who has been exiled, and she represents the homeland to which the exile returns: has she been faithful to the exile, does she await the exile? Here again, woman is figured as nation and, in contrast to the male protagonist, is made ethically responsible for resistance. The film inquires in its gendered allegory as to whether Rosi's dignity is adequate to the situation.

Solanas is not the only filmmaker returned from exile to employ a subplot, concerning the sexual relations between a couple, to express political judgements. For example, in the final scenes of Raúl Beycero's *Nadie, nada, nunca*, based on Juan José Saer's novel of Santa Fe, the conclusion of the main character's affair comes to stand for a deadening of emotions in the face of the atrocities of the dirty war. Also, in Rafael Filippelli's *El ausente*,[20] partially based on a short story by Marimón that analyzes from a leftist critical perspective problems in leftist political practice in the period of the Cordobazo, a formulaic love scene between the labor-leader protagonist and his girlfriend, before the final shot of the outside from the safe house from which he was disappeared, purposefully serves as an inadequate summation of the *militante*'s life and foregrounds a specific incomprehension by the militants, not of the personal danger they faced but of the nature of the war in which they were now designated to be victims. As diverse politically as are Solanas, Beycero, and Filippelli, and as different as their fortunes are in Argentine film culture, their recurrent use of filmic clichés of sexual passion (or lack thereof) to address vital political questions is an indication that, across the political spectrum, there was, from the period 1987 onward, the lack of a new political discourse.

In Caloi's comic strip of August 8, 1989, he referred to the "formadores de gracia," those with the power to have created the economic disaster Argentina faced, those who could be held accountable for increasing the absurdity of the political economy of the nation. The ephemeral record, the discursive transformations on the question of whether the Argentine populace had a determinant role in the formation of its government in the period 1978–89, indicates not only cycles of generalizable pessimism and optimism but also an enduring commitment by large sectors of the populace to resistance to agents and structures of oppression. The mid-1980s brought a return to civilian rule and a return of exiles. The 1990s will tell if, in this period of severe capitalist restructuring, there will be a lowering of the price of humor and a revitalized politics of culture.

NOTES

1. Conversation with Andrés Cascioli.

2. One example of indirect, perhaps even unplanned retaliation for film censorship involved a *Superman* movie from which the scene of the hero moving a bus in New York was cut because on the side of the bus was an advertisement for the broadway musical *Evita*. A short while after the film was shown in Argentina, General Galtieri visited New York. A photographer took a picture of the general and his wife passing below the marquee of *Evita* and that photo, which ran in a popular magazine, was not censored.

3. See Jean Franco's "Killing Priests, Nuns, Women, Children," in *On Signs*, ed. Marshall Blonsky (Baltimore: Johns Hopkins University Press, 1985), 414-20.

4. *Respiración artificial* won the Premio Boris Vian; *Tiempo de revancha* has won best film awards at the Cartagena, Biarritz, and Havana film festivals. See, for analyses of literature of the period, David William Foster's "Argentine Sociopolitical Commentary, the Malvinas Conflict, and Beyond: Rhetoricizing a National Experience," in *Latin American Research Review* 22, no. 1 (1987), 7-34; Marta Morello Frosch's "La ficción de la historia en la narrativa argentina reciente," in *The Historical Novel in Latin America: A Symposium*, ed. Daniel Balderston (Gaithersburg, Md.: Ediciones Hispámerica, 1986); or René Jara and Hernán Vidal, eds., *Ficción y política: la narrative argentina durante el proceso militar* (Buenos Aires and Madrid: Alianza Editorial, in conjunction with the Institute for the Study of Ideologies and Literature, Minneapolis: University of Minnesota, 1987).

5. See the analysis of "the cult of fear" in Juan E. Corradi, *The Fitful Republic: Economy, Society, and Politics in Argentina* (Boulder and London: Westview Press, 1985).

6. *A House Divided: Argentina, 1880-1980* (London: C. Hurst & Co., 1984), 431.

7. Tim Barnard, ed., *Argentine Cinema* (Toronto: Nightwood Editions, 1986), 60-61.

8. *Transitions from Authoritarian Rule: Tentative Conclusions about Uncertain Democracies* (Baltimore and London: Johns Hopkins University Press, 1986), 8.

9. *State, Power, Socialism*, trans. Patrick Camiller (London: NLB, 1978).

10. *Nunca más: Informe de la Comisión Nacional sobre la Desparición de Personas* (Buenos Aires: EUDEBA, 1984).

11. For a bibliography on the accounts of torture, see Andrew Graham-Yooll's *A State of Fear: Memories of Argentina's Nightmare* (London: Eland Books; New York: Hippocrene Books, 1986).

12. Translated by Paul Riviera and Omar Rivabella (New York: Random House, 1986; London, Penguin Books, 1987).

13. This point is developed in Jean Franco's "Death Camp Confessions and Resistance to Violence in Latin America," in *Socialism and Democracy*, no. 2 (Spring/Summer 1986), 5-17.

14. Translated by Alicia Partnoy, with Lois Athey and Sandra Braunstein (Pittsburgh and San Francisco: Cleis Press, 1986).

15. See Horacio Verbitsky's *Rodolfo Walsh y la prensa clandestina, 1976-1978* (Buenos Aires: Ediciones de la Urraca, 1985).

16. I am indebted to Mary Louise Pratt for this comparison. See her article "Women, Literature and National Brotherhood," in *Women, Culture, and Politics in Latin America*, ed. Seminar on Feminism and Culture in Latin America (Berkeley, Los Angeles, and Oxford: University of California Press, 1990), 48-73. See also Marina Warner's *Monuments and Maidens: The Allegory of the Female Form* (London: Weidenfeld & Nicolson, 1985).

17. Daniel López, ed., *Catálogo del nuevo cine argentino* [vol. 1, 1984-86; vol. 2, 1987-88]. See also Jorge Abel Martín, *Cine argentino: diccionario de realizadores* (Buenos Aires: Instituto Nacional de Cinematografía, 1987).

18. John Hess, "Tribute to Argentine Cinema in San Francisco," *Cine Acción News* 3, no. 3 (Fall 1987), 8-9.

19. Poster, "Contemporary Argentine Cinema," The Ontario Film Institute, March 17-April 30, 1986.

20. This film has not yet been released in Argentina, but was shown at the Los Angeles and Havana film festivals in 1989.

Cortijo's Revenge: New Mappings of Puerto Rican Culture
Juan Flores

It was the best joke of the week. Imagine, naming the Centro de Bellas Artes after Rafael Cortijo. El Centro Rafael Cortijo para las Bellas Artes, the Cortijo Center for the Fine Arts! The very idea of it, our country's cultural palace, its halls bearing the venerable names of Antonio Paoli, Rene Marqués, Carlos Marichal, and Sylvia Rexach, baptized in honor of the street musician par excellence, the unlettered, untutored promulgator of *bomba y plena*! And yet, farfetched as it might seem, people began treating as a fait accompli what was only a proposal by an aspiring political candidate, or actually not even a proposal but the threat of a proposal. The message was "vote for me and I'll propose it." And though within a few days the whole issue passed into hasty oblivion, for that week in mid-August 1988 el Centro Rafael Cortijo was the talk of Puerto Rico, filling the newspapers with rumors and recriminations in all directions and generating a debate that would have made not only Cortijo but Antonio S. Pedreira turn over in his grave.

And many, indeed, were the echoes of Pedreira's lofty concerns. As one commentator wrote in *El Mundo*, "This event makes us ask ourselves, once again, who we are — that philosophical exercise which has so long been a constant in our daily lives. If we can clear away all the triviality, opportunism, and backbiting it has generated, this move to honor Rafael Cortijo serves to transform the Palace of Fine Arts from a majestic architectural structure into an ongoing metaphor and reminder of the path to take when it is clear exactly where we stand."[1] Here we are, back again to that historic questionnaire initiated by the journal *Indice* in 1929, the provocative "who are we and how are we?"

("¿qué somos y cómo somos?") that led, after a flurry of responses from some of the island's leading intellectuals and some years of gestation, to that most extended and influential of all reflections, Pedreira's *Insularismo* (1934). Not that we are just returning to that existential preoccupation some sixty years later, with the comfortable advantage of hindsight. For as dated and derivative as Pedreira's thinking may strike us today, the groping search that he undertook has never really abated and has remained with us, in modified versions and with changing emphasis, through the decades. Whether it was Vicente Geigel Polanco, Tomás Blanco, René Marqués, José Luis González, Luis Rafael Sánchez, or Rosario Ferré, writers of each subsequent generation have addressed the same issues as those that inhabited the pages of *Insularismo*, and they have ultimately met with similar frustrations.

But the hubbub over the appropriate legacy of Rafael Cortijo signals the continuing relevance of *Insularismo* in especially sharp relief, and at a time when the very interrogation of culture and identity, the "master narrative" of any collective cultural history, has come under grave suspicion. It took the towering presence and symbolic passing of a black popular musician of the uncontested stature of Cortijo to force the questions of African and working-class culture onto the agenda of everyday Puerto Rican life. It may have occasioned laughs and irony at the time, and exemplified partisan opportunism at its most cynical, but the threat to sanctify the name of Cortijo and the ensuing reactions from all quarters of the cultural establishment bring into rare focus the still-unfinished business involved in exposing the theoretical confines of *Insularismo*.

And the rejoinders in the Cortijo cross fire were as telling as the seemingly outlandish suggestion itself. What about the other stellar figures in the history of Puerto Rican music, the first line of argument went, as the names of Juan Morel Campos and Rafael Hernández were quick to surface; isn't it, after all, as Pedreira had claimed, the *danza* and the international standard *boleros* and *canciones* that represent the backbone of the national music? And if it's about memorializing illustrious black Puerto Rican artists, what about the great eighteenth-century painter José Campeche; or what about the renowned black singer Ruth Fernández, who has the added asset, in "affirmative action" terms, of being a woman, and is even alive to perform at the inaugural? And then, if the occasion is one of acknowledging the *plena* as the authentically national popular music, what about Manuel Jiménez ("Canario"), the first to extend the *plena*'s popularity through recording; or what about John Clark and Catherine George, those children of immigrants from the English-speaking islands who were the first known practitioners of *plena*? (Or, we might add, since his name went unmentioned, what about Joselino "Bumbún" Oppenheimer, who was instrumental in establishing the *plena* as a musical form and practice?)

But the cries of "why Cortijo" went further than the unveiling of other names, which extended from Manuel Alonso to Enrique Laguerre, and included Luis Palés Matos, Julia de Burgos, Juan Tizol, Felipe Rosario Goyco ("Don Felo"), Rafael Ithier, Juano Hernández, Carmelo Díaz Soler, and Francisco Arriví. Beyond the catalog of the just-as-deserving, and of greater theoretical interest, objections were raised as to the anomaly of naming a center of "fine arts" after an exponent of the "popular arts," no matter how unequaled a master. The "Centro de Bellas Artes," the thinking goes, "was built because of the need for theaters in which to hold concerts, drama, ballet, opera, and *zarzuela*."[2] There may also be a need, of course, for a center for popular art, especially since "we now have to hold *salsa* and rock concerts in coliseums and stadiums with poor acoustics, unbearable heat, foul smells, and a host of other inconveniences"; but to appropriate the space intended for the fine arts is not the answer. After all — and here the reasoning gets interesting — presentations of the fine arts tend to be very expensive, and because they are absolutely needed "for the greatest cultural good of the people," they require subsidy from the government and the public sector, "so as to keep prices reasonable for the audience." Sites catering to the popular arts, on the other hand, are generally "private businesses that can only cover their expenses by enjoying the affluence of the public." The commentator ends by acknowledging that "it's often not possible to draw a clear line between popular and fine arts," but his final thought, following from this rather convoluted account, is that "there's a right place for everything." The bottom line, it seems, and ultimate justification for assigning the popular arts to the business sector, is "quality"; as the then-director of the Instituto de Cultura Puertorriqueña, Elías López Sobá, reminded us, "this is a palace of the fine arts. It is for those who have a contribution to make in the field of dance, theater, music, plastic arts, mime, and pantomime."[3]

Behind the aesthetic and fiscal objections, of course, lurk the moral ones. It is interesting that on these grounds the strongest position was voiced not so much by the upholders of the "high arts," but by the prominent folklorist Marcelino Canino. In Professor Canino's view, "though musicians of the stature of Mozart found inspiration in the dances and tunes of the common folk, Cortijo's music can only be described as 'vulgar' and 'lumpen.'"[4] Rather than exalting the black race, he said, Cortijo's songs only denigrated it further. "It was music for the masses that never became folkloric because it has not lived on in the memory of the people." Such language has a sadly familiar ring to it, for it was typical of the early reaction to most forms of twentieth-century popular music, from jazz and the blues to samba, *son*, and calypso. The epithets *vulgar* and *lumpen* accompanied the *plena* for the first three decades of its existence, and here they are once again, in 1988, in the assessment of Cortijo. Not only is he excluded from the ranks of the country's fine arts, but even those of the national folklore. He is also rejected ad hominem: the noted constitutional lawyer Federico A. Cordero, who spoke out immediately and vehemently against the renaming of the Centro, argued that Cortijo set a bad example for the country. "Puerto Rican society is today deeply concerned over the problem of drugs, so that to speak under these conditions of Cortijo, who was part of the drug subculture, is not a good example to follow."[5]

The objections to the idea of a "Centro Rafael Cortijo para las Bellas Artes" thus amounted to a broadside, coming from many political and social quarters and especially from among the prevailing voices of the cultural elite—which is indeed why they won out, squelching the threat long before it could become a proposal on the floor. When the dust settled, a position prevailed that, despite all the disclaimers and quite beyond the issue of renaming the Centro de Bellas Artes, continues to deny the consitutive role of African and popular expression in the national culture. In other words, it was a victory for racism, as members of the Cortijo family and countless other Puerto Ricans, including many intellectuals and musicians, were quick to point out. Not only did they clear the record of personal defamations, but they clearly identified the racist motives behind the political opportunism of the Popular Democratic Party (PPD). It seems that the Populares were trying to save face in the wake of an infamous remark made a few months earlier by Rafael Hernández Colón on a visit to Spain. There, in the Hispanic "madre patria," the PPD governor took the occasion to refer to the African contribution to Puerto Rican culture as a "mere rhetorical adscription" (*una mera adscripción retórica*). Floating the idle threat of honoring Cortijo was thus a defensive maneuver that, ironically, could only result in still another mandate for that familiar Eurocentric mentality. Just how Eurocentric it was is clear even from Hernández Colón's effort to answer the resounding criticism of his comments. By considering Puerto Rican culture "essentially Spanish," he only meant to refer to "the racial integration of our people around its common Hispanic roots."[6]

It was against this still dominant mentality — the mentality, we might add, of Pedreira in his time — that the most vocal proponents of Cortijo spoke out. While not necessarily bemoaning the defeat of the effort to rename the Centro, Cortijo's longtime friend and fellow musician Tite Curet Alonso argued strongly for the immense stature of Cortijo in Puerto Rican music. In direct response to the charges of Marcelino Canino, Curet Alonso states the key point: "Rafael Cortijo made our most vernacular rhythms, the *bomba* and *plena*, known throughout the world. . . . And if nobody remembers Rafael Cortijo, why such concern over him and why the idea of lending his name to the Center for Fine Arts according to law? No, my dear professor, no sir! Cortijo was great and continues to be great, as you well know beyond the shadow of a doubt."[7] Curet Alonso ends by calling attention to the seamy aftermath of the whole Cortijo affair: they actually went so far as to dig up his body, six years in the grave, for an autopsy. "Our poor friend! And after so many of our civic and political leaders come to mourn for you, with tears in their eyes, at the Cemetery of Villas Palmeras!"

In true *plena* tradition, it was Rafael Cortijo's funeral on October 6, 1982, as much as his musical breakthroughs in 1954, that marked a turning point in Puerto Rican culture and its theoretical reflection. Thanks, in large measure, to Edgardo Rodríguez Juliá, whose brilliant chronicle *El entierro de Cortijo* (Cortijo's funeral, 1983) anticipated in uncanny ways the whole uproar over Cortijo in 1988. At one point, his narrator even fantasizes whimsically about the eventual admission of Cortijo into the hallowed halls of the country's high culture: "Maybe some Leticia del Rosario will come along one day, in twenty years or so, and establish a Rafael Cortijo Theater, under the administration of González Oliver's son, and thereby enact a grotesque kind of poetic

class justice."[8] "The revenge of Cangrejos" ("la venganza de Cangrejos") is what this same inversion of the class hierarchy was called
in 1988. (Santurce, where the Bellas Artes is located, was called Cangrejos in Cortijo's time, and the deepest irony of the whole case is that
Cortijo was born and raised in a house at the very address where the
Centro de Bellas Artes now stands.) On the occasion of his funeral,
Rodríguez Juliá built a real memorial to Cortijo, while his narrator
reflected on the meaning of immortality in the age of mediated popular culture. "But you will live on, Cortijo," he wrote,

> even if nobody listens to you anymore; there will stand your
> monumental work, silent but patient, and always ready to spring back
> to life. To be immortal is not so much to go on living as to be sure of
> resurrection. Cortijo is for the "cocolos" and the *salsa* lovers what
> Canario is for me—a daring leap over two decades. But don't worry,
> mi Cortijito, you'll see that we won't forsake you even though this
> damned historical memory of ours only extends back as far as what we
> have forgotten. (37)

Generation after generation, stage after stage in the history of the
country, the concept of the national culture penetrates progressively
deeper to its black, working-class roots. "This idea of class revenge,"
one commentator noted in 1988, "evokes a sense of pride in Puerto
Rico. Here every one of us has a secret ancestor in the closet."[9] The
very idea of a "Centro Rafael Cortijo para las Bellas Artes" is part of "a
long voyage toward the integration of our Puerto Rican identity in
view of that key link which is our African heritage," another step in the
unveiling of that ancestral secret.

The path out of and beyond "insularismo" has been first of all this
extended journey inward, and deeper than Pedreira could have imagined in 1934. It began back in the nineteenth century, in the writings
of Salvador Brau, Alejandro Tapia y Rivera, and others, and gained
further impetus from the lesser-known working-class writer Ramón
Romero Rosa, in his 1903 article "A los negros puertorriqueños."[10] In
Pedreira's times, it proceeded forward in the essays of Tomás Blanco,
especially his "Elogio de la Plena" ("In Praise of the Plena") (1935),
and in the poetry and poetics of Luis Palés Matos. A new juncture was
marked off in 1954, with the release of Cortijo's "El Bombón de Elena"
and the publication of José Luis González's story "En el fondo del
caño hay un negrito" ("At the Bottom of the Ditch There's a Little Black

Boy"). The mid-1970s saw the publication of Isabelo Zenón's two-volume *Narciso descubre su trasero, Narcissus Discovers His Behind*, the first extended exposé of racism in Puerto Rican culture and politics. But it was in the 1980s, most prominently in *El entierro de Cortijo* and in José Luis González's controversial essay "El país de cuatro pisos" ("The Four-Story Country") (1984; originally 1979), that the balance finally tipped, and the new Afro-Caribbean horizon has come into full view.

For the long introspective quest leads not so much to some hidden "essence" of our identity, some primordial "¿qué somos?," but to a sharper understanding of the dynamic within Puerto Rican culture and its place among the cultures with which it most directly interacts. If it is to be more than a "mere rhetorical adscription," the recognition of blackness necessarily points beyond the shores of the island to the rest of the Caribbean and Latin America and to the cultural dynamic in the United States. In this respect, the Eurocentric, elitist view, in the manner of Pedreira, constituted the very intellectual insularity that his book called upon his compatriots to overcome. Discovering and valorizing African "roots" has comprised a second stage, after the first one marked off by Insularismo, in the theoretical definition of Puerto Rican culture, and that stage has only come to full articulation over the past decade. Yes, there is a national culture, as Pedreira did affirm, after all, with all his gloomy reluctance, but it is grounded on the popular, African-based traditions of that culture.

The 1980s, though, has also been the decade of wariness, in much contemporary cultural theory, over the dangers of essentialism in defining "identities" of any kind, be they class, national, racial-ethnic, or gender. And here, I think, we might see a stretch of the voyage ahead. On this count, the writings of Rodríguez Juliá and of other contemporaries like Ana Lydia Vega, Rosario Ferré, and Luis Rafael Sánchez seem more helpful than José Luis González's architectural construct in "El país de cuatro pisos," though that essay would certainly best qualify as the most direct sequel to Pedreira's *Insularismo* in recent years. For despite its often welcome strokes of historical revisionism, González's work ultimately has recourse to an essentialist stance, most evident in his explosive claim that the "first Puerto Ricans were black Puerto Ricans." Rather than originary, authentic "roots" of a cultural tree, or the ground floor of a cultural building, our African background needs to be assessed as a guide to the culture's dynamically changing placement in the surrounding cultural geography. Maybe Pedreira's navigational image of the "thematic compass" (*brújula del tema*) is useful after all in countering the still prestigious metaphors of organic growth and the constructivist blueprints designed to replace them.

The most characteristic recent response both to Eurocentric, elitist privileging and to the relativism of the syncretist model seems to be what we might call a relational one, which would aim to identify not some ur-identity but the contacts and crossings experienced by the culture as social practice. It is not the popular, African component in itself that goes to define the "real" Puerto Rican culture, but its interplay with the non-African, elite, and folkloric components. Similarly, with respect to the national culture it is not the shores of the island that demarcate the "¿qué somos y cómo somos?," but the expanses of sea, land, and air that conjoin our cultural territory with the Other(s). Even the history of *bomba y plena*, which, especially after Tomás Blanco's landmark essay, has gained wide recognition as the most distinctively Puerto Rican musical tradition, attests to the need for such a situational approach: at key stages in that history, the influence of Haitian, Anglophone Caribbean, and Cuban and Dominican styles and practices have been of signal importance. A promising recent example of this method, as applied to the interaction of European elite and black artisan cultures within the Puerto Rican tradition, is Angel Quintero Rivera's work on the *danza*.[11]

But I find that Rodríguez Juliá's writing goes especially far in the direction of a relational, nonessentialist presentation of Puerto Rican culture in its contemporary dynamic. *El entierro de Cortijo*, far from merely paying celebratory homage to the great *plenero* and to Afro–Puerto Rican culture, chronicles the multiple intersections that actually characterize the culture at any given point in time and place. The evocation of the fallen cultural hero gains its particular poignancy from the account given to the simultaneously interacting presence at his funeral of sharply contrasting cultural worlds. The most obvious of these interplays is the running contrast between Cortijo and the early-century *criollo* poet Luis Lloréns Torres, and between that poet himself and the "Caserío Lloréns Torres," the working-class projects where the funeral procession begins. Here is how the mischievous chronicler captures that irreverent collision between signifier and signified:

The name of the poet (who is actually second-rate, though an ingenious versifier) has undergone an ironic transposition: the projects, that anti-utopia created by the welfare state of Muñoz Marín, shares with the myth the virtue of a meaning which is both blurred and perfectly clear. . . . Fuck, as they say in the Motherland, and to think that all this is a whole lot more than the name of a poet. If we leave behind the courses in Puerto Rican literature and the standard manual of Manuel Manrique Cabrera, Lloréns Torres signifies smack, set-ups, *salsa* beats à la Marvin Santiago, drug busts, joints, blow, and needle tracks. My God, this place sure has a bad rep, as my mother would say. (13)

Class and racial differences are thus analyzed by their concrete enactment in the observations of the chronicler, who is himself, of course, very much implicated in the cultural drama: "a white boy with chubby cheeks, a handle-bar mustache and eyeglasses is a disturbing presence in Lloréns" (13).

The narrative form appropriate to this relational method of cultural analysis is the chronicle, while the texture of the story is a kind of stylistic pastiche. The diverse, interacting cultural voices and idioms are not defined, but are contextualized and given utterance. This pastiche effect is evident not only in the language but also in the historical perspectivism, where the narrative present is set into striking proportional relation with earlier cultural stages. (It is interesting that the chronicler here points to the year 1934 as a bench mark of a preceding cultural stage, the 1934 not of Pedreira's *Insularismo* but of the heyday of Canario.) That acute retrospective sense only heightens our awareness that we were in the mid-1980s when the story happens and is told.

In 1954 . . . Cortijo is not only the last of the great *pleneros*; Cortijo is the very flavor of the *plena* of those years, the 1950s, that seem so long ago to us living today, closer in fact to the 1930s of Canario than to these apocalyptic 1980s. But let's figure it out. . . . In 1954 you were twenty years from 1934; in 1984 you'll be thirty fatal years from those shows when Cortijo's group performed at the Taberna India, featuring Reguerete and Floripondia. I was born in 1946, just ten years after the beginning of the Spanish Civil War. . . . On October 9 I'll be thirty-six, and I'll have to explain to my son, who's a rock fan, that Cortijo's very first group still wore ruffle-sleeve shirts. (30)

With that patchwork of chronological measurements as a starting point, the chronicler goes on to set forth, in what must be the most sparkling five pages on the topic, the revolutionary importance of Cortijo in the history of Puerto Rican popular music.

Rodríguez Juliá does not ignore the question "¿qué somos y cómo somos?," the agonizing problem of cultural "definition." True to his relational, nonessentialist approach, though, he insists that the real challenge is not definition but description, not a claim to the idiosyncratic and originary but an account of diversity and complexity. Making no presumption of "objectivity," he relies time and again on the subjective reference so as to bring the historical and cultural Other closer, not only to the narrator himself but to all who cohabit the same or adjacent cultural chronicles. "How to define our people?" he ponders, just at the moment when he catches a glimpse of "the matriarchal presence of Ruth Fernández" among the throngs of mourners.

> To define is easy, but how difficult it is to describe! They're down-home people (pueblo pueblo), my Puerto Rican people, with all their contradictory diversity, like that sickly looking lady with her hair in a bun and wearing sneakers because of her bunions, you know, like the bunions in the *plena* "los juanetes de Juana"; the little beads of greasy sweat remind me of those self-sacrificing ironing women and cooks who used to pass by every Saturday on the streets of my childhood and head off to their working-class places of evangelical worship. (18)

The chronicler defines by way of describing, and describes his "pueblo pueblo" by invoking, through association and memory, an emblem of Puerto Rican nationality. And just at this point, when the narrator directly poses the issue of identity, it is women who inspire and embody the cultural collectivity, black working-class women. Here, the dimension of gender supplements and perhaps even underlies the more commonly emphasized factors of class and race. We need only call to mind a few of Pedreira's unflattering words about women to appreciate how far we have come on this issue as well as on those of class and race. Women are characterized in *Insularismo* as weak and frivolous, and it is clearly the men who are suited to take firm command of the educational and cultural tasks of the country and lead the way out of collective insularity.[12]

As Rodríguez Juliá's emblem of identity indicates, it is women who are seen to comprise the most representative, and potentially most emancipatory, force in the whole cultural pastiche. At the present stage of thinking about Puerto Rican culture, women's perspectives and experience are coming to be recognized as still another path beyond the elitist, ethnocentric, and patriarchal confines of *Insularismo*. Feminist standpoints in Puerto Rican cultural theory and practice are most clearly and forcefully set forth, of course, by women writers and artists themselves, though they also appear in works by male authors, such as Juan Antonio Ramos and Manuel Ramos Otero. Rather than replacing or superseding the dimensions of Africanism and popular culture, women's perspectives typically complement them and foster a critical awareness of their basic importance in the culture.

This interplay of gender, class, and racial-ethnic awakenings is perhaps most evident in the writings of Rosario Ferré. Her *Papeles de Pandora* (*Pandora's Papers*), *Maldito amor* (*Cursed Love*), *Sitio a Eros*, and other fiction, poetry, and essays constitute an extended evocation of black, popular Puerto Rican culture from the experiential vantage point of a woman, and a woman from the white elite at that. She brings the world of *plena* culture to life in her own lyrical voice, summoning its energy in the very cadence of her prose.

Toward the end of *Insularismo*, in a rare personal aside, Pedreira remarks that he first really became aware of being Puerto Rican, and of a distinctively Puerto Rican way of acting and speaking, when he was a student at Columbia University in the early 1920s. In New York, he recalls, "I met many Latin Americans who would easily notice in me traits that are typical of us as a people."[13] It was abroad, away from the island, and in the perception of others that the particular features and contours of the native culture came into view. This experiential paradox, the sense of moving closer because of physical and cultural distance, has recurred among so many Puerto Ricans before and since Pedreira's student days in New York that it is almost archetypal of the emigrant consciousness. For its sheer scale and duration, and because of the obvious psychic impact of this inside–outside paradox, the migration and resettlement process has assumed definitive importance in Puerto Rican culture and its theorization. I once commented that what is most conspicuously missing in José Luis González's rather shaky "four-story country" are the cellar (*el sótano*) and the roof (*el rufo*).[14] What is the Puerto Rican cultural edifice without its Taino foundation? And, as González himself dramatized so well in his story "La noche que volvimos a ser gente" ("The Night We Became Human

Again"), what is a tenement (*un bildin*) without a *rufo*; what is Puerto Rico in our times without the Nuyorican community?

"At the bottom of every Nuyorican there is a Puerto Rican" ("En el fondo del nuyorican hay un puertorriqueño"), a young New York poet recently proclaimed, thus paraphrasing González's best-known story. And in another poem, entitled "Nuyorican," he openly berates his beloved island homeland for being less Puerto Rican than El Barrio:

yo soy tu hijo,
de una migración,
pecado forzado
me mandaste a nacer nativo en otras tierras
por que, porque éramos pobres, verdad?
porque tu querías vaciarte de tu gente pobre,
ahora regreso, con un corazón boricua, y tu,
me desprecias, me miras mal, me atacas mi hablar,
mientras comes mcdonalds en discotecas americanas,
y no pude bailar la salsa en san juan, la que yo
bailo en mis barrios llenos de todas tus costumbres,
asi que, si tu no me quieres, pues yo tengo
un puerto rico sabrosísimo en que buscar refugio
en nueva york, y en muchos otros callejones
que honran tu presencia, preservando todos
tus valores, así que, por favor, no me
hagas sufrir, ¿sabes?[15]

[I am your child,
of a migration,
a sin forced on me
you sent me to be born a native of other lands
why, because we were poor, right?
because you wanted to get rid of your poor folk,
now I return, a boricua at heart, and you,
you reject me, with nasty looks, attack the way I talk,
while you eat McDonalds in American discotheques,
you know I couldn't even dance salsa in San Juan, which
I dance in my barrios rich with all your customs,
so that if you don't want me, I have

a delicious Puerto Rico where I can find refuge
in New York and in many other byways
that honor your presence, preserving all
your values, so that please, don't
make me suffer, you know?]

With this playfully earnest inversion of perspectives, the assessment of Puerto Rican "insularism" has come full circle. For the Nuyorican, Puerto Rico is not "insular" enough, having been overrun by continental values and flavors even more than has been permitted by the Puerto Rican "enclave" on the continent.

The dynamic relation between the island and the "enclave" — the title of another book by the same poet — has held an intense fascination among Puerto Ricans, including its writers and artists, since the 1950s, when the New York community began to assume its immense proportions and when the island's major writers took it up as a central theme in their work. Of equal intensity have been the discussions, and the distortions, of the emigration experience, reflective of the various angles from which it has been viewed. Beyond dispute, though, is that the migration and emigrant community have been the main historical disclaimers of the notion of Puerto Rican culture "insulated" within its territorial confines. The relation of Puerto Ricans to places removed from the island has had a very different effect than was envisioned by Pedreira in *Insularismo*. Responding to a comment, which he cites in English, from a 1930 issue of a U.S. monthly, to the effect that Puerto Rican schoolchildren "have an unusual interest in far away places and like to go to the map," Pedreira only sensed "a melancholy process of perpetual isolation." "The map which we study with such care and affection," he concluded, "is but an escape valve which unconsciously helps to ease some of the pressure to emigrate."[16]

That process, of course, was still only a trickle in those years, and its mushrooming in the ensuing decades has fortunately engendered more creditable analyses of the relation of Puerto Ricans to geography lessons. What has been emerging in recent years is the understanding that it is not a question of division or unity, but of circulation and reciprocity. This new relational concept, articulated most memorably by Luis Rafael Sánchez in his story "The Air Bus" ("La guagua aérea"), derives in part from the increasingly circulatory nature of the migration process itself, and the simultaneously physical and spiritual access of so many Puerto Ricans to both cultural worlds. Under the present conditions of transportation and communication Puerto Rico is part of New York, and New York, like it or not, is present in Puerto Rico.

But another source of this advance beyond earlier dilemmas and distortions is the new direction of thinking about cultural change and contact developed in recent years. Contemporary postmodern cultural theory, with its guiding concepts of decentering, deterritorialization, and the crisis of representation, has been busy refiguring the whole problematic of "borders" and "bridges" that so preoccupied Pedreira and later thinkers. Even the models of mainstream and tributary cultures, of cores and peripheries, primary and subcultures — yes, even dominant and subordinate — which have been so influential since the 1960s, have begun to recede in favor of more interactional, and more carefully delineated, paradigms. And Puerto Rican culture, which had long been such an exemplary case in point for those earlier dualities, is today once again a particularly rich field for remapping cultural theory and testing its new vocabulary.

"We are a border generation" ("Somos una generación fronteriza"), Pedreira moaned, regarding as he did Puerto Rico's situation at the crossroads of two discordant cultures as the origin of its collective disorientation and isolation. The overbearing presence of both has made for a condition of pertaining to neither, a state of cultural "anomie" as that term is deployed by later diagnosticians like René Marqués and Eduardo Seda Bonilla. The "frontier" is an outpost, far removed from the hub of any identifiable and rooted cultural expression.

Recent cultural theory among Chicano writers, whose history revolves around the existence of "la frontera," allows us to think in a new way about cultural collisions, interfaces, and navigable crossings. The border, that site of mutually intruding differences, may be perceived not as a kind of no-man's-land, but as a wellspring of cultural innovation and identification. For the Chicano writer and artist Guillermo Gómez-Peña, "border culture" ("la cultura fronteriza") signifies not exclusion and denial, but inclusion and discovery. "I opt for 'borderness,'" he says, "and assume my role: My generation, the *chilangos*, who came to 'el norte' fleeing the imminent ecological and social catastrophe of Mexico City, gradually integrated itself into otherness. . . . And one day, the border became our house, laboratory, and ministry of culture."[17] The same positive account of the border situation is voiced by the Chicana poet Gloria Anzaldúa in her book *Borderlands / La Frontera*; from a strong feminist perspective she speaks of a "new mestiza consciousness," a migratory spiritual homeland in which "continual creative motion keeps breaking down the unitary aspect of each new paradigm."[18]

Aboard our "air bus," Puerto Ricans have come to inhabit the same fertile borderlands. In his entertaining little tale of the late-night flight from San Juan to New York, Luis Rafael Sánchez notes that the very historical ambivalence of his fellow passengers opens up a new space of creativity and cultural referentiality. "Puerto Ricans," he comments,

> who want to be there but must remain here; Puerto Ricans who want to be there but cannot remain there; Puerto Ricans who live there and dream about being here; Puerto Ricans with their lives hanging from the hooks of the question marks *allá? acá?*, Hamletian disjunctives that ooze their lifeblood through both adverbs. Puerto Ricans installed in permanent errancy between "being there" and "being here" and who, because of it, deflate all the adventurous formality of the voyage until it becomes a mere "ride on a bus" . . . however aerial, so it may lift them filled with assurances over the blue pond . . . the blue pond, the Puerto Rican metaphor for the Atlantic Ocean.[19]

Puerto Rican culture today is a culture of commuting, of a constant back-and-forth transfer between two intertwining zones. "I cannot live in Puerto Rico because there's no life for me there," one passenger remarks, "so I'll bring it with me bit by bit; in this trip, four crabs from Vacía Talega, in the trip before, two fighting cocks, in my next, all of Cortijo's records." As the story ends, "It is the imposing flow of reality with its hallucinating proposal of newer, furiously conquered spaces. It is the relentless flow of a people who float between two ports, licensed for the smuggling of human hopes."

The Nuyorican experience is showing how it is possible to struggle through the quandary of biculturalism and affirm the straddling position. Not with the claim to be both, but as the title of a poem by Sandra María Esteves words it, with a pride in being "not neither." In "Not Neither," the Nuyorican woman poet enacts this drama of confusion and self-discovery:

Being Puertorriqueña Americana
Born in the Bronx, not really jíbara
Not really hablando bien
But yet, not gringa either,
Pero ni portorra, pero sí portorra too
Pero ni que what am I? . . .
Yet not being, pero soy, and not really
Y somos, y como somos
Bueno, eso sí es algo lindo
Algo muy lindo.[20]

In a beautiful little poem, Tato Laviera also gives voice to this new sense of beauty and freedom as it erupts from the interstices and neglected enclave of Nuyorican life. Here, in "tight touch," the cultural rhythms engender a self-confidence and dignity that dispel all lingering traces of the proverbial Puerto Rican "insularism" and "docility":

inside the crevice
deeply hidden in a basement land
inside an abandoned building
the scratching rhythm of dice
percussion like two little bongos
in a fast mambo
quivering inside this tiny ray
of sun struggling to sneak in
the echo of the scent attracted
a new freedom which said, "we are
beautiful anywhere, you dig?"[21]

Pedreira's closing thoughts in *Insularismo* are about music; the last of the many deficiencies in Puerto Rican culture that he chooses to mention are "an acute shortage of composers" and a general lack of musical creativity. "We must help in this effort with a sense of generosity and patriotism," he announces, "and with the sincere hope of filling in our own times this gap we may notice today in one area of our nation's culture."[22] This alarm was sounded in the early 1930s, when Canario and Rafael Hernández songs were playing everywhere, and but a few years before Tomás Blanco's "Elogio de la Plena."

But Pedreira's views on Puerto Rican music are well known. Plena was, for him, another form of our folkloric music, along with the *seis*, which in its instrumentation and style incorporates "elements from the three main roots forming our cultural trunk." But despite its deep cultural origins, this kind of music was for Pedreira "our nervous savage music" ("nuestra nerviosa música brava"), which he considered to be basically out of tune with our cultural "climate." In pronouncing the *danza* the national music of Puerto Rico, Pedreira fuses Hispanophilia with that geographical and atmospheric determinism that lies at the heart of his guiding metaphor. The line of thinking here illustrates, perhaps more clearly than anywhere else in *Insularismo*, the openly repressive strategy of cultural elitism. The *danza* arose, he claims, because "our climate could not bear such constant agitation" as that of the "música brava," and we had to find "more intimate and relaxed forms of expression." "The *danza* is for us what the fox-trot is for the North Americans, that sporting, active, and strong people who needed a choreographic exercise consonant with their athletic constitution, gymnastic prowess, and hygienic Alpine character. Puerto Rico, by contrast, being a tropical, anemic country, needed a dance rhythm which was slow and reserved. . . . Our *danza*, unlike the fox, lends itself to light amusement and conversation. Its calm movements, with extended intervals that have a relaxing effect, respond appropriately to the demands of the climate. The *danza* serves as a respite from our wild music (*nuestra música brava*)."[23] Thus, in this view, the *danza* arose, and must persist, in order to counteract and hold down the intense cultural energy of "la música brava."

Pedreira, of course, did not live to witness how "brava [wild]" our music could get by the time Rafael Cortijo got hold of it. What he referred to repeatedly as a period of "transition," an "intermezzo" in the country's cultural history, turns out to have been the threshold of a new economic and political order. Industrialization, a refurbished colonial status, and mass emigration have transformed the geography of Puerto Rican culture, and ushered what had been the "repressed," silenced, and discarded cultural actors and voices to the foreground of the entire cultural field. As in North America, where the fox-trot has been eclipsed many times by even "wilder" steps and rhythms, in Puerto Rico the national culture has been impelled to let down its elitist defenses and make way for the explosive ascendancy of our "nervous," overly agitated forms of popular expression. While the leisurely grace of the *danza* has itself come to assume an antiquarian, folkloric stature, the tradition of *bomba* y *plena*, in league with its cousins *la rumba, el son, la guaracha, el mambo,* and *el merengue,* and with North American jazz and rhythm and blues, has become an integral strain of the popular Latin American music of our times, *la salsa.*

Rafael Cortijo, Ismael Rivera, and Mon Rivera were catalytic in this protracted subversion of the cultural hierarchy, a process that took hold a generation ago, in the 1950s, and which by our times has assumed definitive importance in all thinking about Puerto Rican culture and identity. It may be some time yet before we have a Centro Rafael Cortijo para las Bellas Artes, and perhaps even longer before this new popular, Afro-Caribbean, and feminist cultural subject can emerge as a revolutionary agent in the face of our ongoing colonial condition. But what was the joke of the week in August 1988 was also a landmark, of sorts, in the rewriting of our national history, another advance in our collective defiance of *Insularismo.* It is in this spirit that the Nuyorican poet Tato Laviera, at the request of Cortijo himself, wrote his poem "rafa"; the closing stanzas give eloquent voice to the momentous energy of Cortijo's revenge:

> as he finally exploded 1960
> ismael rivera sounds puerto
> rican charts creating music
> the world over;
>
> as we search through *plena* history
> there's a godfather-*padrino*-figure
> humble but stubborn to his traditions;
>
> as we detail contributions
> so we must all stand
> gracious ovation
> rafael cortijo
> general consensus
> puerto rican people.[24]

NOTES

1. *El Mundo,* Aug. 9, 1988, 33.
2. *El Mundo,* Aug. 13, 1988, 23.
3. *El Mundo,* Sept. 5, 1988, 5.
4. Cited in *El Mundo,* Dec. 11, 1988, 39.

5. *El Mundo*, Aug. 10, 1988, 35.

6. *El Nuevo Día*, June 6, 1988, 53.

7. *El Mundo*, Dec. 11, 1988, 39.

8. Edgardo Rodríguez Juliá, *El entierro de Cortijo* (Rio Piedras: Huracán, 1983), 37. Page references in text are to this edition.

9. *El Mundo*, Aug. 9, 1988.

10. Ramón Romero Rosa, "A los negros puertorriqueños," in *Sources for the Study of the Puerto Rican Migration* (New York: Center for Puerto Rican Studies, 1982), 30-33.

11. Quintero Rivera, "Ponce, La Danza, and the National Question," *Cimarron* 1 (Winter 1986), 49-65.

12. See *Insularismo* (Río Piedras: Edil, 1973), 94.

13. Ibid., 94.

14. See my essay "The Puerto Rico that José Luis González Built: Comments on Cultural History," *Latin American Perspectives* 11 (Summer 1984), 173-84.

15. Tato Laviera, *AmeRícan* (Houston: Arte Público, 1985), 53.

16. *Insularismo*, 110.

17. Guillermo Gómez-Peña, "Documented/Undocumented," in *Multi-Cultural Literacy: Opening the American Mind*, ed. Rick Simonson and Scott Walker (St. Paul, Minn.: Graywolf Press, 1988), 127.

18. Gloria Anzaldúa, *Borderlands / La Frontera: The New Mestiza* (San Francisco: Spinsters/Aunt Lute, 1987), 80.

19. "The Flying Bus," trans. Elpidio Laguna-Díaz, in *Images and Identities: The Puerto Ricans in Two World Contexts* (New Brunswick, N.J.: Transaction, 1987), 17-25. Original text in Spanish, "La guagua aérea," in *Imágenes e identidades: El puertorriqueño en la literatura* (Río Piedras: Huracán, 1985), 23-30.

20. Sandra María Esteves, *Tropical Rains: A Bilingual Downpour* (New York: African-Caribbean Poetry Theatre, 1984).

21. Tato Laviera, *La Carreta Made a U-Turn* (Houston: Arte Público, 1984), 6.

22. *Insularismo*, 157.

23. Ibid., 136-37.

24. Tato Laviera, *Enclave* (Houston: Arte Público, 1981), 64.

Interview with Tomás Ybarra-Frausto: The Chicano Movement in a Multicultural/Multinational Society

Tomás Ybarra-Frausto has written extensively on Chicano art and culture. He is currently associate director for Arts and Humanities at the Rockefeller Foundation.

Latino culture in the United States is extraordinarily diverse and has deeply influenced the entire spectrum of contemporary culture. In an interview with the editors, Tomás Ybarra-Frausto describes the new issues facing the Chicano movement in the 1990s. He begins with a review of contemporary Chicano culture since the 1960s.

The Chicano Cultural Movement

People tend to forget that "Hispanics" occupied parts of the present territory of the United States long before it was occupied by French or British colonizers, in fact, as far back as the Spanish conquest. But the emergence of Chicanos as a "minority" and indeed the adoption of the term *Chicano* was very much of the 1960s and it is there that a review of the movement begins.

In the 1960s and 1970s, Chicano cultural movements tended to be based on alternative institutions and to avoid the mainstream. This marginality was a response to the historical experience of the community rather than a result of theoretical discussion. The key words of the 1960s—*recuerdo* (memory), *descubrimiento* (discovery), and *voluntad* (affirmation of Chicanismo)—are associated with the writer Tomás Rivera. For Rivera, *recuerdo* was the reclamation of cultural practices. *Descubrimiento* was the forging of a new identity. And *voluntad* was mass mobilization for action. Major factors in the affirmation of Chicanismo were the Farm Workers Movement led by César Chávez and the cultural expressions of painters, poets, and writers. The Teatro Campesino, founded by Luis Valdez in Delano, California, in 1965, was at first directly at the service of the Farm Workers Movement and served to embody their politics in dramatic form. Its audience was primarily farm workers and their families. In this initial period, Valdez developed the *autos*, which were short dramatic sketches focused on struggles such as the grape boycott and the unionization of farm laborers. Soon the *autos* included more general social issues such as schooling and health care. In its next phase, Valdez elaborated a series of *mitos*, complementary opposites of the *autos*. These engaged the mythical, spiritual realm, the inward realities. In this formative period, the Teatro Campesino was particularly important in focusing on the *habla*, the vernacular speech.

After 1968, both the Teatro Campesino and Chicano art began a criticism of traditional culture, in particular canonical Mexican art and literature. One example of this is the performance of the traditional *corrido* "Juan Charrasquiado" with the famous refrain "en aquellos campos no dejaba ni una flor" [in those times he left no flower unplucked]. And the actors would perform the *corrido* to illustrate the meaning of the lines that the audience sang without reflection. They thus deconstructed the *corrido*, allowing the audience to recognize that it is about rape rather than about a flower.

The Teatro Campesino was also the genesis of what is now known as *rascuachismo*, an underclass sensibility rooted in everyday linguistic practices and in artistic works put together out of whatever was at hand. When the audience at the Teatro Campesino saw the curtain go up, they saw burlap sacks stitched together. Neither the curtain nor the action were seamless, a continuous piece. This was not only *la cultura de la necesidad*, or "poor theater," but an ironic comment on theatrical convention.

Similarly, Chicano art became critical of the Mexican muralist tradition from which it stemmed. Mexican muralism was too closely linked to government sponsorship and painted on walls controlled by the state. By contrast, Chicano muralists were unsponsored and painted on barrio walls. In the Chicano movement, the mural was intended to become part of the everyday life experience of the people. Like all artistic expression in this stage, it functioned as a social text by mirroring the actual struggles of the movement in pictorial form.

In the mid-1970s, new forms began to be created. Although a lot of this art was realistic, no one claimed it to be the only stylistic possibility. Chicano artists felt free to experiment in any direction so long as they held to the one basic premise: art should be committed and not art for art's sake. Because there were few written manifestos, we have to look at the practice to see how the political was embedded in the art.

In the early stages of Chicano muralism, artists used any materials at hand, even house paint. Later they were increasingly concerned with a professional knowledge of their materials; for example, what paint is most likely to last. But it would be a mistake to think of the first generation of Chicano artists and writers as a bunch of *locos* running around doing art. It was not a question of populist spontaneity. Many of the artists had been trained, some of them in the most traditional and mainstream U.S. institutions. But they rejected their training in search of an iconography appropriate to their own communities. Some, like Carmen Lomas Garza, *chose* to paint in a naive style. In parallel fashion, many writers of the 1950s and 1960s, like Tomás Rivera and Ernesto Galarza, who were trained in orthodox Spanish departments, often with an emphasis on Peninsular literature, or in traditional history departments, turned to the vernacular and to ethnographic narrative.

An important aspect of the new forms in the mid-1970s is the turn to individual experimentation. There is a gradual diminution of communal and large-scale public works. I do not see this as a retreat from the political, but rather as a changing conception of artistic practice. In any case, the understanding of the political itself was undergoing change. Epic and heroic novels like José Antonio Villarreal's *Pocho* (1959)[1] and Rodolfo Anaya's *Bless Me Ultima* (1972),[2] which exemplify an earlier period of the Chicano cultural movement, gave way to explorations of the politics of personal experience. Lyric poetry written by women, like Lorna Dee Cervantes and Bernice Zamora, was particularly important in undermining this patriarchal narrative. At this point, there emerged a larger Latino public and the emergence of an academic culture, with a publishing infrastructure. Nevertheless, public performance of poetic texts in communal settings continued to be important as affirmations of Chicano experience.

Like other classes and groups, Chicanos are increasingly defined by diversity rather than homogeneity. Differences of social class, educational background, regional provenance, sexual orientation, and linguistic ethos came to be emphasized over and above other aspects of identity.

Two competing tendencies—subversion and incorporation—emerged in the 1980s. On the one hand, patterns of consensus were undermined by subversive forms of representation. On the other hand, there was an option toward exchange and partnership with mainstream cultural institutions.

The emphasis on diversity was pioneered by lesbian writers like Anzaldúa and Cherríe Moraga. Their anthology, *This Bridge Called My Back* (1981), represented a real breakthrough and opened up space for another sensibility and subjectivity. This, in turn, enabled discussion of works of literature like John Rechy's novel *City of Night* (1963)[3] and Edgar Pompa's play *The Reunion* (1975),[4] which had never been previously discussed or incorporated into Chicano literature. A lesbian was the first to discuss that work as Chicano literature. Even now, in any anthology, you have a greater presence of lesbian than gay male writers.

In addition to these differences of sexual orientation, other kinds of difference manifested themselves. For instance, the *santero* tradition of northern New Mexico, in contrast to the urban subcultures of Los Angeles; the contrast between barrio bilingualism and academic, standard Spanish or English; the traditional *conjunto* music of Texas in contrast to Latino rock.

With the increasing recognition of cultural pluralism, conflict has arisen between mainstream and community-based institutions for programs that respond to this new multicultural reality. The community-based institutions, where the newest and most exciting work is being promoted, claim that they have been serving multicultural publics for over two decades and should therefore receive equitable support. Because of their outreach to "new publics," the mainstream institutions argue that they should receive the funding. Furthermore, they claim that they can take these cultural forms out of the ghetto and into the mainstream.

One way out of this dilemma is the notion of partnership, where a mainstream institution and a community-based institution work together. The community-based institution receives infrastructural support such as lighting technicians, catalog design, et cetera, while the mainstream institution receives help in developing new publics.

Diversity and *partnership* are likely to be the keywords of the 1990s. Much will depend, however, on whether diversity can hold its ground against the neoconservative backlash and on whether partnering can be equally beneficial to minorities as it is to mainstream institutions. Given the record of mainstream institutions, it seems unlikely. Already community-based institutions are claiming that the mainstream organizations only respond at the level of educational departments, but what is really being contested is getting the Latino perspective at the conceptual, curatorial level, where decisions about representation are made.

The Internationalization of the Chicano Movement: Looking toward Mexico/Mexico Looking Back

Ethnic movements in the United States tend to be thought of as local and regional. The Chicano movement, although nationalistic at times, has always had an international dimension right from its inception. And not only because Chicanos had a special relationship to Mexico. The posters (circa 1965) of Rupert García, a visual artist from San Francisco, for example, comment on the wars in Angola, Vietnam, and other Third World countries. Jesús Treviño, a filmmaker, went to the biennial film conference in Cuba and spoke on Chicano cinema to participants from Peru, Bolivia, and many other countries within and outside of this hemisphere.

As for the Chicano's relationship to Mexico, Octavio Paz's *Labyrinth of Solitude* (1950)[5] posited for Mexicans a homogeneous representation of Chicano culture. For Chicanos, however, it was perceived as thrusting them into marginality and portraying them as schizophrenic and anguished over their own identity. This attitude changed radically after 1968. In that year, the massacre of student protesters in Tlatelolco, Mexico City, led to a widespread questioning of Mexican nationalism. This also marked the beginning of Mexicans' recognition of the Chicano, of the potential that every Mexican may be a Chicano.

At this time, Mexico had begun to decentralize its cultural institutions; there were even regional centers in Arizona and Texas. This provided Chicanos with a conduit to Mexico and, by extension, to

Latin America. Chicano writers and artists residing in San Francisco and Los Angeles now began to read *La Jornada, Cambio, Proceso*, and other Mexican publications.

Some of these publications even carried feature stories on Chicanos. Mexican intellectuals' interest in Chicano literature and culture is evidenced by the permanent seminar on Chicano studies in Mexico at the Convento in Coyoacán. UNAM [Universidad Nacional Autónoma de México] has published books and monographs on Chicano literature and continues to do so.

To be frank, however, such interest is quite circumscribed and may have been a means of political manipulation. Among Mexican intellectuals, the real interest in Chicano culture is slight. In fact, there is a class bias and a cultural chauvinism that negates the role of U.S. minority cultures and women. The problem stems from the fact that most Latin American intellectuals who have relations with the United States are from the elites (writers, artists, social scientists, and so on) and have a difficult time understanding U.S. minority intellectuals who come mainly from working-class backgrounds. Furthermore, on key questions like language, it is difficult for Latin Americans to understand how, for example, Spanglish is acceptable and positive rather than a sign of lack of education.

The position of Chicanos in relation to Mexico is comparable to the Puerto Rican case. When Puerto Rican Studies programs were established in the late 1960s and early 1970s, there were no home-grown professors to staff them. They were recruited from the island; *independentistas* and other standard bearers of Puerto Rican culture came to spread their gospel of authenticity. This disjuncture around the question of authenticity is becoming more generalized as other Latin American migrations increase. We must beware of Latin Americans bearing banners of ancestral authenticity. They are not our authentic voice. Many groups of Dominicans, Chileans, Colombians continue with their literary and cultural events, reproducing the trappings of their native situations. But this has little to do with U.S. Latino writing. At what point does the backward-looking exile become transformed into the observer of a new landscape and begin to look forward?

Nuyorican novelist Nicolasa Mohr, for example, wrote that her work had nothing to do with that of island writers. She felt a greater affinity with Alice Walker and women writers of color. The alliances that are now being established among U.S. Latino cultural workers are setting a new cultural agenda. Writers, painters, musicians, and dancers are creating a new spectrum of commonality and difference.

Changes in the political and ethno-cultural landscape will begin to have an impact on U.S. literary institutions, selecting which Latin American artists and writers are to be published and exhibited here. In many respects, women have taken the lead. Women writers of color have established a strong tradition in the United States and their prestige within alternative networks opens the way for women of color from Latin America to reach a wider public.

For years Octavio Paz and the upper-class literary mafia have had access to our cultural markets through their contacts with the U.S. publishing elite. Because of the international relations between U.S. minorities and the rest of the hemisphere, alternative networks have been created by Chicanos and other Latinos, which provide opportunities for writers, artists, filmmakers, and video artists unknown in the United States.

Increasingly, there is a deeper and denser dialogue between Latinos and the United States and their cultures of origin. Whereas at one time U.S. Latinos might have felt inclined to seek recognition and approval from their cultures of origin, Mexico for Chicanos and Puerto Rico for Nuyoricans, in the 1990s the exchange has become more reciprocal.

Ethnicity, Tradition, and Experience

The position of Chicanos, Nuyoricans, and other Latinos at the "border" means having to look in two directions at once and bringing two different realities into association. The issue of authenticity makes clear that there are sharply divergent concepts of tradition and of the relation between tradition and change. Latino cultural expression offers countless examples of a kind of counterpoint or negotiation between past and present, between inherited tradition and contemporary innovation. In the performative arts, for instance, we have the fascinating reworking of the old Spanish *pastorela*. This medieval nativity play of Spanish origin came to the Southwest via Mexico. Chicano versions, with their introduction of new characters, scenes, and themes, and the modification of conventional components, are good examples of tradition and change. The traditional *hermitaño*, in the

Texas version of the *pastorela*, establishes a lively and very topical interaction with the contemporary audience, commenting and dialoguing on events and problems facing the local community.

Thus, while traditions are maintained for the sake of historical survival, it is also the case that the "real" tradition is to break with tradition, to desacralize and to actualize it. The past is thus revitalized, and inherited cultural trappings are recontextualized to suit present needs and functions. This process of recontextualization may be seen with particular clarity in the Puerto Rican *casitas* in New York City. As faithfully as they may be modeled after the rural dwellings that history left behind in Puerto Rico, the new structures in the South Bronx and El Barrio assume a very different purpose and use of social space. The *casitas* are not lived in, but serve a variety of other purposes: cultural activities, political meetings, community gatherings. They are typically decorated with heterogeneous signs and images both of the familiar New York surroundings and Puerto Rico.

In U.S. minority cultures there is a stepping out of the sanctioned roles within the tradition. Like the *hermitaño* in the Texas *pastorela*, a new character emerges who systematically contraverts the tendency to marginalization. It's like dubbing in reggae or in rap: the character acts as an intermediary between tradition and innovation, negotiating between them like *el pelado* [the down and out], the subaltern who is allowed to speak. This new mediating character deploys different and often divergent cultural repertoires.

The practices of the underdog are the tactics of parody, pastiche, and ironic refiguring, which make up a whole panoply of commentaries on the master discourse. It is, of course, important to differentiate such tactics from the way they are described and used in postmodern discourse. For in Latino culture the signs that parody, and are parodied, are not free floating, fractured, or evidence of the schizophrenia that Jameson attributes to postmodernism. I have used the term *rascuachismo* to describe an underclass sensibility that uses parodic expression and is rooted in particular forms of community culture. You may thus see all the operations of postmodern culture in the minority cultures, but for different reasons, and with different meanings and outcomes. For if you can take a tradition and actualize it, you may begin to recognize that the same process may also occur in relation to institutions. The hidden goal of *rascuachismo*, as for "signifying" in African American culture, is overcoming the fear of using the tools of irony in order to gain empowerment or the possibility of new social power.

Along with the invention of new characters defying the decorum of tradition, there are even new names — like Chicano or Nuyorican — which subvert the authority of accepted meanings. It is interesting that the appropriation of "marginal" Latino culture in mainline museums and the academy has not been able to accept defiant "counter" work, like *placas* [spray-painted signatures] and street graffiti.

Along with this different cultural practice goes the need for theorizing from within. Contemporary minority culture demands a revision of mainline cultural theory and practice since it no longer accommodates traditional genres, forms of expression, and aesthetics. This challenge even addresses the question of elaborated theoretical language itself. Minorities use the vernacular against the elaborated language. The vocabulary of contemporary cultural theory is confronted with the vernacular discourse, in such a way that what is placed in question is not only the language but what it is saying about identity, tradition, etcetera. We come to recognize that academic theorizing, however sophisticated, is not as textured and nuanced as the practitioner's theorizing. Alternative expressive practice of this kind engenders a new vocabulary, a countervocabulary, which the artist does not need to invent because it is already there in the practiced culture. And embedded in these "marginal," alternative forms, of course, there are new power relations, which accounts in part for why dominant theory has no words for them.

NOTES

1. New York: Doubleday, 1959.
2. Berkeley: Tonatiuh Quinto Sol International, 1972.
3. New York: Grove Press, 1963.
4. This play was performed in 1975.
5. México, D.F.: Cuadernos Americanos, 1950.

Contributors

Vinícius Dantas is a poet, critic, and translator. He has written numerous articles on poetry and literary theory, including "Oswald de Andrade e a poesia" (*Novos Estudos CEBRAP* 30: July 1991).

Juan Flores teaches Latin American studies at City College, and sociology and cultural studies at The City University of New York Graduate Center. He is the author of *Insularismo e ideología burguesa en Antonio Pedreira* (1979), *Divided Borders*, and numerous articles on cultural politics, popular culture, and Puerto Rican literature and culture. He is a member of the *Social Text* collective.

Jean Franco is a professor in the departments of English and comparative literature at Columbia University. She is the author of *Plotting Women: Gender and Representation in Mexico* (1989).

Néstor García Canclini teaches in the anthropology department at the Universidad Antónoma Metropolitana in Mexico City. He has published widely on cultural politics, border culture, cultural studies, postmodernity, and the institutionalization of popular culture. His most recent book is *Culturas híbridas: Estrategías para entrar y salir de la modernidad* (Mexico City: Grijalbo, 1990).

Randy Martin teaches in the department of political science at the Pratt Institute. He is the author of *Performance as Political Act: The Embodied Self*, and his work has appeared in *Social Text, Socialism and Democracy, The Drama Review, Minnesota Review*, and the *Journal of Dramatic Theory and Criticism*, among others.

Kathleen Newman teaches Latin American and Chicano cinema at the University of Iowa. She is one of the coauthors of *Women, Culture,* *and Politics in Latin America* and is working on a book on State theory and cultural studies.

William Rowe is a reader in Spanish American studies and coordinator of the Centre for Latin American Cultural Studies at King's College, University of London. He is also an honorary professor at the University of San Marcos, Peru. His most recent books are *Juan Rulfo: El llano en llamas* (London: Grant & Cutler, 1987) and, with Vivian Schelling, *Memory and Modernity: Popular Culture in Latin America* (London: Verso, 1991).

Iumna M. Simon teaches in the literary theory department at the Universidade Estadual de Campinas (UNICAMP). Her books include *Território da Tradução* (UNICAMP, 1986) and *Drummond: Uma Poética do Risco* (1989). Among her recent essays is "Esteticismo e Participação: as Vanguardas Poéticas no Contexto Brasileiro" (*Novos Estudos CEBRAP* 26: March 1990).

Howard Winant teaches in the sociology department and is director of the Latin American Studies Center at Temple University. He is the coauthor, with Michael Omi, of *Racial Formation in the United States: From the 1960s to the 1980s* (New York: Routledge, 1986). A recent contribution to the changing character of identity politics is "Postmodern Racial Politics," *Socialist Review* (1990).

George Yúdice teaches Romance languages at Hunter College and cultural studies at The City University of New York Graduate Center. He is the author of *Vicente Huidobro y la motivación del lenguaje* (1978), *Literatura y valor: A partir de la postmodernidad* (forthcoming), and numerous essays on literature, theory, and cultural politics in Latin America and the United States. He is a member of the *Social Text* collective.

Index

Compiled by Eileen Quam and Theresa Wolner